M000304905

THE REAL

BUSINESS

OF

BLOCKCHAIN

THE REAL
BUSINESS
OF
BLOCKCHAIN

HOW LEADERS CAN
CREATE VALUE
IN A NEW DIGITAL AGE

DAVID FURLONGER
CHRISTOPHE UZUREAU
GARTNER, INC.

Harvard Business Review Press

Boston, Massachusetts

HBR Press Quantity Sales Discounts

Harvard Business Review Press titles are available at significant quantity discounts when purchased in bulk for client gifts, sales promotions, and premiums. Special editions, including books with corporate logos, customized covers, and letters from the company or CEO printed in the front matter, as well as excerpts of existing books, can also be created in large quantities for special needs.

For details and discount information for both print and ebook formats, contact booksales@harvardbusiness.org, tel. 800-988-0886, or www.hbr.org/bulksales.

Copyright 2019 Gartner, Inc.
All rights reserved
Printed in the United States of America

10 9 8 7 6 5 4 3 2 1

No part of this publication may be reproduced, stored in or introduced into a retrieval system, or transmitted, in any form, or by any means (electronic, mechanical, photocopying, recording, or otherwise), without the prior permission of the publisher. Requests for permission should be directed to permissions@harvardbusiness.org, or mailed to Permissions, Harvard Business School Publishing, 60 Harvard Way, Boston, Massachusetts 02163.

The web addresses referenced in this book were live and correct at the time of the book's publication but may be subject to change.

Library of Congress Cataloging-in-Publication Data

Names: Furlonger, David, 1951- author. | Uzureau, Christophe, author.
Title: The real business of blockchain : how leaders can create value in a
    new digital age / David Furlonger and Christophe Uzureau.
Description: Boston : [Harvard Business School Publishing Corporation],
    [2019]
Identifiers: LCCN 2019020310 | ISBN 9781633698048 (hardcover)
Subjects: LCSH: Blockchains (Databases) | Business planning. | Leadership.
Classification: LCC QA76.9.B56 F87 2019 | DDC 005.74/1—dc23
LC record available at https://lccn.loc.gov/2019020310

    ISBN: 978-1-63369-804-8
    eISBN: 978-1-63369-805-5

The paper used in this publication meets the requirements of the American National Standard for Permanence of Paper for Publications and Documents in Libraries and Archives Z39.48-1992.

*For Brigette and Wing, who made this
book better, as they do with everything else in life*

CONTENTS

PREFACE

January 3, 2019, marked the tenth anniversary of the first blockchain transaction. Within days of that inaugural transaction, we started having conversations with business executives about the potential of blockchain to create digital opportunities. Those conversations number by now in the thousands. We have also heard hundreds of technology providers promote their view of the technology. Those interactions made clear to us that senior executives like you face difficult choices.

Those among you who are just starting to explore blockchain may feel that the technology is so specialized and complex that it belongs in the domain of technology specialists. You might struggle to see how it is relevant to you and your business function, and thus see little incentive to move from a position of observation to one of experimentation. Others among you may be blockchain veterans, sold years ago on the technology and its promise for bringing about world peace and abolishing hunger. You may feel disappointed that, ten years later, those promises have not been realized.

Whatever your level of experience with this disruptive technology, understand that blockchain's promise of providing a way to do business with anyone or anything in the world at any transaction size and without an intermediary between you is as powerful as ever. The question is not if the technology will deliver, but when, and what role do you play in making sure its promise is realized? Furthermore, business leaders like you must ask yourselves whether you're ready to accept and adopt the changes that blockchain will require of your organization. And are these changes worth the returns?

The answers to these questions are far easier to come by with accurate, ground-level, unbiased, and business-oriented information on what blockchain is and what makes it powerful. You need to understand where it can accelerate your digital transformation, how it interacts with other technology platforms in your enterprise, and how it could affect organizational and societal constructs. You need a reliable road map for tracking the evolution of blockchain and planning how you can capitalize on it.

We wrote this book to provide you with that information, along with the insight you need to capitalize on this world-changing technology. We define blockchain in the clearest business terms possible and describe what it enables you to do that is not possible today. From that foundation, we give you the strategic tools, vision, and confidence you'll need to make sound and timely decisions for yourself and your organization.

These decisions will reverberate outside the walls of your business, since blockchain, by definition, is not contained within an enterprise or ecosystem. How you apply the technology has implications for society and the future role of technology in the human experience, in the expansion of financial enfranchisement, and on issues of trust, identity, privacy, value, and democratization.

In short, we wrote this book for business executives and policy makers to assist them as they cut through the hype and focus on the core value propositions that blockchain may unlock, and what it will take to succeed.

THE REAL
BUSINESS
OF
BLOCKCHAIN

CHAPTER 1

THE REAL BUSINESS OF BLOCKCHAIN

On a recent flight to Dubai, David sat next to the CEO and chairman of a European company investing in blockchain. Over the eight hours, the CEO talked about transforming his family's business from its twentieth-century origins as an industrial extractive company into a real estate developer, and then diversifying into cloud computing and now blockchain. This classic tale of creative destruction executed from inside an organization would seem, on the surface, the least likely move for a company like his, given its old money and old-world history.

That's how it happens with blockchain. It has captured the business imagination. Many see it as the solution for bringing trust and transparency to digital environments. In doing so, it could expand trade, enable new markets, and provide better tools to manage expensive, opaque processes that cost firms millions of dollars. This promise has made blockchain one of the most popular subjects among clients at Gartner, the global research and advisory firm where both of us work.

Companies in industries as diverse as finance, sports, health care, retail, oil and gas, and pharma are engaging in a wave of blockchain experiments. They're hoping to solve intractable issues such as counterfeiting and fraud, inefficiencies caused by opaque or manual processes, and perennial challenges with data quality and data management. Startups are also developing solutions, for example, to innovate movie financing, social media engagement, hospitality, and the gaming industry.

Here are just a few organizations that we spoke with while researching this book:

- The Australian Stock Exchange (ASX) and the Depository Trust and Clearing Corporation (DTCC) are developing blockchain platforms to modernize the mechanisms used for asset clearing and settlement.

- Taipei Medical University Hospital is developing a blockchain solution to facilitate cross-organizational access to patient records, with the patient's consent.

- The Union of European Football Associations (UEFA), organizer of the Champions League and Euro football tournaments, is working with IT solution provider ELCA to develop a blockchain solution to prevent fraud and price gouging—major problems with tickets sold on the secondary market—and to maintain security oversight at tournament venues.

- Volkswagen and Renault are separately using blockchain to create an immutable "passport" that captures vehicle history and maintenance records to prevent odometer tampering and other costly forms of fraud.

- The city of Austin, Texas, is creating an ID system to help homeless people access medical care and other services.

Expectations for blockchain are well founded. With our colleagues at Gartner, we have estimated that blockchain could generate as much as $3.1 trillion in new business value by 2030, half of it by 2025 with applications designed for operational improvement.[1]

Yet these returns will not come for free. One of our aims with this book is to substantiate the claims made for blockchain, clarify what is real and what isn't, and help you as a business leader understand what you will have to do to secure your share of the value. With that in mind, we want to emphasize that the way enterprises are talking about and using blockchain today is just an initial step. Beyond operational improvements and increased efficiency, fully mature blockchain solutions will allow you to reengineer business relationships, monetize illiquid assets, and redistribute existing data and value flows in ways that could reinvent how your business engages in a digital world. That is the *real* business of blockchain.

To describe how you can begin to unlock your share of that value, we will first clarify what blockchain is and what it enables you to do that can't be done with other technologies.

THE FIVE CORE ELEMENTS OF BLOCKCHAIN

Formally, blockchain is a digital mechanism to create a distributed digital ledger on which two or more participants in a peer-to-peer network can exchange information and assets directly without the need for a trusted intermediary. The blockchain authenticates the participants and validates that they own the assets they want to exchange and that the transaction can take place. The blockchain records the information pertaining to the transaction on a digital ledger, a copy of which is independently held and updated by each participant in the network. Records are unchangeable, time-stamped, encrypted, and linked to each other in blocks; each block is a cluster of about two thousand transaction records grouped together.[2] The ledger grows as participants transact.[3]

But informally, what does that definition mean? It means you can theoretically do business with an unknown partner located anywhere on the planet and trade any asset at any transaction size and not need

FIGURE 1-1

The five elements of blockchain

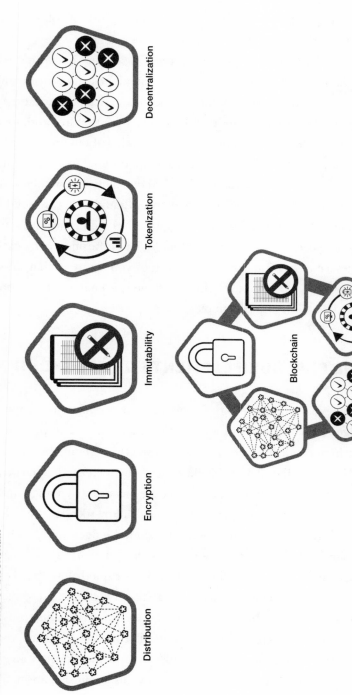

Distribution

Encryption

Immutability

Tokenization

Decentralization

Blockchain

a lawyer, a bank, an insurance company, or any other intermediary making sure both of you follow through on what you've promised to do. Such a solution vastly expands the range of assets that a business could trade. The arrangement also greatly increases who or what a business could directly trade with, without needing a third party (which would take a piece of the value).

Blockchain combines existing technologies and techniques into a novel architecture composed of five elements (figure 1-1):[4]

1. **Distribution.** Blockchain participants are located at a physical remove from each other and are connected on a network. Each participant operating a full *node* maintains a complete copy of the ledger, which updates with new transactions as they occur. Nodes are the machines owned or used by participants and equipped to run the consensus algorithm described below.[5] Any participant can review any part of the ledger but cannot change it except under prescribed circumstances.

2. **Encryption.** Blockchain uses technologies such as public and private keys to record the data in the blocks securely and semi-anonymously (participants have pseudonyms). The participants can control their personal identity and other information and share only what they need to in a transaction.[6]

3. **Immutability.** Completed transactions are cryptographically signed, time-stamped, and sequentially added to the ledger. Records cannot be corrupted or otherwise changed unless the participants agree on the need to do so. Such an agreement is known as a *fork*.[7]

4. **Tokenization.** Transactions and other interactions on a blockchain involve the secure exchange of value. The value comes in the form of tokens.[8] Digital markets can function more effectively with tokens and need to create them (tokenization) for various reasons. Tokens might function as digital representations of physical assets, as a reward mechanism to incentivize network

participants, or to enable the creation and exchange of new forms of value. They also allow private and corporate participants to control their data.

5. **Decentralization**. Both network information and the rules for how the network operates are maintained by multiple computers, or nodes, on the distributed network. In practice, decentralization means that no single entity controls all the computers or the information or dictates the rules. Every node maintains an identical encrypted copy of the network record. A consensus mechanism operated by each full node verifies and approves transactions.[a] This decentralized, consensus-driven structure removes the need for governance by a central authority and acts as a fail-safe against fraud and bad transactions.

Together, these five core elements of blockchain allow two or more participants who don't know each other to safely interact in a digital environment. Our insistence on all five elements is not semantics. When a blockchain is missing one or more of these elements, its value is limited or even negated.

There are, however, opposing views on this subject. New technology often goes through a period when opportunistic actors try to define the market in ambiguous or self-serving ways. The use of the word "database" to describe blockchain is an example of this. Blockchain *isn't* a database. Although vendors sometimes falsely describe it as one, the mechanism has several key differences. For instance, unlike databases, blockchain is not a general store for information. Moreover, blockchain is immutable; it is not read, written, deleted, and changed the way that databases are. Most importantly, while a database can be distributed to various parties, only one central administrator controls it. In block-

---

a. *Consensus mechanisms* are algorithmic rules defining and describing the data exchange between network nodes. Consensus is achieved through majority agreement, which allows for data to be factually agreed on and recorded on a ledger.

chain, administration is through consensus.[9] Central control is contradictory to the very idea of blockchain.

We see misleading language in other contexts as well. There is rampant "blockchain washing" by vendors trying to sell packages or services that use some blockchain-enabling technologies and only a subset of blockchain's design elements. Likewise, some tech-savvy companies are implementing solutions they are calling "blockchain," and then requiring supply-chain partners to integrate with them as a way to embed these partners deeper into their ecosystem.

Then there is the simple reality that blockchain is immature and organizations don't know how to use or extract value from it yet. Many are therefore experimenting with only the elements they understand and have the skills to manage. Consequently, most of the so-called blockchain solutions currently in development, a few of which we listed at the start of this chapter, use only some of the five elements of blockchain. The companies may not have even needed blockchain to achieve the same ends. According to our research, traditional data architecture could have done as well as, or better than, blockchain in 85 percent of these projects.

HOW BLOCKCHAIN UNLOCKS VALUE FOR YOUR BUSINESS

We cannot overstate the amount of new commercial activity that blockchain could enable. To get a sense of the opportunity, consider the amount of data produced today by mobile devices, GPS, internet of things (IoT) sensors placed in physical environments, and dozens of other enabling devices that are rendering both digital and physical assets visible to networked environments. Almost unfathomable, this network of devices captures more than 2.5 quintillion bytes of data created daily.[10] Leaders like you want to monetize these new data assets for your company and trade them with willing buyers.

But the centralized infrastructure you rely on to execute commercial transactions and manage risk—payments systems, insurance, delivery and logistics services, and legal contracts—was not designed to handle the kinds of machine-to-machine transactions possible today with digital or digitalized assets. Digital transactions don't have a minimum size the way transactions do in the analog world. Units of data, cryptocurrency, reward points, and pieces of an asset (as opposed to the whole) are just a few new forms of value that digitalization makes tradable in single units. Individually, the units could be worth less than $0.01, but they can be traded by the millions or trillions. The burgeoning trade in these digital assets is big business, exploding as we write this book. Amazon has a patent for a streaming data marketplace.[11] Digital industries like gaming are embracing microtransactions for in-game purchases. And new markets are forming daily to trade data, single watts of energy, carbon credits, and other digitally represented assets. The cryptocurrency and initial coin offerings (ICO) craze that took hold in 2017—followed by a deep crash and movements toward regulation—has not curtailed the enthusiasm to experiment with finance. This enthusiasm points to the mainstreaming of token-driven business models that are enabled by a blockchain to finance and capture digital opportunities.

Traditional centralized mechanisms for establishing trust, identity, and payment were not built to autonomously handle these microtransactions by the trillions in a distributed machine-centric environment—and they can't handle them, certainly not securely and efficiently. Businesses need a different way to deal with new digital assets and interactions without involving an intermediary that can collect data on every party in the transaction and take a piece of the value. You need blockchain.

Blockchain can also redirect *existing* value flows. It does this by reducing control over four business currencies by central market powers—including large multinational corporations, digital platforms, and large intermediaries. The business currencies are: data, access, technology, and contracts. We revisit them at various points throughout this book. Suffice it to say for now that data is the anchor currency because of how customers leave behind a data trail, like Hansel and his breadcrumbs. Powerful market intermediaries such as large retailers, financial services firms, government agencies, and digital platforms can pick up this data essentially for free and analyze it to improve user experiences and to drive product development. Organizations that can capture plenty of data at very low cost and analyze it thus have an advantage over others in the value chain.

Blockchain starts to break that advantage by redacting the data trail. Instead of leaving data behind as you search and interact with a person or an organization, the data related to both you and the other parties on a blockchain can, under specific design conditions, be kept under participant control and shared as needed for a transaction. This shift in control prevents a central actor from capturing an outsize share of value and ushering it off-chain or using undue influence to nudge customer behaviors in particular directions. In this way, blockchain also reopens existing markets to new competition.

GOING BEYOND THE HYPE

The potential to create new value and unlock existing value flows makes blockchain one of the most revolutionary technologies available today. But in its current state, blockchain is, from an enterprise perspective, still young and evolving. It has yet to prove itself in a hardened business context, and some of its elements—decentralization and tokenization, in particular—are radical enough to make many business leaders pause. More sophisticated application will come through experimentation and ongoing maturation of the technology and the businesses that use it.

In the meantime, a great deal of contradictory information is floating around the market. On the one hand, many observers applaud blockchain as *the* solution to an impossible range of problems. On the other hand, we hear anecdotes about enterprises that launched blockchain pilots but couldn't convert them into operational deployments, resulting in limited cost savings or value. Combine unrealistic expectations and real-world disappointments with the cryptocurrency crash of 2018, and you get what we have been predicting since at least 2016. In Gartner lingo, blockchain is moving toward the "trough of disillusionment" or, more colloquially, the blockchain winter.[12]

It is normal for technologies at blockchain's stage of evolution to be touted for a period of time and then experience a near-complete backlash during which people dismiss the high expectations as hype, resulting in the slide into the trough. The backlash can be especially strong for technologies with the potential to solve a wide range of complex problems or create vast amounts of value. We saw a similar dip in enthusiasm with the dot-com crash of 2001 and the more recent challenges enterprises are having with digital transformation.[13] Blockchain's inevitable slip into the trough doesn't signal that you should do less with the technology, however. On the contrary, you will want to do more with it now. Despite changes in attitude about blockchain, its technologies are maturing and use cases for the enterprise are beginning to show impact. It is in this period of evolving maturity that you will more easily find the use cases and design elements that solve *real* problems and unlock a technology's true potential. After the trough of disillusionment comes the plateau of productivity; after winter, spring.

THE GARTNER BLOCKCHAIN SPECTRUM: MAPPING YOUR FUTURE

Blockchain will evolve from its early application today to realize its full potential to enable a wide range of new digital transactions. We created the Gartner blockchain spectrum (figure 1-2) to illustrate the evolutionary path from the late 2000s, when many of blockchain's enabling technologies reached mainstream awareness, to the current-day solutions that use only a few elements, to blockchain's longer-term potential to enable microtransactions and unlock digital value flows. The spectrum reflects the experiences of organizations, including hundreds of our clients, engaged in the real-world development and application of blockchain technologies and design principles. Using

FIGURE 1-2

The Gartner blockchain spectrum

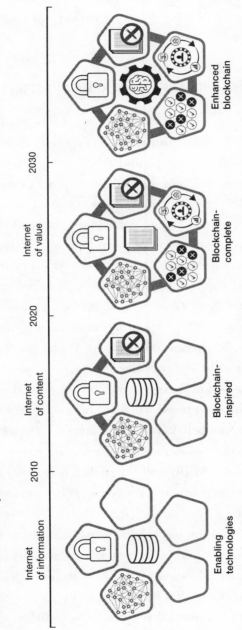

the spectrum as our guiding framework for this book, we reveal how blockchain will evolve from what it is today to what it will be by 2030. As seen in the figure, we expect this evolution to unwind in three phases.

PHASE 1: BLOCKCHAIN-INSPIRED

The first phase of the blockchain spectrum began to pick up momentum after 2012, when business leaders started exploring the technology through proofs of concept and pilots. We expect this phase to last through the early 2020s. Blockchain-inspired solutions use only three of the five elements—distribution, encryption, and immutability. These solutions often aim to reengineer existing manual processes specific to an individual organization or to an industry. High-profile blockchain-inspired examples include a solution developed by Alibaba to facilitate tracking and tracing of food products, including milk products from Australia and New Zealand, and honey and wine from around the world. The global shipping and logistics company Maersk also launched a blockchain-inspired solution called TradeLens for managing documentation flows in supply chains.[14]

There are several reasons why the solutions developed during the blockchain-inspired phase will focus on only three of the five elements. The explanations boil down to the maturity of the technology, the enterprises' readiness to embrace each element, the ease of implementation of each element (internally and externally), regulatory considerations and the propensity to deal with a limited set of known, and therefore trusted, participants.

As it pertains to blockchain technology, each of the underlying elements—distribution, encryption, immutability, tokenization, and decentralization—has a separate set of technologies associated with it, and each technology has its own maturity path. The technologies also need to interact in ways that are scalable, reliable, and secure. Despite this challenging work, it is well under way, and Gartner analysts expect that the major technical challenges of enterprise-scale blockchain will be resolved by 2025. Meanwhile, the market has hundreds of experiments in progress but few full implementations. Only 3 percent of the 2,871 chief information officer (CIO) respondents to Gartner's 2019 CIO survey say they have a live and operational blockchain for their business, and an additional 8 percent of respondents are in short-term planning or pilot execution. Few to none of these implementations use all five elements of blockchain.[15]

The challenge is not just technical. There are also organizational challenges. To benefit from blockchain solutions that go beyond the efficiency and process improvement focus in the blockchain-inspired phase, organizations must embrace decentralization, the most difficult of the five elements. Decentralization means that every full node in a blockchain network gets an equal vote on whether a participant and a transaction are valid, and every node has access to and full viewing rights over the ledger. Many business leaders are as troubled by the notion of full transparency (albeit in an encrypted form) as they are by letting lines of code execute business decisions, especially if such execution is outside their full control. Technology infrastructure providers and market intermediaries stoke those fears. These actors make money on centralized technology and processes and have a vested interest in having you continue using their methods.

Blockchain's technological immaturity, coupled with the conservatism inside many organizations, combine to create the current market for blockchain-inspired solutions in *centralized* environments. You can identify these solutions by the words *closed*, *private*, *permissioned*, *enterprise*, and *proprietary*. Some of the solutions also incorporate tokens, but in a limited way. By definition, blockchain-inspired systems are centralized and hence cannot allow unmediated trade in data and other forms of assets.[16]

PHASE 2: BLOCKCHAIN-COMPLETE

Blockchain-complete solutions deliver the full value proposition of blockchain. The big upgrade from blockchain-inspired solutions comes from tokens operating in a decentralized environment using smart contracts.[b] Tokenization allows you to create new assets and represent illiquid assets in a form that can be autonomously traded. Decentralization uses consensus to authenticate potentially untrusted users, assets, and transactions and ensures that no central provider can own or control the underlying mechanisms of trade in these assets. Deployed with all five elements of distribution, encryption, immutability, tokenization, and decentralization, blockchain-complete solutions enable trade in new forms of value and unlock monopolies on existing forms.

Few mainstream enterprises or governments that we know of are building blockchain-complete solutions yet. Many startups are doing so, however, and some of them will gain market momentum by the early 2020s, with more scale apparent after 2025. Though not immediate, the proliferation of blockchain-complete solutions will push organizations to explore new ways of operating with greater degrees of decentralization than they have now.

PHASE 3: ENHANCED BLOCKCHAIN

Sometime after 2025, complementary technologies such as IoT, artificial intelligence (AI), and decentralized self-sovereign identity (SSI) solutions will converge and become more integrated with blockchain networks.[c] The resulting enhanced blockchain solutions will expand the types of

---

b. A *smart contract* is a computer program or protocol that typically runs on a blockchain. The program facilitates, verifies, or executes business processes triggered by events, on-chain transactions, or interactions with other smart contracts. A smart contract is a digital and autonomous representation of the traditional contract process, including contract formation, creation of enforceable and immutable rights and obligations, and execution of performance.

c. Self-sovereign identity (SSI) allows individuals or organizations to own their digital and nondigital identities and to give express consent to share that identity with others to engage in commercial transactions. Decentralized identity services enabled by an identity trust fabric can immutably store the proof of identities and their profile attributes cryptographically. Organizations, people, or things can then extract and share part or all of that identity record as needed for an interaction. In this way, SSI adds security and flexibility to individuals or organizations that want to share their data or ID on a per-interaction basis.

value that can be tokenized and exchanged and will enable a greater number of smaller transactions to occur and be supported by smart contracts than would be possible with traditional mechanisms. Enhanced blockchain will eventually allow microtransactions to take place between mutiple autonomous computerized objects without human intervention. From these capabilities, new markets will emerge to monetize previously unmonetizable or illiquid assets such as intellectual property (IP), data, physical objects, and other high-volume or high-value assets.

Decentralized, self-sovereign identity solutions will bring particular benefit to enhanced blockchain networks. These technologies allow participants to secure their personal data in a digital wallet or another storage mechanism and share it according to rules set up for this purpose. (The participants will also be able to selectively share data on blockchain-complete solutions by consenting to the tokenization of personal data they want to share with third parties.) When combined with AI, SSI dynamically enforces the rules established by the data owner and automatically requires the owner's consent before data can be shared or used. After they agree to share their data, the participants can also trace and document who saw it and who used it. This transparency enables broader monetizing of, and accountability for, the use of personal data while also ensuring privacy.

As new forms of value come online with enhanced blockchain solutions, businesses will likewise innovate new business models using decentralized operational structures. Organizations will be technically able to delegate economic decision making to "things," which would act autonomously and according to the terms defined in a smart contract that runs on the blockchain. These enhanced things could remove humans from the transaction and eventually move blockchain networks toward completely autonomous transactions and ultimately the establishment of decentralized autonomous organizations (DAO).[d]

---

d. A decentralized autonomous organization (DAO) is a digital entity that can engage in business interactions with other digital agents and corporate entities without conventional human management. DAOs rely on smart contracts to manage and execute interactions. By definition, DAOs operate independently and can span multiple geographic and legal jurisdictions and institutional boundaries.

The Gartner blockchain spectrum articulates how blockchain adoption will evolve over time to include decentralization as a design element. This evolution will create a new path to digitalize your industry and organization.

THE PROGRAMMABLE SOCIETY

As blockchain—and business—evolves, what is at stake is no less than your ability to participate in a fair and accessible digitally-enabled world economy and society. In such an environment, a diverse range of businesses, individuals, and things interact, operate, earn profits, and create value on their own terms. This world is not a foregone conclusion.

Figure 1-3 illustrates the directional options in today's increasingly tech-enabled world. The y-axis represents the environment of evolving digital capability, from web enablement to full programmability. *Fully programmable* implies that smart things or autonomous agents have attained legal authority to make independent decisions to produce or consume assets. To illustrate with a simple example, a sensor in a programmable building could decide on the amount of energy a room needs for the lighting system and then could "buy" the necessary energy from the sensors managing the micro-wind turbines installed on a neighbor's roof. In a fully programmable environment, these value exchanges can take place with or without human involvement. The y-axis is blockchain independent. Business and society will become more programmable with or without blockchain technology as IoT, AI, and advanced computing paradigms such as edge and quantum become more dominant.[e]

e. *Edge computing* describes a distributed computing environment in which data processing takes place close to the things or people that produce or consume the data. The goal is to reduce latency (delays) by keeping unnecessary traffic from the center of the network. Edge computing also establishes local hubs for interconnections between interested peers. *Quantum computing* is an advanced form of computing whereby various aspects of quantum mechanics, including superposition and entanglement, perform operations on data. Quantum computing can significantly increase the efficiency and speed of calculations. See Wikipedia, s.v. "quantum computer," last modified February 12, 2018, https://simple .wikipedia.org/wiki/Quantum_computer; and Neil Gershenfeld and Isaac L. Chuang, "Quantum Computing with Molecules," *Scientific American*, June 1998, 66–71.

The x-axis represents the continuum from full centralization of the governance structure to full decentralization. The idea of a continuum is critical, since decentralization is itself a dynamic condition—even in blockchain. Some industries and corresponding businesses are highly centralized today as a function of their structure. Others are naturally more fragmented. Even given that variation, any significant movement along the x-axis is blockchain dependent, since organizations that want to digitally transform and operate under decentralized governance *need* blockchain or some other form of digital ledger technology to allow all economic participants, including autonomous things, to transact with each other and earn due economic returns. Only decentralization *enabled by blockchain* makes transactions without an intermediary possible in a networked environment.

Thus, while the figure depicts four quadrants, the inevitable increase in programmability realistically limits an organization's directional options to two: organizations will either move north to become more digital under centralized governance, or they will move northeast to become more digital under decentralized governance.

The prevailing emphasis for the past two decades has been to drive toward "digital transformation." In terms of figure 1-3, the progression has moved organizations north from the lower left corner—where most business in most industries operate as relatively centralized and mostly analog—over the line into the upper left quadrant. While some legacy businesses have realized positive results from this approach, far more organizations struggle to realize value through the digital transformation of their current models.[17] Legacy infrastructure, investments, processes, partners, organizational cultures, profit models, and other aspects of these businesses are a source of competitive advantage, but are also extremely difficult to adjust without risking critical relationships and current sources of income. Because digital native platforms do not have these limitations, they can grab territory in the northwest quadrant (digitally sophisticated, centralized business), and, with that position, draw in customers. A diverse and relevant product set, an intuitive user interface, uncomplicated payments, and convenient delivery cultivate customer loyalty, enabling further centralization.

FIGURE 1-3

Planning for digital capability and level of decentralization

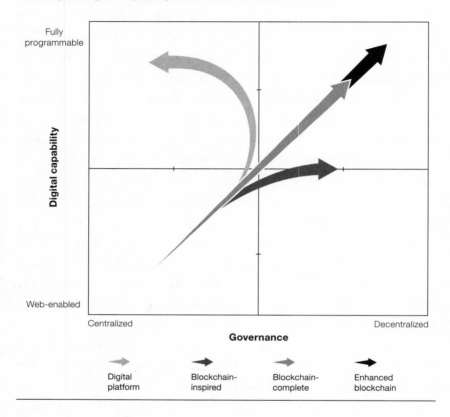

Nondigital native platforms vying for the same customers and using the same techniques lack the proficiency the native platforms enjoy.

Organizations that choose to move north will thus see increased programmability and will continue along the same trajectory they have followed for the past two decades under the control of a few large, digitally capable businesses (and government agencies) using the increasingly centralized infrastructure we rely on today. Allowing digitalization to progress in this way results in an outsized share of value accruing to a few powerful organizations—including large digital platforms, banks, insurers, telecommunications companies, logistics giants, and central governments. These organizations would have unlimited control over the data and value produced in a programmable world, allowing them to dictate the terms of how other businesses access markets and technology and how they benefit. Absolute control would enable these programmable entities to become even more centralized over time.

Alternatively, organizations can choose a north-east trajectory to become more digital and more decentralized. A few companies have already decided to tackle the northeast quadrant to compete in their markets with relatively decentralized, digitally enabled business models. We say "relatively" because the multifaceted nature of business also means that a company can be quite centralized in some ways but decentralized in others. Some examples of companies embracing decentralization in aspects of their business or operating models include car-sharing providers like Zipcar, which enables decentralized car ownership, and LO3 Energy, which uses blockchain to support personal energy generation and exchange without the involvement of a centralized utility. Apparel brands such as Betabrand and Everybody World have open-source and crowdfunded product development models. And crowdfunding from the likes of Kickstarter, Indiegogo, and Ulule provides decentralized financing for independent ventures.[18] These examples and dozens of others show how decentralization of certain operational functions can deliver value. The companies themselves may be small, but they are among the fastest-growing firms in their respective sectors.

These are the available paths as the world becomes more programmable: move north and compete directly with digital native platforms and other central actors; move northeast, and you open the potential to step around the digital native platforms and other centralizing forces and set new terms of engagement. Along this northeast path lies, first, blockchain-complete solutions designed with the five defining elements and, later, enhanced blockchain solutions built on networks that include "things" as participants and use AI in the design protocols.[f]

---

f. We use the word *things* to describe computerized and network-enabled machines. In today's internet of things (IoT), these machines function mostly to capture data about the device or environment in which they are embedded and transfer it to a central

MOVING ALONG THE
DECENTRALIZATION CONTINUUM

The very notion of the consensus-driven decision making that is inherent in the design of blockchain-complete and enhanced blockchain solutions is antithetical to most organizations and business leaders. You and other leaders might be tempted to simply focus your energy on the blockchain-inspired phase, hence limiting your movement to the lower edge of the northeast quadrant of figure 1-3 and ignoring the later phases of the spectrum.

Yet we encourage you to keep the long view in mind as you experiment with blockchain-inspired solutions. We positioned movement along the decentralization continuum as a choice you face in an increasingly programmable world and society, but we don't believe each of the available options is equally appealing. Millions if not billions of internet nodes and networked objects have spent the last two decades capturing communications; recording conversations; and keeping track of movements and transactions, relationships, objects used, and objects under consideration for billions of networked humans and organizations around the globe. Increasingly, the companies and governments that control this data are not just collecting but are also interpreting it, communicating it back, nudging people, and influencing behaviors.

This is reality—our reality. A handful of organizations worldwide hold vast reams of customer and company data. We handed it to them in exchange for added convenience and cool new gadgets. They don't need to have nefarious goals à la Big Brother for centralization of those resources to have unappealing economic and societal consequences.

store. As internet-connected things become more intelligent—as they become embedded with if-then algorithms or eventually with more-sophisticated forms of AI—they will be able to buy, sell, and request service. This increased sophistication will open new opportunities for revenue, efficiencies, and customer relationship management. Smart things represent new customers that organizations can sell to and that governments can tax. Humans have already enabled some things to negotiate, buy, and sell.

Our economy and society are not going to become less digital and programmable in the coming years. On the contrary, they are on a clear path toward continued adoption of AI and ongoing expansion of IoT to the point that nearly every asset, environment, process, and interaction will be fully programmable within just a few decades, just as Alan Turing described more than fifty years ago. You now need to decide what kind of a programmable society you want to live in. Do you want one in which interactions, transactions, and the data related to them are controlled by a small group? Or do you want a society with widespread access, privacy, engagement, and value exchange?

The latter society requires an embrace of blockchain with eventual adoption of all five elements. To build such a society, you and other business leaders must actively collaborate to reconceive your enterprises as dynamic and increasingly autonomous participants in a larger network. The benefits will accrue to you, your organization, the economy, the business community, and society as your ways of exchanging value align with the increasingly intelligent and things-driven environment in which we live.

YOUR REAL BUSINESS LENS

WHAT DID YOU LEARN?

Blockchain is a computerized way to allow two or more participants in a network to exchange assets without needing a third-party intermediary, which would take a share of the value. Blockchain as we define it includes five core elements: distribution, encryption, immutability, tokenization, and decentralization. Together, these elements create a trusted environment in which to create and share value. These elements are not equal in terms of how easy they are to implement. Decentralization is the most challenging, as it also requires a business-level embrace of some degree of decentralized governance.

WHAT SHOULD YOU DO ABOUT IT?

As a leader, you should develop a vision of how increased decentralization could benefit your business. The timelines are short, as blockchain-complete solutions with all five elements will begin to gain market traction around 2023. Only slightly further out lies a future business and societal environment that includes IoT and AI, in which autonomous and intelligent things own assets and trade value. You need to know how you can prepare to interact through IoT and AI without needing a central actor to mediate the interaction for you.

WHAT'S NEXT?

The evolution of blockchain cannot be ignored. Dozens of case study interviews and thousands of client inquiries at Gartner over the last few years reveal that countries, industries, governments, enterprises, and consumers are taking steps to understand its use and application. The impact of the technology will be significant. You have to decide what, where, and how you will participate. Let's begin by delving deeper into the current blockchain-inspired phase of the spectrum.

PART ONE

BLOCKCHAIN- INSPIRED SOLUTIONS

CHAPTER 2

SEEKING VALUE

Blockchain-inspired solutions include three of the five design elements of blockchain: distribution, immutability, and encryption. Organizations are using these solutions to improve record keeping and transparency and to modernize cumbersome or manual processes, including those that cross enterprise boundaries. Through 2023, the majority of solutions inside established organizations and called "blockchain" will be blockchain-inspired and developed for one of these purposes.

Applied in the right context, blockchain-inspired solutions could, for example, improve efficiency; reduce back-office costs; speed up confirmation, settlement, and traceability; and improve data quality and management.[1] An example of a high-potential solution that fits these criteria is currently in development at the Australian Stock Exchange (ASX) to replace its twenty-five-year-old Clearing House Electronic Subregister System (CHESS), a computer system that records shareholdings, manages share transactions, and facilitates the exchange of title or ownership when people sell financial products for money. Today, CHESS handles as many as two million trades per day.[2] The system is a true workhorse, but twenty-five years is a long time in the world of technology. Dan Chesterman, CIO of ASX, explained that he concluded in

2015 that the exchange had reached the natural limit of what it could do to improve CHESS's capability and efficiency.[3]

Sticking with the status quo was not an option, given the opportunities and challenges pressing on the ASX. CHESS runs a proprietary messaging protocol, which makes it difficult for the ASX to attract listings from the AsiaPac and the Middle East. The Australian government also opened competition in clearing and settlement of equity trades.[4] ASX does not have a credible competitor in Australia, but technological advancement could change that. For those reasons, the organization will need a new system to maintain its status in Australia and be a viable global partner beyond the continent. In 2016, ASX presented its roadmap to replace CHESS with a "distributed ledger technology" (DLT) solution—in other words, CHESS as a permissioned blockchain.[5] However, the roadmap also stipulated that ASX will build an ISO20022 messaging option for ecosystem participants that don't want to use the DLT capability. With this announcement, ASX established itself as one of the first national securities exchanges hoping to use blockchain technology for its mission-critical financial settlement systems.

The ASX and others developing blockchain-inspired solutions see benefit in using this new technology, even without tokens or decentralization as part of the design. Starting with equities, the ASX plans on incorporating other securities asset classes and new products. Eventually, this vision could be a building block in revolutionizing the Australian markets and others. There are risks, however. We clarify those benefits and risks for you in this chapter and give you tools to evaluate the solutions you see in your market.

To be clear, we firmly believe that blockchain-inspired solutions do not deliver on the full promise we see for the real business of blockchain. Still, these solutions are not without value. For the right application in the right context, they could enable improvements in document management, traceability, and fraud prevention and create other efficiencies. Using a taxonomy of blockchain-inspired archetypes, we discuss ways to distinguish the high-benefit solutions from those with low benefit. But before we describe the archetypes, let's revisit the matter of centralization in blockchain-inspired solutions and how it affects the four business currencies (data, access, contracts, and technology) that form the core of the blockchain-inspired benefit-risk calculation.

BUSINESS CURRENCIES WITH BLOCKCHAIN-INSPIRED SOLUTIONS

To recap, the four business currencies are major sources of value and competitive advantage in digital, not just blockchain, environments. In the simplest interactions, users "pay" for free access to software or a digital solution with the details they reveal about their interests and habits; the digital platforms in turn use this data to attract advertisers, develop new products and features, and increasingly steer customers to take certain actions. The lack of an explicit and multilateral contract between the user and the digital platform provider means there is no limit to how much data the provider can collect or how often it uses the data and in what situations.

All centralized digital platforms exert control over the data that runs through them. This means that blockchain-inspired solutions exert centralized control over data just as digital platform do. Furthermore, because blockchain-inspired solutions are not designed to be decentralized, they instead operate with some level of central coordination and governance of the network. Centralization is achieved by including aspects of database management mechanisms as part of the information architecture; the database mechanisms determine which entity acts as a transaction authenticator and validator and therefore decides what gets written to the ledger. Although, as we explained earlier, a blockchain is not a database and lacks a central authority, blockchain-inspired strategies blur those distinctions. Some would argue that a "centralized blockchain" is a contradiction in terms and that a blockchain that includes a database is not a blockchain at all. Ignoring these semantic arguments, we call these solutions that exploit database technology *blockchain-inspired*.[6]

Most important, a centralized solution has a single authority and does not use a decentralized consensus algorithm to validate the identity of participants and authenticate the transactions. Also, a centralized architecture with a single authority creates a single point of failure for the network. Put simply, all the promises you hear about blockchain as more secure and reliable than traditional data architectures are not true *if the design is centralized.* Security is not the only consideration, either. Without tokenization and decentralized consensus, a blockchain-inspired solution cannot enable participants who do not know each other to exchange value without a third party validating the exchange.

Ownership over a blockchain solution becomes a major issue with solutions under central control. With decentralized blockchains like Bitcoin, there is no owner and access is open to anyone (pseudonymously) who wants to participate and has the infrastructure to do so. Blockchain-inspired solutions, in contrast, usually have one owner or a limited group of owners, and membership is restricted to the parties invited by the owner to participate. For that reason, blockchain-inspired solutions are also referred to as *closed, private* or *permissioned* blockchain networks.

These dynamics of technological and business control have a direct impact on the competitive opportunities and threats a given solution can enable. Figure 2-1 reprises figure 1-3, which mapped the degree of digitalization or programmability and the degree of decentralization operating in the business environment. In figure 2-1, blockchain-inspired solutions are represented by the shaded area, with clear boundaries based on the degree of centralized control.

This figure offers a strategic view of what centralization means for a blockchain. Any given blockchain-inspired solution will capture a smaller band of territory in relation to the degrees of digitalization and decentralization. Some blockchain solutions, such as ASX and its CHESS replacement, provide a highly controlled and centrally operated and governed solution to a market problem. The rationale for this choice is sound. As Chesterman explained during an on-stage conversation at Gartner IT Symposium/Xpo October 2018 in Australia, "We aren't solving a trust problem. People do inherently trust the ASX to be the

FIGURE 2-1

The blockchain-inspired benefit zone

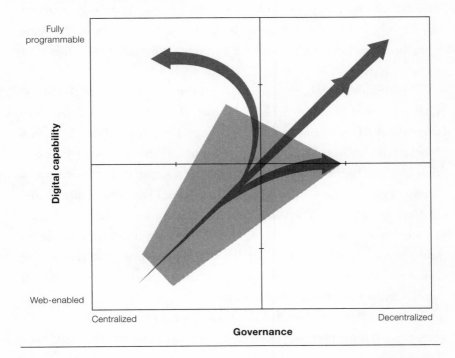

source of truth for the data that is in CHESS. We're solving a data synchronicity problem."

Other solutions that are similarly led by one company or a small group of companies may aim to exert control over others in the value chain. Eventually some solutions hope to evolve toward decentralized collaboration over time. The distinction can often be seen in how a solution trades in the four business currencies. Let's examine each currency, with an eye on how it operates in the blockchain-inspired phase of the spectrum.

DATA

Data is an important currency at all stages of the blockchain spectrum, but it is most vulnerable during the blockchain-inspired phase.[7] This vulnerability is especially apparent with blockchain-inspired solutions designed to facilitate interorganizational interactions in a value chain. If your organization participates in one of these blockchains, and the governance of that blockchain allows a single actor or subgroup to access or control all the data that flows through it, then you may be exposing your business information without receiving commensurate insight or value in return.

To demonstrate what we mean, we'll use the example of the blockchain collaboration TradeLens. Launched in August 2018 by shipping giant Maersk and global technology firm IBM, TradeLens is a blockchain-inspired logistics solution designed to streamline information sharing in the supply-chain industry.[8] Daniel Wilson, director of business development in Maersk for the TradeLens collaboration, told us that the solution came out of a larger exploration of digital solutions for the logistics industry. "There is a dire need in our industry for digital transformation, such that all participants have reliable and predictable information flows. We saw that a blockchain platform would go at least some way to remedying those pain points."

For context, more than five thousand container ships sail the earth's oceans, and some of these vessels carry as many as twenty thousand containers of worldly goods.[9] The shipping industry needs air-tight records to manage those volumes, but much of this record keeping is still paper based. If the documentation is incomplete, is written in the wrong language, or is lost, goods can be held up, creating additional costs.

TradeLens aims to digitalize the process by capturing the necessary shipping information on a blockchain-inspired platform that allows the actors involved in a transaction to access the record when they need it. The TradeLens network had over one hundred global logistics sector participants at its August 2018 launch, and by October 2018, the platform had managed 154 million shipping events, with daily volumes reaching 1 million. Maersk reports that the network of onboarded TradeLens participants represent 20 percent of the addressable global shipping market, and promoters highlight the potential of blockchain to cut the time spent on shipment administration by 40 percent.[10]

The promise is there. Yet the centralized approach gives some industry actors pause. Executives from German transportation company Hapag-Lloyd, for instance, have publicly expressed their resistance to participating on a platform owned and controlled by a competitor. "Technically the solution could be a good platform," CEO Rolf Habben Jansen said, "but it will require a governance that makes it an industry platform and not just a platform for Maersk and IBM. And this is the weakness we're currently seeing in many of these initiatives, as each individual project claims to offer an industry platform that they themselves control. This is self-contradictory, without a joint solution, we're going to waste a lot of money, and that would benefit no one."[11]

When we asked Wilson about the issue of governance, he said, "The perspective of many in the industry is that having a platform that facilitates standards for information sharing would be an unalloyed good, but they have concerns about the governance model. And we've changed the governance in the last twelve months to reflect that industry feedback. We are listening to the market. We haven't heard anything negative in a material sense about the technical approach."

On the technology, Wilson added, "We are working through various forums for the discussion of standards. We are using open-source technology; all the data structures are open. Someone else could take the same technology and build their own platform, but why would they do that? The value is having all the information in one place, having a one-stop shop."

Meanwhile, a rival shipping industry blockchain-inspired solution has been announced. The Global Shipping Business Network has nine shipping industry signatories, including COSCO and the Shanghai International Port. The network has declared its intent to develop a blockchain solution, though what the solution will look like in practice is not yet clear.[12]

The data access and commercial concerns expressed by Hapag-Lloyd come up with any solution built with centralized technology governance and central ownership. The concerns are exacerbated for information-intensive solutions. When blockchain-inspired solutions allow a single large company with superior AI analytical capability to view and access the data and influence the flows from every party in the system, the benefits could accrue disproportionately to that actor, with the disparities multiplying over time. The lack of tokens in blockchain-inspired solutions reinforces the centralization of power, since there is no mechanism to allow participants to control their information, provide consent, or trade it as an asset.

Thus, when we say data is a currency, we mean that the form, ownership, and governance structure of blockchain-inspired solutions can give participants more or less control over the data they input. Know what and how you're "paying" before you sign on to such solutions.

ACCESS

The business that owns a blockchain-inspired solution controls access to a process or a portion of the market. Businesses that want to participate pay for that access explicitly through fees or a subscription, but they also pay implicitly by locking themselves into the solution or exposing their competitive information.

In contrast, the concept of permissioned access doesn't exist in blockchain-complete solutions. Any participant or node can join a blockchain peer-to-peer network. The blockchain design in fact favors participation because decentralized consensus-based decision making gets stronger and more trustworthy when more nodes are involved. Access and participation define the ethos, grounded in the idea that transparency drives adherence to the rules. The concept is similar to eBay's early use of member reviews to allow people to call out bidders or sellers who didn't honor the terms of an auction. Make it open, transparent, and accountable, and everyone will play nice.

The theoretical benefits of open access are clear, but the reality is more complicated. Open access is a challenging concept for many leaders used to seeing boundaries inside and beyond their organization. For them, a blockchain-inspired solution, with its permissioned access, defined interactions, and known actors, is more familiar and comfortable and can be applied today within their organization.

Yet there is risk in these familiar waters. Taken to an extreme, blockchain-inspired solutions trade on scarcity rather than availability. Solution creators make these forms of blockchain useful so that "customers" and "partners" see short-term benefits. But this "value" could be coerced in the right circumstances. For instance, a major customer or channel partner could make participation in its centrally controlled blockchain a condition of ongoing partnership. In these situations, access to the blockchain solution will be synonymous with access to the market. If you refuse, you lose the ability to connect with your end customer.

CONTRACTS

Contracts specify the terms and conditions of doing business. In blockchain, those terms are captured in the technology of the blockchain itself, either as a *smart contract*—lines of code that capture and execute the business rules and agreements of a blockchain—or in the underlying technology stack.[a] The rules allow the blockchain to execute transactions without human intervention.

But who defines these rules, and who decides on modifications to them? If one actor defines the rules and owns the blockchain, then there is reason to be wary. In contrast, if decisions are community based and the smart contracts and their maintenance are transparent, they could serve as equalizing forces that keep the rules and their consequences visible. You therefore need to understand the source of the smart contracts, who is in charge of the maintenance of the related code, and who bears the liability in the event of an error. Smart contracts and the rules

a. Gartner defines a *smart contract* as a computer program or protocol, typically running on a blockchain-based technology platform, that facilitates, verifies, or executes business processes. These business processes could be triggered by events, on-chain and off-chain transactions, or interactions with other smart contracts. Business rules are defined in the smart contract, which automatically enforces the rules by allowing the performance of a transaction without third parties, making a smart contract self-executing. A *technology stack* is a combination of system software components and tools used in the creation and support of an application. It includes related programs, runtime environments, frameworks, and programming languages.

they execute should never be regarded as a technical issue. It's a business issue, as control of the contract gives control over the value produced and exchanged by the blockchain.

TECHNOLOGY

There's a battle under way in the technology sector to define the dominant systems used to build blockchain solutions. The stakes are as high as those of the past, the combatants both familiar (IBM, Oracle, Intel, SAP, Microsoft, Samsung SDS, etc.) and new (Ethereum, R3, Quorum, NEO, Digital Asset, Fisco, and over a hundred other potential platforms). The familiar competitors stake their authority on worn positions: trusted source versus open source, stability versus flexibility, and so on. Vendors are going hard after enterprise blockchain budgets. Some have designed specific solutions to common industry issues. Others claim that they can build anything.

Many of the solutions that are already live are transitional; their primary purpose has been to fulfill an immediate need or opportunity. They should be viewed as learning platforms, not as long-term solutions, since blockchain technology is continuously evolving and maturing. The ongoing maturation of blockchain technology is important, particularly with blockchain-inspired solutions, since solutions built with centralized governance cannot be easily (if at all) decentralized later. The technology designed for a centralized architecture cannot be used for decentralization, and vendors have no incentive to enable it, especially if the blockchain uses *their* system and technology stack. Open solutions built from the outset to handle some degree of decentralization will allow you to upgrade faster and evolve in that direction over time.

BLOCKCHAIN-INSPIRED ARCHETYPES

The four business currencies offer a lens for evaluating the hundreds of blockchain-inspired solutions in development right now. How does a solution handle data? Who gets access? Who defines the contracts?

Who develops the technology? Answers to these questions clarify the balance of benefits and risks in blockchain solutions on offer from trading partners or vendors. Having these answers could also help you decide in advance what qualities you want in the solutions you build or buy.

You'll be asking these questions often, given the explosion in blockchain activity we see in the market. The hundreds of blockchain-inspired proofs of concept, pilots, and implementations under way vary in how they deal with the four currencies. In light of those differences, we have identified five blockchain-inspired archetypes (figure 2-2). Some of them keep open the possibility of evolving to a decentralized, tokenized model over time; they can migrate from blockchain-inspired to blockchain-complete if design principles permit. Other archetypes reinforce centralized operational approaches that are incompatible

FIGURE 2-2

The blockchain-inspired archetypes

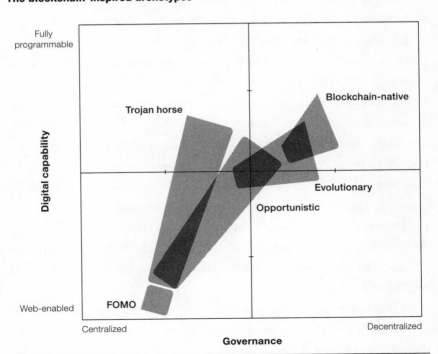

with blockchain-complete solutions. You incur risk in adopting any new technology, but you will benefit from taking a first step. To help you decide how, we present a closer view of the five archetypes.

FEAR OF MISSING OUT (FOMO) SOLUTIONS

In a recent conversation Christophe had with leaders of an auto insurance company seeking to develop a blockchain solution for automotive claims handling, we asked a question common to these kinds of client interactions: Why blockchain? The leaders wanted to capture and store information about the driver, the vehicle, and the context of an accident, believing this data could streamline accident investigations through a more transparent process. Yet none of what they described requires blockchain. In fact, blockchain in this closed, centralized context could be more expensive, complex, and higher-risk than alternatives built with standard database and messaging technology. Christophe told the leaders what he thought, but they shrugged and said their senior leadership had told them to find a way to use the technology. The company's desire to use blockchain is less a reflection of the technology's relevance to the problem than it is a reflection of pressure on organizations to keep up with digital trends.

We regularly hear from organizations developing blockchain tests or pilots to address an in-house problem that could be solved better, faster, and more cheaply with an established approach. For some leaders, the hype around blockchain creates tunnel vision that makes them unable to consider alternatives. Other leaders know that they should compare different options but see no value in doing so; their boss, under the influence of blockchain FOMO, has said go blockchain or go home. As the CIO of a regional financial services firm told David at Gartner's Middle East Symposium in 2018, "You don't understand; my CEO told me to do blockchain."

FOMO-driven blockchain projects are unlikely to save costs or create value. They are not pointless, however. Exploring an advanced digital solution like blockchain could send a message to the market that your organization is innovative and on top of current trends. That message can cause prospective customers to give you a second look. It can also force competitors to invest time and resources for similar FOMO reasons.

Yet leaders need to be wary of developing a false sense of security about their knowledge of blockchain and carefully control the money they spend on these kinds of solutions. If a project fails to produce value, some leaders will believe they tried blockchain and failed, when they simply had the wrong use case. Too many FOMO blockchains damage the credibility of blockchain in the business. In addition, when businesses insist on preemptively implementing blockchain solutions in the enterprise, these solutions often burden the existing systems and processes and create additional costs that bring no increase in efficiency.

TROJAN HORSE SOLUTIONS

For this archetype, one powerful actor or a small group of actors develops a blockchain-inspired solution and invites—or sometimes requires—the ecosystem participants to use it. These solutions are by definition blockchain-inspired because they have a single owner or a small collective of owners who are known to each other. Though some providers with centralized solutions will use words such as *decentralization* and *consensus* (a feature of decentralized systems), the archetype's central ownership strongly indicates that the system design is centralized as well.

We've dubbed these solutions *Trojan horses* because they look attractive from the outside. They have a respected brand behind them, they enjoy seemingly strong technological foundations, and they address known, expensive, and wide-reaching problems in an industry. Yet the price of admission is potential exposure of proprietary data and process and commercial activity without equal access to the same. Viewed through the lens of the business currencies, Trojan horse solutions require the participants to relinquish some control over their data and contracting terms in exchange for access to markets and technology.

Walmart's food-tracking blockchain appears to fall into this category.[13] This solution was developed to track the produce supply chain. Walmart was reportedly motivated by the desire to prevent foodborne illness and reduce the costs of produce contamination. In the non-blockchain environment, it can take weeks or longer to pinpoint the exact farm or processing plant responsible for a contamination, and dozens of people can fall ill in that time. Such an outbreak occurred in the United States in late November 2018 involving romaine lettuce, which disappeared from store shelves for more than a month after the incident.[14] These events waste uncontaminated produce and damage brand reputation. Complete, accessible records will allow stores like Walmart to more quickly pinpoint the origins of a contamination and stop it at its source.[15]

Undeniably, the industry needs better ways to stop food contamination. Yet once supply chain partners input their data to a centralized system, those companies risk getting locked in to sharing their data with that system but without due compensation for that information.

The potential long game for Trojan horse blockchain-inspired solutions follows the path of market disintermediation—a path cut by powerful channel partners since the beginning of the industrial age. At first, these dominant firms encourage trade partners to participate by offering a solution to an existing problem and access to a desired end customer. But once in the system, the participants are locked in— the platform owner can refuse to do business with them unless they stay or accept new terms and conditions.[16] Over time, these Trojan horses can analyze the platform data and shift sourcing to the lowest-cost or lowest-leverage actors in the network. They can also gradually pressure producers to increase quality, reorient production, and lower costs so the platform owner can attract more customers, which encourages still greater polarization of volume. Customers benefit at first in the form of greater convenience, improved products, and lower costs. Eventually, however, the consolidation of power in the market decreases competition, which risks making the supply less reliable, less diverse, less influenced by customer choice, and more expensive. Put directly, Trojan Horse solutions drive deeper centralization.

OPPORTUNISTIC SOLUTIONS

The Depository Trust and Clearing Corporation (DTCC) is the post-trade clearing and settlement intermediary for the US financial system. Like the ASX in Australia, the DTCC manages post-trade processes and serves as a single source of record for trading activity in the US market. In 2006, the DTCC built a mainframe solution called Trade Information Warehouse (TIW). As Robert Palatnick, managing director and chief technology architect for the DTCC, described it, the mainframe was supposed to be "the central golden record of credit default swaps."[17]

"There were a lot of manual and paper-based processes which the mainframe addressed when the solution was launched in 2006," Palatnick said. "But since the financial crisis, a number of exchanges have been created and the volume of over-the-counter trades is down. With the mainframe due for an upgrade and the size of the market decreasing, we found the cost to be too high. So we came together with technology providers, experts, and our clients, and decided TIW represented a good opportunity to do something significant and impactful with blockchain." The company is currently working to design its TIW using distributed ledger technology and cloud-based solutions. When we spoke with Palatnick, the TIW was in structured testing with fifteen participating banks, and managed roughly $10 trillion in outstanding positions.

Like the CHESS replacement in Australia's stock exchange, TIW falls into the category of opportunistic blockchain-inspired solutions. These solutions address known problems or opportunities, and the initiating company has qualified the risks of using untested technology, the costs associated with blockchain as compared with other technological options, and the benefits that are likely to accrue. The solution is blockchain inspired, but there is no pathway to increased decentralization (nor would a central authority like the DTCC want it).

Opportunistic blockchain-inspired efforts offer value through improved record keeping or process-level efficiencies. The Australian stock exchange also saw the potential to derive additional value from market expansion to customers outside its main geographic area.

Organizations also gain useful experience with opportunistic block-chain-inspired solutions. These efforts lend credibility to the technology and to the implementing team and give everyone experience with some of the cultural and technical challenges of distributed data sharing.

For the former CIO of a Middle Eastern bank who went live with a blockchain payments initiative in early 2017, the benefits of oppor-tunistic blockchain-inspired solutions were worth the effort. The solu-tion was designed to connect a defined group of high-volume customers operating in different countries to execute cross-border payments without the intermediary SWIFT (Society for Worldwide Interbank Financial Telecommunication). The system was taken offline after six months, however. According to the CIO, there was "a lack of ROI." Talks with a large overseas partner that planned to use the system col-lapsed, and without those volumes, the system was not worth the costs.

Still, the CIO spoke positively of the experience. He said his bank gained confidence in blockchain as reliable for that specific use case, and his technology team learned how to build and operate a blockchain system. "We got good experience of how it all worked, we spent [very little], we discovered that working in even the smallest of consortia was painful, and our tech exit strategy maintained the client experience." He added, "It was good PR for the bank!"[18]

Put again in the perspective of the currencies, opportunistic block-chain-inspired solutions present some loss of control over data and contracts. But as the bank CIO acknowledged, the solutions do offer some payoff in market access and technology experience.

EVOLUTIONARY SOLUTIONS

The technological immaturity of blockchain *today* makes complete solu-tions difficult to implement in an environment with mission-critical sys-tems. Nevertheless, some organizations are exploring blockchain-inspired solutions that they intend to evolve toward blockchain-complete as the technology matures. To maintain the possibility of a future transition, owners must, from the outset, make architectural and operational decisions that enable decentralization and tokenization, even if those elements are not used in the initial deployment.

Sweden's effort to build a blockchain real estate registry offers a useful example of a solution with evolutionary potential. In much of the developed world, private citizens hold a majority of their wealth in their homes, which people may use as collateral to secure low-interest loans. Despite the economic relevance of property as an asset, buying and selling real estate is an onerous, technical process that is limited in form. Owners, buyers, and real estate agents trade copious documentation at the point of sale, sharing the paperwork with mortgage companies, banks, and legal entities involved in verifying ownership and reviewing contracts and financial arrangements. Each actor may receive, fill out, or review the documentation digitally, but the number of process steps and the volume of people who touch each transaction can stretch the process by weeks or months and introduce error, more so when paper is involved. Additional delays follow after "closing" once the paperwork goes to the government registry office, where it can languish for weeks before officials record the sale and issue a formal title. Those time lags can be costly, limiting opportunities in the real estate market, creating numerous parallel and inconsistent systems, and allowing fraudulent owners to apply for loans or make business deals on properties they don't own.

Sweden's Lantmäteriet, the government mapping and land registry office responsible for regulating real estate, is testing a blockchain solution to clean up the process and potentially save $106 million annually. It formed a partnership with SBAB Bank; Landshypotek Bank; Telia Company, a telecommunications firm; Kairos Future, a management consultancy; and ChromaWay, a blockchain technology vendor. As Lantmäteriet Chief Innovation Officer Mats Snäll stressed, "The goal is to develop a blockchain ledger on which real estate transactions will run, with nodes eventually distributed and ideally decentralized across organizations in the ecosystem."[19] The Lantmäteriet blockchain network could eventually include mortgage lenders, real estate brokers, law firms, real estate agents, property developers, and private buyers and sellers. The aim is to enable a more efficient and transparent record than exists with today's public register of real property.

The first transaction took place in the network in June 2018. In its nascent, "inspired," form, the system operates as a closed or permissioned network running on a limited number of nodes. Each party to the property exchange uses a separate interface to access the network, and the system uses a combination of technologies, including a centrally-managed database instead of a ledger. No digital tokens are included within the initial design. A smart contract validates the process, but the contract is currently not self-executing: it merely validates that an exchange happened; it doesn't execute the exchange.

The Swedish Lantmäteriet must resolve several issues before it can reach scale. Some matters are administrative (e.g., Swedish law requires ink signatures on real estate transactions while European Union law allows for e-signatures), and some are operational (the various participants in real estate transactions have different business cases for participation, not all of which are aligned). The blockchain solution might also surface cultural problems. For example, customers may need time before they accept a decentralized, digitalized process for exchanging their primary source of wealth. Financial questions, such as who pays for the solution and who benefits from it, must also be addressed. Finally, the Lantmäteriet must consider the regulatory governance of multiparty networks. What's more, a group of banks and real estate companies are developing a competing online web portal system that could divide the market or become a better short-term solution. These challenges notwithstanding, promoters of the blockchain land registry assert that the solution could evolve into a network that connects all the actors in an ecosystem in a "permissionless" way. The business currencies in such a solution would trade at a low to moderate risk level for participants.

BLOCKCHAIN-NATIVE SOLUTIONS

The fifth and final blockchain-inspired archetype are the solutions "born on the blockchain." Developed by startups or greenfield innovation efforts, these solutions create a new market or a disruptive approach to an existing business model using blockchain as a foundational element. Some solutions in the native archetype are still blockchain-inspired due to the immaturity of the core elements of decentralization and tokenization, but their development separate from existing enterprise environments will allow them to evolve toward blockchain-complete solutions over time.

One sector with significant blockchain-native activity is higher education. Woolf University, for example, is a native blockchain entity that hopes to become the first blockchain-powered educational institution. Founded by a group of academics from Oxford and Cambridge, it aspires to be a nonprofit "borderless, digital education society," a decentralized Airbnb for degree courses. Woolf University connects professors with students via secure contracts and captures a record of the learning exchange so that the student can get credit and the professor can get paid. The WOOLF is the native token used in the smart contracts, but instructors can choose to be paid in WOOLF or in their country's fiat currency. Woolf University will seek EU accreditation and anticipates a global platform launch in 2019.

Native blockchain-inspired solutions will insert new business models or approaches into legacy industries. Untested technology will be the major currency risk. These solutions will appeal to participants who want to control their own data and experiment with decentralization.

BLOCKCHAIN-INSPIRED SOLUTIONS ON THE PATH TO DECENTRALIZATION

The five archetypes of blockchain-inspired deployments clearly illustrate the wide world of exploration in blockchain. The designs and business motives underlying each archetype dictate both the costs of participation and what you get from it. Solutions based on FOMO can offer some opportunities to learn but rarely advance an organization's digital capabilities or degree of decentralization. A Trojan horse carries its participants steeply north on the grid in figure 2-2, enabling stronger digital capabilities but within a centralized model. Opportunistic solutions carry implementing organizations in a northeasterly direction, but hit a hard limit because of their lack of decentralization. Evolutionary and blockchain-native solutions have the greatest potential to prepare organizations for decentralization and future blockchain-complete deployment.

The majority of businesses that derive measurable value with limited risk will do so with an opportunistic, evolutionary, or blockchain-native archetype. Trojan horse blockchains will gain market attention and possible traction, but are unlikely to bring long-term value to anyone but the platform owner. If time and market pressure were to change Trojan horses' ownership structures, then these prototypes could evolve toward an evolutionary model.

YOUR REAL BUSINESS LENS

WHAT DID YOU LEARN?

Blockchain-inspired solutions will dominate the market until around 2023. These solutions take advantage of three of the five key blockchain design elements and usually address known challenges involving intra- or interenterprise data sharing and workflows. Well-designed solutions will bring benefits, but you need to weigh the risks and costs involved. Because blockchain-inspired solutions lack decentralization as a design element, participants who do not know each other cannot trade or exchange value without a third party validating the exchange. Instead, these solutions usually have one owner or a limited group of owners, and membership is restricted. In this context, the business currencies of data, access, contracts, and technology could be controlled by a single actor or subgroup, depending on the design and purpose of the solution. The five blockchain archetypes reflect varying degrees of centralization: FOMO-based solutions (most in-house projects), Trojan horses (e.g., Walmart), opportunistic solutions (e.g., ASX), evolutionary efforts (e.g., Sweden's Lantmäteriet), and blockchain-native solutions (e.g., Woolf University).

Organizations cannot use blockchain-inspired solutions to create or exchange new forms of value, as new digital native forms of value require tokens operating in a decentralized environment. Thus, the blockchain-inspired phase of the spectrum is not an end game but rather a way station en route to the blockchain-complete phase.

WHAT SHOULD YOU DO ABOUT IT?

As a leader, you will want to review and benchmark your blockchain development against the four business currencies of data, access, contracts, and technology to understand the mid- to long-term value propositions and risks. Ask the following questions with your executive team: How will your organization pursue blockchain initiatives? What archetypes best fit with your strategy? How will you manage your business currencies? If you're already involved in blockchain pilots, proofs of concept, or full implementations, are the solutions inspired? If they are, where does the network data reside? Who has access to it? And who writes the contracts?

WHAT'S NEXT?

Organizations pursue blockchain initiatives for internal use and through partnerships and consortia efforts in a specific market, geographic location, or value chain. Indeed, consortia have been the driving force behind much blockchain activity. Consortia also present a significant challenge for organizations, despite the potential benefit of sharing risk with like-minded partners. You should remain wary of ceding control to a powerful central power or to competitors. To consort or not to consort? That is the question we address in the next chapter.

CHAPTER 3

CONSORTING WITH THE ENEMY

Consortia are playing a critical role in blockchain development. Like the blockchain-inspired solutions they have helped bring to market, consortia take many forms. Some align organizations in a genuine collective model to pursue common goals; others represent the vision of a single, powerful entity exerting influence over industry subordinates. Although some people may view the latter as a partnership or joint venture more than they see it as a consortium, we take an expansive view of a consortium, that is, any group of companies or organizations working toward a goal that individual members cannot achieve on their own. From this perspective, consortia are behind the majority of enterprise blockchain solutions planned or in development.

Blockchain consortia have particular credibility as developers of solutions to address an industry problem or a geographic one. Consider the solution in development by Isabel Group in Belgium. Formed in 1995 as a consortium of four Belgian banks, each of which owns 25 percent of the current organization, Isabel Group is a technology service provider that manages activities like multibanking, and provides solutions to enable know-your-customer (KYC) compliance. KYC is a regulatory requirement that aims to curb money laundering.[1] KYC rules require all banks to collect and regularly update identifying information for customers involved in financial transactions. Compliance can cost banks millions of dollars, yet it brings no competitive value. Other services Isabel Group provides include online identity management, payment management, and security.

Typical KYC practice requires each bank to separately capture information from corporate customers, manage it locally, and update it regularly (typically every six months). Since corporations can have relationships with multiple financial institutions (sometimes dozens), however, this approach creates redundancy across the financial system and leads to inconsistencies that cause payment delays or rejections and disrupts capital flows.[2] Isabel Group believes blockchain can provide a more efficient alternative and is building a blockchain-inspired solution designed to capture and verify KYC credentials for businesses *once* each renewal cycle, regardless of how many bank relationships the businesses have.

Frank Verhaest, Isabel Group's program manager for innovation and blockchain, characterized the solution during a teleconference with the authors in September 2018 as a self-sovereign identity-management tool for corporations.[3] Once its identity is captured, the corporation, which will get access to the blockchain solution for free, can reuse its record with other banks as well as with third parties such as insurance companies or nonbank payment providers, effectively creating a digital corporate passport. The identity records could enable Isabel Group to offer complementary services such as e-invoicing and fraud management. Verhaest estimated the KYC functionality alone could reduce by 50 percent the €335 million annual cost of KYC compliance incurred by Belgian banks.

Those are compelling numbers. But does Isabel Group need blockchain to achieve them? "We could have used an encrypted database for this initiative," Verhaest admitted. "But banks see an advantage in blockchain, because each bank only has access to the data of its own customer and, as a consequence, it enforces a broader scale of trust across the consortium."

Verhaest's comment gets to the heart of both the benefits of consortia and their risks. Leaders like you benefit from sharing ideas and the costs and risks of solution development. Yet you also worry about relinquishing control or exposing proprietary information to enterprises that are effectively your competitors. The benefits appear to be winning in the current market, resulting in the rapid formation of blockchain consortia across all industries. As a leader, you cannot afford to ignore the influence these consortia have on blockchain developments in your industry. Instead, you need a strategy for participation: Why to consort? When to consort? How to consort in a way that brings benefits and limits risk? In this chapter, we'll give you the tools you need to answer those questions.

BLOCKCHAIN CONSORTIA: A CONTRADICTION IN TERMS?

For many blockchain leaders, consortia seem like a natural fit with blockchain. Peer-to-peer networks that enable direct transactions need the resiliency of many distributed nodes operating the consensus protocols that enforce the network rules. As multientity organizations, consortia could pilot solutions from the outset with a core volume of participants. If designed to progress toward decentralization, these solutions would fall under the evolutionary form of blockchain-inspired solutions described earlier.

Despite the apparent affinities between blockchain and consortia, there are also differences. Consortia often form to consolidate market resources for the purpose of developing and promoting standard operating procedures. Examples of consortia formed for that purpose are SWIFT for cross-border payments, the Organization of the Petroleum Exporting Countries (OPEC) in the oil and gas industry, Dairy.com in the agriculture market, or Hulu in entertainment media. These consortia exist to centrally address an industry need, sometimes dictating market terms in ways that benefit large, powerful members, with mixed impacts for smaller players and for the economy as a whole. Such centralization directly conflicts with the promise of blockchain to enable equal participation and access for anyone.

When multiple consortia focus on the same problems in different ways, the issues of centralization become more complicated. Multiple blockchain consortia are attempting to solve the challenges of KYC compliance and trade finance, for instance.[4] Among KYC efforts, there is Isabel Group, as mentioned, and the Nordic KYC Utility, a joint venture in development by five Nordic banks with plans to serve third parties. R3 has also conducted a KYC blockchain pilot, with thirty-nine banks operating in nineteen countries.[5] Blockchain consortia in trade finance include we.trade, Marco Polo, Voltron, and eTradeConnect, each with a slightly different approach, depending on different blockchain protocols, such as Hyperledger (Linux's open-source tools for distributed ledgers on blockchains) and R3's Corda (another open-source blockchain platform).

What would the implications for competition be if multiple consortia gain traction while focusing on the same issues? From the centralization perspective, having just a few consortia options nonetheless creates an environment of limited competition that protects the status quo. In this view, blockchain consortia are seen as an attempt to protect market power by locking participants into blockchain-inspired solutions promoted by central intermediaries. It's the blockchain-as-Trojan-horse model meant to lure unsuspecting leaders with the promise of a "gift" that will ultimately limit their independence.

An alternative is for collaboration between consortia to drive new standards. Having standards without central authorities could encourage market entry, further competition and innovation, and establish the building blocks for interconnected and decentralized systems. According to this view, consortia could facilitate the transition from blockchain-inspired to blockchain-complete and, eventually, blockchain-enhanced solutions. They would challenge the status quo.

Both scenarios of blockchain as consolidating and blockchain as decentralizing are possible. Some consortia will aim to centralize market power, and some will become obsolete as the blockchain market matures. While some groups will merge (like we.trade and Batavia), disband or run aground because they cannot resolve governance and commercial conditions, others will develop systems and strategies to decentralize and evolve to blockchain-complete.[6] During the blockchain-inspired phase and probably beyond, all types of consortia will be at the center of countless initiatives. Let's take a look at the kinds of consortia forming in today's market.

KEEPING YOUR ENEMIES CLOSER

By our count, there were more than one hundred blockchain-focused consortia in 2019, with more forming all the time. The links between consortia members vary widely and include industry, geographic, technological, and business affiliations. Many enterprises belong to more than one consortium.

INDUSTRY-CENTRIC CONSORTIA

Some of the best-known consortia in blockchain are based on industry linkages. For example, the Energy Web Foundation, based in Zug, Switzerland, identifies and develops blockchain use cases across the energy supply chain. The Blockchain Insurance Industry Initiative, originally a European project, was formed to assess blockchain innovation in the reinsurance industry. The Mobility Open Blockchain Initiative includes members of the automotive value chain, and the Blockchain in Transportation Alliance focuses on developing standards for blockchain use in the logistics and transport industries. Industry-based consortia are usually focused on a shared problem. They gather to address industry-specific challenges such as KYC, trade finance, logistics, certifications, and standards. In many cases, these consortia also create an open forum for discussing these issues.

GEOGRAPHIC CONSORTIA

Some consortia also focus on challenges specific to a country or geographic region. These geographic consortia may also have industry connections. Isabel Group, for example, has its origins in the Belgian banking market but hopes its blockchain efforts will help it become a pan-European supplier. The Russian FinTech Association is another country-focused consortium that formed under the oversight of the Central Bank of Russia. The organization branded its Masterchain blockchain, on which it has built and tested solutions for payment processing reportedly to enable cross-border payments with and across the European Union in a way that bypasses the SWIFT network.[7] The Russian FinTech Association highlights how consortia in other locations get involved in geopolitics such as recent consortia activity in China (with the Financial Blockchain Shenzhen Consortium), Luxembourg (Infrachain), Japan (the Blockchain Collaborative Consortium), and the United Arab Emirates (the Global Blockchain Council).[8]

TECHNOLOGY-FOCUSED CONSORTIA

Technology consortia rally around a platform or another technological approach as a first principle for solution development. Hyperledger, spearheaded in 2015 by the Linux Foundation, and the Enterprise Ethereum Alliance, which began in 2017, are two of the best-known examples of technology-first blockchain consortia.[9] Both formed with the goal of enabling interorganizational collaboration, and both promote the need for interoperability between ledgers.[10]

A third technology-centered consortium is R3, which was born out of an initial partnership between financial service institutions and technology providers. R3 is the creator of the (now) open-source Corda platform. As one of the first participants in the Hyperledger project, and because of its financial services industry affiliation, R3 enjoys a certain amount of influence. The organization has been involved in multiple high-profile proofs of concept and pilots in financial services, including a collaboration with HSBC, ING, and Cargill to capture and share trade finance letters of credit, as well as initiatives with the Bank of Thailand and Central Bank of Canada.[11] Because multiparty enterprise-scale implementation has been extremely hard to achieve, however, some original R3 consortium members have lost faith and moved on.[12] (Defections and turnover have also afflicted Hyperledger.[13])

BUSINESS PROCESS CONSORTIA

Business process consortia aim to develop blockchain solutions to reduce costs, friction, or risks involved in business activities. In the maritime industry, the Lloyd's Register has provided financing for Maritime Blockchain Labs, a consortium looking at ways to improve security in the selection of ship crews and improve crew documentation and certification.[14]

Ant Financial, Alibaba's financial services arm, in cooperation with four Australian and New Zealand food production companies, as well as with China's customs agency and logistics company Cainiao offers another good example of a business process–focused consortium. Food fraud has been a huge issue in China, given the country's large and growing import market. In 2008, for example, three hundred thousand infants fell ill, and six died, after drinking formula made with contaminated milk.[15] Ant Financial has an operational blockchain traceability solution, which has been implemented on the Tmall e-commerce platform for a variety of products, including imported milk powder and formula, honey products, organic rice, wine, and liquor, with more than 150 million traced items as of November 2018.[16] A representative from Ant Financial specified to the authors in October 2018 that "each traced item is issued a unique blockchain certificate that allows consumers to look up the provenance, supply-chain, and quality assurance information through the Alipay mobile app. Small producers can also differentiate their products from lower quality copycats on the market thanks to the traceability solution."[17]

WHY CONSORT?

Members of blockchain consortia usually collaborate around a common interest—industry, geographic location, technology, or business process. Yet these interests are clearly not mutually exclusive. A finance-focused consortium may also standardize on a particular technology, for example. Or members may come from the same country but have a common goal of enabling geographic expansion for participants.

Agreement on basic concerns or approaches is rarely enough to motivate long-term collaboration, however. On the contrary, blockchain consortia undergo a great deal of churn. Enterprises and business leaders join one or several consortia, participate for a time, and then depart again, usually to join a different consortium within a few months. Several advantages of collaboration may encourage members to remain connected in the longer term.

LEARNING

Business leaders are often motivated to join consortia to exchange ideas and gather information—sometimes even to collect competitive intelligence. Though ideas will flow from firm to firm organically, consortia make this sharing more efficient and legitimize the information. Leaders also claim that belonging to a consortium gives them PR opportunities that assuage FOMO pressure from superiors in their organization. Buzz, or the illusion of it, buys them time to get at the substance of blockchain for their firm.

Even strong learning benefits are not usually enough for leaders to maintain membership over the long term, however. When asked to increase a commitment—for example, by investing in or integrating to a consortium-built solution—leaders may decide that there isn't enough direct benefit to take that next step. Those who maintain participation often do so on the basis of more-quantifiable benefits.

BLOCKCHAIN AS A GREAT CONVERSATION STARTER

Leaders in some sectors often have common experiences and ideas for collaboration, but they don't always find ways to come together to share them. People in highly regulated industries in particular may hesitate to meet with others in their industry for fear that doing so will cause them to run afoul of antitrust laws.

"Blockchain allowed us to get in a room and talk, and we discovered there are areas we could agree on for a digital way of working," said Rebecca Hofmann, an executive in operations and technology excellence at the Norwegian energy firm Equinor.[18] Her introduction to blockchain came in 2014 at a conference, where various people she knew in the energy sector told her about the need for an energy blockchain forum to facilitate understanding, collaboration, and the exploration of sector opportunities. Within a few months, Hofmann had founded the US Oil & Gas Blockchain Forum. Members now include Equinor as well as Chevron, ConocoPhillips, ExxonMobil, Repsol, Pioneer Natural Resources, and Hess.

Hofmann believes that blockchain opened the door for the companies to come together in a way they couldn't in the past to discuss both blockchain-specific and other needs. "To me," she said, "that is more significant than the blockchain technology itself, though without blockchain we wouldn't have all been able to get in the room." They had tried to collaborate before. "We have many nonprofit standards boards that have tried to bring additional efficiency to the industry," Hofmann said. "We just have never trusted each other so processes between the parties have stayed fragmented. We are all competitors, but we are also partners, and we have a stigma on us that we don't trust each other. Blockchain promises a centralized trust factor. I think it is allowing people to say, 'Wow if there is a place where all the companies could interact in real time and we all get a copy of that one source of truth, and we can trust that source because it's cryptographically locked, that is very interesting.' That has opened a door for us to say, 'Let's talk about this.'"[19]

Since she founded the forum in February 2018, it has split into two operating groups: the original US Oil & Gas Blockchain Forum, which is focused on continued learning and networking around blockchain technology for the energy industry, and, in January 2019, the OOC Oil & Gas Blockchain Consortium, which focuses on collaborative development of blockchain solutions. Each of the four solutions in development when we spoke to Hofmann focuses on integrating and transforming processes in the oil and gas industry. In this industry, some processes, such as seismic data management, truck ticketing, approval for expenditures, balloting, and joint venture billing exchange, are highly fragmented with paper-based documentation.

The energy sector does not appear to be alone in its desire to foster better collaboration and alignment opportunities. Jean-François Bonald, Blockchain project leader at RCI Bank and Services, which provides financing and services for the customers and dealership networks of Renault-Nissan-Mitsubishi, expressed views similar to those that motivated Hofmann to form her group. "By definition," he said, "you cannot make a distributed ledger on your own. The consortium enables us to group with other banks . . . [A]s part of it we are forced to agree first on the rules of engagement and be in agreement on how decisions are made." The collaborative aspects, he believes, are critical. "If one party takes over, the blockchain will not work. This is about breaking existing monopolies and developing a new ecosystem. It's about defining new perimeters, new protocols, a new competitive environment."[20]

RISK MANAGEMENT

New technology brings a variety of risks, including retirement of legacy systems, infrastructure costs, integration costs, system failure, security vulnerability, scalability, and speed. Every organization, even companies with strong IT talent, faces these risks. Consortia make it easier to both pool the risks and limit them by group-funding proofs of concept, application development, and beta implementations. A subset of consortium members participates according to rules set up by the consortium, but all members share the outcomes, lessons, challenges, and best practices. The Blockchain Insurance Industry Initiative (B3i) formed initially as a consortium to collaborate on technology solutions in this mode. The organization has since become a private software company, B3i Service AG, owned by sixteen insurance market participants. It plans to deploy a blockchain-based trading solution.[21]

Consortia also limit risk by promoting standards that facilitate technological maturity and thereby reduce industry costs. The SWIFT network for cross-border payments exemplifies how standards help. The network gives bank members one process and mechanism for sending money to each other. Because of SWIFT, a bank in Singapore can lend $10 million to a counterpart in New York after Singapore markets close and get it back before the opening bell the next day, all at far lower cost and safer transfer than could happen with proprietary systems. Standards literally keep money flowing.

In blockchain, a large and complex range of standards will be needed over time. Among these are business standards for legal terms and conditions; funding standards; technology standards for data governance; and interoperability standards to enable communication between solutions. An initiative from the European Commission—the EU Blockchain Observatory and Forum—that is trying to promote blockchain innovation and development recently issued a report highlighting the significance of standards.[22] Similar initiatives are being explored by the International Organization for Standardization and by Standards Australia.[23] During the blockchain-inspired phase, standards development will focus first on common issues within industries or functions. As the technology matures and businesses evolve to enable blockchain-complete solutions, the standards will need to expand to the granular level of the various technologies used to build blockchain solutions and the contracts that run on top of them. None of this will be easy or rapid with significant challenges existing in terms of governance and commercial liability.

Standards also apply to standards of practice. As explained earlier, the future of blockchain comes from decentralized blockchain-complete and enhanced blockchain solutions running on peer-to-peer networks with nodes spanning across the value chain. If your trading partners, clients, and down-market supply-chain participants are pursuing incompatible approaches, the lack of standards hurts everyone. With standards of practice in place, everyone uses the same technology and methods. The standardization encourages participants to test and use the system. With more participants, the consortium can iterate on the solution and improve it in faster cycles, adding new functionality that draws still more participants. (This same process could also drive increased centralization as transaction volumes polarize around a given solution. If the consortium operates in a highly regulated industry and receives approval from government regulators, its ongoing relevance is all but ensured.)

The last benefit of standards for risk management applies to technology vendor validation and consolidation. When consortia develop single solutions for use by multiple members, there are fewer individual buyers of the technology applications and systems. To compete for these projects, vendors must professionalize their development processes and fix weaknesses in their solutions. The "buyers' market" that could result from consortia cooperation explains why so many large enterprise vendors are participating in various consortia. They want to ensure that they are included in the ultimate solutions.

CONSORTIA-DRIVEN SOLUTIONS: FROM INSIDE OUT TO OUTSIDE IN

All organizations have both an inward and an outward focus. Although blockchain-driven solutions work for some back-office problems, you as a leader need to also consider the power of blockchain to provide solutions to challenges that your customers, suppliers, and the greater community face.

INSIDE-OUT SOLUTIONS

In September 2018, the RiskBlock Alliance, a blockchain consortium for the insurance industry, announced its first solution: Mortality Monitor.[24] Designed for the life insurance sector, Mortality Monitor scans social security data to verify a policyholder's death and passes the information to the relevant life insurance company. The goal is to digitalize, streamline, and validate the process so that next of kin can receive life insurance payouts faster and so that fraudulent claims can be intercepted.[25] The solution also protects family members who may not have known that their loved one had a life insurance policy.[26]

Mortality Monitor is just one of the blockchain-inspired solutions RiskBlock plans to build and make available to members of its blockchain platform, Canopy.[27] The vision, as the RiskBlock Alliance communicated it to us in a recent meeting, is to establish the definitive blockchain platform for the insurance and risk management industries and then develop interoperable solutions to run on top of it. RiskBlock already has a number of pedigreed insurance companies among its members, including Geico, Liberty Mutual, Munich Re, and Nationwide.[28]

We highlight RiskBlock not only for the ambition of its vision, but also for the focus of its initial solutions. Like Isabel Group's planned solution for KYC compliance, RiskBlock's first application focuses on back-office issues that create costs for everyone. That is very common. In our review of consortia activity for this book, we see significant, current emphasis on back-office processes, for good reason. Fraud-vulnerable, paper-based processes are clear pain points for organizations. Solving them can produce widespread benefits in the form of back-office efficiency. Leaders under pressure from new digital entrants, however, might not want to limit their experiments to process-based challenges. Instead, they could diversify the solutions they explore to include those with direct impact on the customer. They'll need to shift their gaze from the inside out to the outside in.

OUTSIDE-IN SOLUTIONS

Outside-in solutions address an unmet customer need through superior product design, improved customer experience, or a new business model. Consortia don't typically focus on these solutions, because members view them as differentiators crucial to their competitive advantage. Firms don't want consortia mediating those relationships.

Despite the obvious challenge, we believe nonetheless that neither individual businesses nor consortia can afford to focus exclusively on back-office, inside-out issues. There is too much startup activity and competitive pressure from digital natives to ignore.

Let's use the automotive industry as an example. Blockchain efforts are under way in various silos of the automotive value chain. The efforts included the aforementioned developments at Renault and Volkswagen to capture vehicle history and at various auto insurers to improve claims processing. Both sets of efforts might reduce direct costs for companies, with possible pass-on cost reductions for customers. But the way each of these examples focuses only on a piece of the automotive value chain is telling. Insurers are motivated to reduce inefficiency in their part of the ecosystem; manufacturers in their part. But do those efforts help the customer—the driver?

Drivers view all the issues related to driving through one lens—that of the traveler trying to get where he or she wants to go. From that perspective, the car manufacturer, the auto repair shop, the insurance company, the gas station or electric-vehicle power station, the transportation authority that maintains the roads and collects tolls, municipal parking garages, and other actors are part of the same system. As long as each silo is independent and lacks IoT integration to a network, no part of the value chain can do much to facilitate operations in another. But as each piece gets smarter, transportation becomes more integrated and the separate participants have to collaborate if they hope to stay relevant to the market.

This smart automotive future is very close. Within a decade, the intelligent sensors in a car will be able to communicate with sensors located along a driving route to exchange information. The German firm Bosch launched a startup called StreetProbe with support from the German government to realize one version of this concept.[29] Data points such as driving conditions (*Slow down; it's icy!*); distance traveled (*That's $3.60 for your tolls if you stay in this lane, $5.00 if you switch to the fast lane*); and parking availability (*There are three available spots near your destination; would you like to reserve one of them?*) could be fed to vehicles and their drivers to facilitate decisions. Some of these exchanges already happen through siloed processes mediated by humans. For example, drivers can learn about accidents en route from their in-car navigation systems, and in-car transponders allow toll booths to register car data and charge the correct tolls. Those systems don't interact with each other, however, and they still need a great deal of human intervention to work (you have to plug your destination into the navigation system, for example). Human input won't be necessary as IoT matures; municipalities are already preparing for that future.[30]

When these sensors are equipped to execute transactions, an enhanced blockchain network could facilitate payments and other value-driven interactions such as reserving and paying for parking and drawing electricity off the grid. The network becomes even more necessary when autonomous self-driving vehicles shuttle between multiple owners or operate in a ridesharing network.[31] In that shared environment, the car's information systems will access the identity for each rider; document how many miles the person traveled at what time; allocate energy expenses, congestion taxes, insurance-by-the-hour premiums, toll payments, and accident claims; and execute the transactions.

The recently formed Mobility Open Blockchain Initiative is pointing toward that future with its list of use cases, including ridesharing, usage-based insurance, and autonomous machine payments. Its membership includes insurance companies, car manufacturers, and blockchain technology providers. We mention this initiative less for the solutions it is developing (there are no live systems that we know of at this point) than for its outside-in focus on the ride experience through engagement by the broader automotive ecosystem. As the initiative's CEO, Chris Ballinger, told CoinDesk in May 2018, "What is required to move [blockchain solutions] forward is a decentralized business network. You really have to have common standards and common ways for cars to communicate, to identify themselves and make payments. But if each auto company is trying to develop its own car wallets or its own way of paying tolls, or providing a ridesharing service, it just doesn't work; it's the Tower of Babel."[32]

Ballinger points to an inevitable evolution if consortia are to play a role in blockchain beyond the blockchain-inspired phase. Just as organizations will have to look toward blockchain-complete solutions that can tap into digital opportunities, so too will consortia—if they are to stay relevant—have to facilitate an organizational transition toward decentralization.

WHEN CONSORTIA MEMBERS STILL TREAT EACH OTHER LIKE THE ENEMY

So far in this chapter, we have focused on the role consortia play in the development of blockchain-inspired solutions. We have also suggested that they could facilitate the market transition to blockchain-complete solutions. In reality, however, organizations of all kinds face undeniable challenges in consorting. To put it mildly, businesses that compete directly with each other in an industry don't have a strong history of playing nicely. On the contrary, if you look to the past for positive consortia examples, the trend leans more often toward failure than success.

The experience of the Indian lending industry is instructive. Lending models that bring many banks together to provide capital on large-ticket loans had once been touted as a way to extend credit while limiting risk. Real-world experience showed, however, that the banks did not share information with each other in a timely way. For example, when one bank learned that a borrower was in default, it did not always share the information with consortium members. The failure to share information resulted in fraud, credit default, and other events that increased risk for participants.[33]

Information hoarding like that experienced by the Indian banks often explains why consortia fail. The issue comes down to trust. If some participants withhold information or other assets—such as access to technology, patents, resources, or talent—then the consortium cannot function equitably. Of course, sharing is not always institutionally or technically easy. Consortia in highly regulated industries like oil and gas or financial services have to abide by strict customer privacy laws. Because these industries have in the past drawn unwanted attention from regulators concerned about antitrust collusion, leaders may feel that the effort to find a middle ground between sharing and overstepping regulatory boundaries is too difficult to bother with.

Even when regulation is less of an issue, organizations find it hard to collaborate in the long term. Our colleague Dwight Klappich shared with us his experience promoting cooperation in the supply-chain industry:

I was with a vendor that built a transportation system in 1992 that could simultaneously optimize inbound and outbound freight. Twenty-six years later, companies have been very successful optimizing outbound freight, but a very small percentage of companies have successfully automated inbound freight. Why? Inbound transportation is an ecosystem enablement and governance challenge where there are potentially thousands of suppliers and hundreds of logistics service providers spread across many geographically scattered locations. On-boarding these participants on to a common platform is hard enough, but how do I get suppliers to consistently do what they are supposed to do, when they are supposed to do it, how they are supposed to do it, and in a timely and consistent way? It is nearly impossible. On and on. It's very hard to do initially, and it remains difficult to hold the supply chain together long term because established relationships are fragile, requiring constant care and feeding. Technology is not the issue. Again, we had the technology in 1992, and even better systems exist today, and still there's very low adoption, and even lower success largely due to ecosystem enablement issues.[34]

The choice may be taken from you in the future, in the sense that IoT, AI, and other tools enabling automation may drive businesses together earlier than they would choose on their own. Firms could be forced to integrate their products or services in a way that reflects the experience of the customer—either integrate or capitulate to central powers capable of disintermediating providers. Why not tackle the challenge proactively? Consortia offer a way to collaborate within a structured environment. To make the most of the relationship, leaders need to understand several key business issues.

IN SEARCH OF CLARITY

Leaders should consider the likely archetype that any developed blockchain solution will fall into and, from that context, ask questions about the issues reflected in figure 3-1. These issues could affect leaders' experience for each blockchain archetype and vice versa. The bars reflect the degree of risk inherent for each archetype as it relates to each issue. For example, a consortium designing a blockchain because of FOMO has no clarity of purpose (its level of risk on this issue is therefore greatest). And a consortium with a blockchain-native solution has an excellent level of clarity of governance (low risk). Your answers to the questions about these issues, individually and in combination, allow you to choose relationships that minimize risks and maximize opportunity.

WHY ARE YOU THERE? CLARITY OF PURPOSE

Does your organization have a vision of what blockchain means for customer strategy? Do you know how you differentiate yourselves in the market? Which new opportunities do you want to pursue? Different consortia will be better or worse at helping you realize enterprise goals,

FIGURE 3-1

The degree of risk of consortia created by lack of clarity, by blockchain archetype

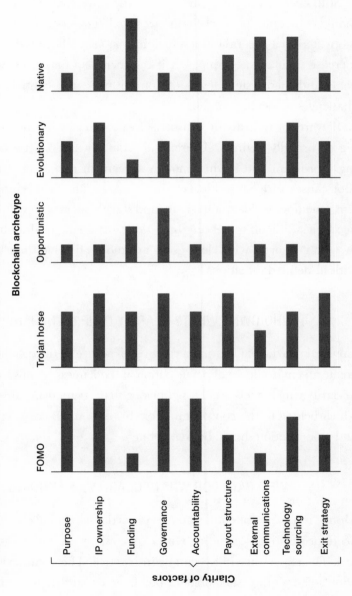

so you should know the answers to these questions before you join a consortium.

Still, even if you and your organization are clear about your goals, many consortia in blockchain aren't. These consortia seem to be motivated by a general interest in doing *anything*. They might still quickly increase their membership, but if the members have widely divergent goals and inconsistent levels of commitment, the consortia will face challenges achieving consensus.

Beware as well about consortia focused on problems that are too big or broadly defined. There is an enormous gap between identifying a problem and having enough agreement about the nuances and root causes to explore blockchain as a solution. With complex problems, members reluctant to share, and stakeholders with wildly different needs, it's difficult to get anything done. As a rule of thumb, narrowly focused consortia with clear goals are more effective than broad ones with ill-defined intentions.

WHO OWNS WHAT? CLARITY OF IP OWNERSHIP

Consortia participants bring a range of expertise to the collaborative. To create an environment of participation and openness, a consortium needs to clarify which intellectual assets belong to participant organizations and which belong to the consortium. For this reason, IP creation, donation, and monetization should be well defined.

WHO PAYS FOR WHAT? CLARITY OF FUNDING

Money is a constant challenge for consortia, which have to balance the need for sustainable funding with expectations around access and control. The experience of R3 can be instructive. The organization started with a few equity stakeholders but later expanded to a subscription model that allowed membership to expand to more than three hundred members and partners.[35] Having that many members gave R3 more funding options, but with these options came a more diverse stakeholder group with more varied skills and goals. Consider, for example, what role technology vendors and professional service firms should play in consortia involving end users. How do you assess the value of different member contributions and recognize or compensate them? What should the payout structure look like? Balancing financial flexibility with auditability is critical.

WHO DECIDES WHAT? CLARITY OF GOVERNANCE

Consortia need clear governance rules. Do all members have equal voting rights, or is there a tiered membership? Do voting members pay for their position in the voting pool, or do leaders get elected to voting positions? Are the rules based on a majority, a plurality, or unanimity? Who is in charge of running the consortium operations? To whom is the management team accountable? How is the board structured? Is it a nonprofit or a for-profit enterprise? How are objections or concerns arbitrated? How are regulations taken into account? Which industry's and jurisdiction's regulations must be considered? Do the rules apply across the entire consortium, or do some rules apply only to some teams or initiatives, as is the case with the Hyperledger project? How are the rules updated as business and technology contexts change? Regardless of the answers to these questions, a consortium could use a blockchain solution in various ways to operate the organization, document the rules, and enforce them.

WHO IS ACCOUNTABLE FOR WHAT? CLARITY OF ACCOUNTABILITY

It is important to understand who is in charge or has a say in a consortium. How are decisions made? Who gets a vote? And who is accountable if decisions or processes run afoul of government regulators or activist stakeholders? Blockchain consortia, as we have said, can sometimes operate as centralizing actors. They allow multiple parties to combine resources to create a common digital solution. It is not clear, however, whether they also centralize liability. Does the joint development of a process also produce joint liability if that process fails? Over what or whom does a regulator have oversight: over the consortia, or over the balance sheet of the member organizations? Blockchain-inspired solutions will not sort out the accountability conundrum for you, though their records will be valuable for handling dispute resolution and to clarify the rules of accountability.

WHO BENEFITS? CLARITY OF PAYOUT STRUCTURE

It is similarly important to understand how benefits are distributed in a consortium. Who gets first access to solutions developed by consortia? If a solution generates profits, what are the payout or reinvestment rules? How do the rules relate to the question of who pays? The multiple models that exist for allocating benefits vary with business and industry situation, the type and size of the firms, which members use the solution, and other issues. Equal allocations of cost savings and "profits" may be the most effective and perhaps even the most equitable approach, but such a distribution may not be realistic if the members' use of the solution varies widely. In practice, total equity between participants is unlikely, particularly in groups with a large membership. In light of these complex, changing considerations, you should, before participating in a consortium, understand the present rules on benefits and the policies for adjusting them in the future. You must also recognize how the rules could change, especially with a Trojan horse consortium, which could be generous with benefits at first to attract users and to encourage lock-in.

WHO GETS TO TALK OR TAKE CREDIT? CLARITY
OF EXTERNAL COMMUNICATIONS

Members need general rules on communication about the consortium. Where do public relations and marketing materials originate, and who needs to know about them or sign off? If an individual member is involved in a use case, can the member talk about it? What information can the person share? With whom and how do they clear what they will talk about with the people designated to represent the consortium publicly? The issues to consider have to do with liability, compliance, and the quality controls enforced by different member organizations. While doing research for this book we spoke to members of consortia who did not agree 100 percent with what other members were saying about the organization. Such mixed messaging can damage the trust fabric of the consortia and can have legal and commercial ramifications besides. Be sure you know what the rules of communication are.

HOW ARE TECHNOLOGY DECISIONS MADE? CLARITY OF TECHNOLOGY SOURCING

Blockchain consortia often conduct tests or pilot projects, and many of these efforts involve third-party technology vendors or service providers. The need for outside expertise raises important questions about how technology will be selected and paid for, and how to avoid vendor bias by powerful members. How will the consortium share implementation lessons and best practices with all members? Who pays for solution integration at an individual enterprise level, and how will solutions accommodate existing systems and processes? What obligations do members have to use a consortia-developed solution? How will upgrades and other changes to the solution be agreed on? Which technology standards will apply? What implications will the technology selection have on an individual enterprise's security policy? Perhaps most critically, will an individual enterprise's technical debt increase?[36] When consortia-built technology does not fit into the broader architecture of individual members, the members incur additional costs and operational issues.

HOW DO YOU GET OUT? CLARITY OF EXIT STRATEGY

Consortia rules usually define how members participate, but they rarely clarify the exit path for members when a consortium's goals no longer align with a member's goals. Leaders need to understand both the entry and the exit rules so that they can decide whether the risks of potential lock-in are worth the gains of participation.

Exit strategies also allow you to define the boundaries of your financial, technological, process, and data commitment to the consortia, and what to do when the goals of the consortia no longer fit with your priorities. If there is no roadmap for exiting, consider this omission a red flag.

YOUR REAL BUSINESS LENS

WHAT DID YOU LEARN?

Consortia are playing an active role in the development of blockchain-inspired solutions. Organizations turn to consortia to consolidate market resources and limit liability as they engage in early exploration of blockchain. Members of consortia enjoy active engagement with others in their industry, when they normally view any other groups as competitors. For some members, this engagement establishes a spirit of collaboration and enables a broader level of trust.

Scores of consortia have formed in just a few years to promote the interests of certain industries, countries, and technology platforms. Powerful firms with vested interests in protecting centralized operations and value chains will establish consortia to achieve market dominance and to promote Trojan horse solutions that lock in the participants.

WHAT SHOULD YOU DO ABOUT IT?

Consorting with the enemy requires careful consideration, depending on your vision for your organization and how you aim to exploit blockchain. First, make sure your organizational strategy regarding blockchain fits in with the intentions and engagement model of the consortia in your industry or geographic area. Second, categorize the prospective consortia by their blockchain-inspired archetypes—FOMO, Trojan horse, opportunistic, evolutionary, or native—and decide which types you are likely to explore. Third, maximize your opportunities by gaining clarity about nine important considerations for the relevant consortia: purpose, IP ownership, funding, governance, accountability, payout structure, external communications, technology sourcing, and exit strategy.

WHAT'S NEXT?

We expect consortia and the solutions they develop to evolve along the decentralization continuum. As they mature, consortia will consider how tokens and tokenization could improve their solutions. In the next chapter, we explore tokenization and how it will drive new forms of digital value and growth.

PART TWO

BLOCKCHAIN-
COMPLETE
SOLUTIONS

CHAPTER 4

GAME ON FOR TOKENIZATION

Tokens enable the exchange of value and have done so for centuries. They date back two to three millennia to the use of cowry shells as a form of payment in the trade networks of Africa and Asia. The shells had inherent value as physical adornments, as did the gold and silver coins that succeeded them. As currency and banking systems evolved over centuries, tokens with inherent value were replaced by fiat currencies, whose value was defined by governments.[1]

Fiat has brought widespread benefits in the form of economic stability and safety, but it has limits. Among the most relevant drawbacks to digital environments are its physical form and denomination—fiat transactions have a literal low end (in US denominations of $0.01) and a practical low end somewhat higher because of the centralized nature and costly infrastructure underlying the global payments system.[2] Yet small transactions are becoming more common as devices and sensors enable the exchange of individual pieces of data, watts of energy, or minutes of attention. These digital, machine-based microtransactions, which need to be executed in real time at a macro scale, are not something traditional payment systems were designed to do.

These limits began driving an embrace of digital tokens long before blockchain came to the fore. Beginning in the 2000s, urban dwellers in sub-Saharan Africa began sending cell phone minutes instead of cash to family members living in remote rural villages.[3] Years later in Zimbabwe, after hyperinflation had severely devalued the national currency, store owners began giving minutes instead of change.[4] When used as units of trade, cell minutes became tokens of value, useful beyond their original purpose.

This flexibility is an attractive quality for users of tokens, if not for their issuers. The Chinese social media and gaming giant Tencent saw how users seek flexibility firsthand in the mid-2000s, when packs of Q coins began appearing for sale on Taobao, China's answer to eBay. Q coins are a virtual currency issued by Tencent as payment on its messaging and gaming service, Tencent QQ. Officially, gamers were supposed to use Q coins to buy resources for their avatars. But shortly after the tokens launched in 2002, people started to use them outside the Tencent ecosystem. First, other online gaming companies began accepting them. Then Q coins became an alternative peer-to-peer payment mechanism. Later they appeared as a payment option for black-market services such as gambling or prostitution. The trade in virtual currency had reached $2 billion per year in China by 2009, when the People's Bank of China stopped allowing the use of Q coins for purchases of real goods and services and eventually stopped all Q coin trading between QQ account holders.[5] But the message from the market was clear: Q coins revealed the demand digital users have for a safe and flexible way to exchange value in digital environments. The explosion in interest in tokens—including cryptocurrencies—shows that demand has only grown.

This chapter illustrates why and how business leaders interested in blockchain must embrace tokens, regardless of the noise and potential concerns surrounding enterprise use of cryptocurrencies. In discussing the real business of blockchain, we offer a broader argument for the value of multiple kinds of tokens. We focus on how tokens and tokenization—the creation and representation of assets using tokens—function in blockchain to create benefits for the creators and participants. We show how tokens drive digital business transformation, capture new sources of funding, and create new markets. Likewise, we highlight tokens' flexibility as a means of payment, a mechanism of exchange, and as a tool to reward and motivate participants to allow them to control and monetize personal assets such as data. But buyer beware: tokens are also a helpful tool for digital platforms and further market consolidation. To clarify why tokens could both enable digital transformation of nondigital native companies *and* enhance the power of digital platforms, we begin with an explanation of the different types of tokens that already exist in digital environments and demonstrate how their ongoing development as part of blockchain will drive digital value.

THE SHAPE OF TOKENS

In theory, there could be as many token types in digital environments as there are sources of value. To define tokens generally before we explore their specific use in blockchain, we present the following four categories:

Fiat tokens represent centrally issued government currencies such as the euro, the US dollar, or the Chinese renminbi and are used to facilitate the exchange of goods and services. These tokens are best known for their physical forms, including cash notes and coins, precious metals, and commodities. This physical form limits their direct use in digital environments.

Process tokens extend the reach of fiat by encapsulating a process necessary to use them in digital environments. For example, EMVCo tokens often reside inside smartphones and represent bank or debit or credit card account information; these are used to facilitate transactions in remote environments. Likewise, Facebook access tokens are issued to third-party apps when users click the "Sign in with your Facebook login" function; these tokens similarly encapsulate user sign-in credentials.

Complementary tokens act as a medium of exchange in closed or otherwise limited contexts. Examples include reward points from airlines, hotel loyalty programs, or known brands like Starbucks Stars and Uber cash. Other examples are digital currencies such as Amazon coins or Q coins. Towns such as Brixton in the United Kingdom have also issued complementary currencies—in this case, the Brixton pound—to support local small businesses. Another geographic example of a complementary currency is the *fureai kippu* in Japan, a social service currency that people earn when performing an act of volunteer charity. Complementary tokens historically have filled in gaps where fiat tokens did not provide sufficient incentive over the terms and conditions of doing business to the issuer, and for economic and regulatory rationales.

Cryptocurrencies are digitally native currencies that replace fiat and process tokens and can be used to create new forms of assets. Cryptocurrencies come in several forms. *Utility tokens* are intended as a crowdfunding method to finance the development of a product or service and as an access mechanism to the resulting solution. *Security tokens* give their holders a share in the issuing entity, much as a stockholder has a share in a publicly traded company. *Stablecoins* are cryptocurrencies whose value is pegged to a second asset (a fiat currency, for example), a publicly traded commodity, or another cryptocurrency.

The ten-year history of cryptocurrencies has been marred by speculation and manipulation, usually in the context of security tokens and Initial Coin Offerings. The high-profile existence of fraud should not poison the entire category, however. Cryptocurrencies are necessary to enable the creation of new forms of digital assets and thus new markets. For example, cryptocurrencies enable participants to represent illiquid physical assets in digital form, tokenize them, and trade them. Cryptocurrencies can also trade units of data, certifications, or IP. The cryptocurrency category includes all types of tokens issued or exchanged via a blockchain solution; we will note when a given example of a cryptocurrency presents a misleading impression about the whole category.

TOKENS IN ACTION

To see how the different token types operate in a digital environment, let's look at a real-world situation as common as planning a vacation (figure 4-1). Imagine that a digital platform like Travelocity or Expedia, or even Facebook, would use tokens to support vacation planning. If that were the case, planning would start as it does now, with the customer making basic decisions about when, where, and who to travel with. The customer might likewise consider other details such as hotel or airline preferences, favorite kinds of food or restaurants, and interesting excursions. In the brick-and-mortar world, travelers share this information with their human travel agent. On the internet, they use the templates available on travel brokerage websites. These sites function as data brokers, since they use customer information to attract marketers in the various travel silos and generate revenue. In our tokenized environment, the information about the traveler's plans goes to one of these data travel brokers (step 1 in figure 4-1).

On receiving the customer's data, the data broker would take the information and capture it in a tokenized form, thus creating data tokens. In our illustration, the tokens are stored in a digital wallet under the control of the data broker. There could be different tokens representing different combinations of data needed by the vendors providing travel services, including airlines, hotels, restaurants, tour providers, and the like. Those vendors would respond in tokenized form with product offers. The vendor-issued tokens are captured in the wallet managed by the data broker (step 2 in the figure).

In step 3, the traveler begins paying for and consuming the services, using the vendor-issued tokens while on the trip, for example, checking into the hotel and consuming services there. Tokens could continue to play a role while the traveler is on vacation (as in step 4). For example, when the traveler accepts an offer of an extra night from the hotel, the offer could come with extra tokens to use for room service, for a drink at the hotel bar, or for a room upgrade. In these contexts, the tokens encourage travelers to stay within the provider's commercial ecosystem.

FIGURE 4-1

Tokens in a centralized digital context

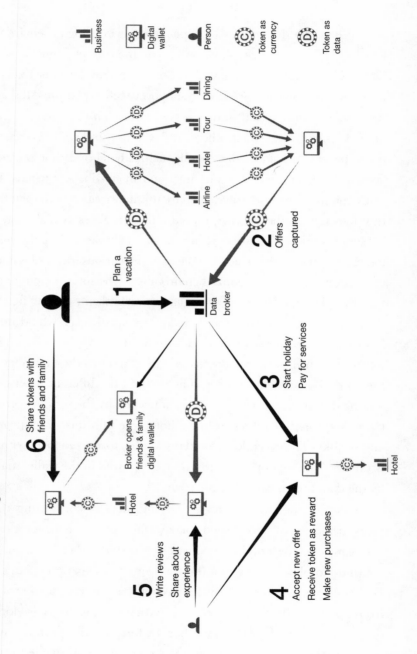

Both on vacation and after returning, the traveler might upload pictures, restaurant reviews, and tour raves to various social media feeds, which could include the data broker (step 5). The data broker coordinates with the vendors to encourage these word-of-mouth reviews by tokenizing an offer of a free night or a free meal in exchange for a review. The traveler can save these tokens for another trip, use them at a different location owned by the provider, or share the tokens via the digital wallet with friends who decide to follow in the traveler's footsteps (step 6).

WHEN TOKENS MEET BLOCKCHAIN

Thus far, we have focused on the various forms that tokens take in digital and physical environments absent the benefits of blockchain. When tokens are used in a blockchain, furthermore, they are designed to fulfill at least one of three purposes.

First, they can *maximize existing value* for the issuer. When a token's purpose is to maximize value, the token encourages customers to take actions that directly or indirectly benefit the issuer. Reward points, identity tokens, and tokenized KYC information are all examples of how a company might tokenize an existing resource and manage it within a blockchain to easily issue it, track it, and allow owners to use it. The goal is to increase customer convenience or reduce friction to enable more loyalty or trade. In the vacation example, when the hotel provides tokens as a reward to travelers who accept additional offers such as a room upgrade, those tokens maximize value.

Second, a token can *represent value*. Cryptocurrencies can be thought of as representations of value. Most literally, bitcoin represents the value of electricity and computational resources used by bitcoin "miners"[a] that

a. *Bitcoin mining* is the computational process whereby, via distributed consensus, transactions are authenticated, verified, and secured on the blockchain. Miners perform this task by solving a computational problem known as the *Nakamoto consensus*, or proof of work. As a reward for the electricity and computational resources they have used, miners receive bitcoins from a token pool of twenty-one million bitcoins that was created at the inception of the network. These tokens can then be used for other purposes in the bitcoin ecosystem.

run the algorithm that authenticates users and validates transactions.[6] With bitcoin, because tokens are also the incentives for miners' participation in operating the network, tokens also maximize value.

While bitcoin is also an accepted mode of payment on some digital commerce sites, most bitcoin trading is done by currency speculators who value the currency for what it's worth in relation to the US dollar or other foreign exchange currencies—in other words, for what it represents in fiat.[7] Beyond bitcoin, the cryptocurrencies that allow blockchain network participants to transact a real-world asset or a share in one (such as an energy co-op, an investment security, or a real estate property) represent value. Turning again to the travel example, when the vendors tokenize offers such as a hotel room package, they are creating tokens that represent value for their holders, since the tokens are tradable for an asset or a service.

Finally, tokens can *create a new type of value* with a blockchain. For example, tokens can allow participants to monetize formerly unmonetizable or illiquid assets. As Roman Cheng, the president of Taipei Fubon Bank, stressed, "Blockchain creates an ability to introduce asset-backed tokens such as with the account receivables due to the various tiers of suppliers of a large corporate buyer's supply-chain ecosystem. And [it] therefore creates powerful financial tools for these [small and medium-sized enterprises]."[8] Another timely example of tokens that fulfill this purpose can be seen in emerging digital asset markets focused on the exchange of data. Some of these markets will allow users to tokenize their personal or corporate data and actively sell it according to its market value or share it with approved parties.

Edgecoin, for example, has a blockchain solution for education credentials that allows universities to digitalize their student records and provide graduates with a certified tokenized copy to share with employers or other education institutions. Another blockchain provider using tokens to facilitate the exchange of data assets is ClimateCoin, a nonprofit working to make the carbon offset markets developed for institutions and governments accessible to individuals. The ClimateCoin CO2 token can be purchased by anyone, and its proceeds are used to invest in companies involved in carbon offsetting activities, such as renewable energy generation.

Whether their purpose is to maximize value, represent value, or create a new type of value, tokens are, for many enthusiasts, the main point of blockchain, since demand for a particular form of value (what the token represents or the value it creates) motivates the creation of a network and participation in it. Neither the size, the liquidity, nor the worth of a tokenized asset is bound at the high or low ends, and participants in the network can be machines. Tokens thus enable economic activity to expand dramatically to theoretically include every human and machine in existence and every tradable resource.

BEYOND DIGITAL MONEY

The various types and purposes of tokens at play in a transaction as simple as vacation planning should make clear that tokens are far more diverse than you might guess from looking at the current market focus on cryptocurrencies as a replacement for fiat money. We understand the instinct to conflate the many kinds of tokens, given that the Bitcoin blockchain was the first distributed ledger to garner mainstream attention and the first operational blockchain-complete solution. But cryptocurrencies designed to replace fiat money are just one type of token that will be useful in digital environments.

Nevertheless, the hype around initial coin offerings (ICOs) has added to the confusion and warrants a brief mention. An ICO purportedly raises funds in an open-source environment for a blockchain-based initiative. As part of the ICO, a company issues tokens on a blockchain platform and uses smart contracts—lines of code that automatically execute the terms of an agreement—to manage the coin offering and define the rules. Although currency speculation and scamming have been a factor in many ICOs, those launched with genuine intent come with the expectation that token holders will get access to the platform or capability under development. In this way, the token plays a dual role for the issuer: it represents value, since buyers pay for them with fiat currency, and it can create value in the way it attracts users to a blockchain solution. We go into more detail on ICOs and the decentralization of finance in chapter 6.

Stablecoins, or stable cryptocurrencies, are another source of confusion. They aim to match the digital benefits of a cryptocurrency, but without the volatility that plagues market-traded cryptocurrencies such as bitcoin and that deters enterprise users wary of risk. Stablecoins try to mitigate volatility by pegging their value to a fiat currency, such as the US dollar, and holding off-chain a certain amount of reserve currency. Issuers of stablecoins must adjust the supply of tokens to match the reserve. Fiat-currency-backed stablecoins tend to be centralized, because their target monetary variable is centralized. And their use augments one central legacy actor (the government or its agent, a central bank) with another—and one that may be less stable or less reputable and therefore less credible than a central bank. To avoid inherent centralization, a stablecoin might peg its value to a portfolio of cryptocurrencies via smart contracts. Another option is to replicate the actions of a central bank with an algorithm and smart contract to manage trading in a way that decreases volatility.

Though they have their advocates, stablecoins have not been successful to date at maintaining perfect price parity with their underlying fiat currencies. The latest casualty is the Tether coin, which lost parity with the US dollar because of market suspicion that the network lacked the US dollar reserves it claimed to have.[9] The market is not yet giving up on stablecoins, however. New exchanges were launched in late 2018, promoting alternative ways to manage volatility.[10]

TOKENS FROM BLOCKCHAIN-INSPIRED TO BLOCKCHAIN-COMPLETE SOLUTIONS

Now that we have laid the groundwork around the different types and purposes of tokens in a blockchain, let's look at how tokens and tokenization will evolve along the Gartner blockchain spectrum.

Blockchain-inspired solutions in the market rarely include tokens. When tokens are part of blockchain-inspired design, however, they usually serve a limited purpose and could consolidate power for the issuer. This limitation diminishes the tokens' effectiveness, because ideally, tokens should not be static; their promise lies in their adaptability. A business might issue tokens with one purpose in mind and expand that purpose over time as adoption and transaction volumes increase. Customer initiatives could drive the expansion, as demonstrated by the Q coin example above. Or issuers might design tokens to be used under different conditions from the outset.

In the vacation example shown in figure 4-1, the reward tokens acquired at the hotel in combination with a room stay became the currency used by the traveler to pay for a product or service. If that hotel has partnerships with other providers in the same city, the tokens might also be accepted as currency at other locations. You could already imagine such a scenario in the context of one of the simplest token environments: airline reward programs, which can be traded today for services from the reward issuer and from program partners. Inside a blockchain-inspired solution, such a token could be efficiently tracked and stored. The blockchain could even allow program partners to participate as nodes in the network and allow reward token holders to redeem their tokens for any of the constituent services, subject to the business rules stipulated by the network.

Singapore Airlines is developing a private blockchain along these lines to make its KrisFlyer miles more relevant for the travelers who hold them and to involve redemption partners. The traveler can exchange their miles into KrisPay tokens to fund a digital wallet and then use the wallet to pay for services at partner locations.[11]

The intent is for tokens to serve as the reward settlement currency across providers and product categories. Customers benefit from more-flexible redemption rules, including the potential to transfer rewards to family members and friends, implying increased fungibility of the token. Merchants, in turn, benefit in the form of new business and, with insight into customer demand, potential new product development. In this way, tokens in a blockchain become a dynamic and versatile medium of exchange. Such tokens could be used in evolutionary blockchain-inspired solutions to facilitate the transition to blockchain-complete solutions. Beyond reward tokens, the travel industry has shown significant interest in blockchain technology. The International Air Transport Association is exploring how to create the Travel Grid blockchain platform as a service on which a variety of aviation-related applications could operate. Examples include retail applications in airports, airline ticketing, supply chain management, and other functions. The intent is to improve passengers' experience and favor ecosystem participation in the $2.7 trillion aviation industry.[12]

The travel sector is not alone in its exploration of tokens to facilitate increased decentralization. E-sports is also embracing tokens—we'll examine it next.

TOKENS TO AID DECENTRALIZATION

The gaming industry has long served as a testing ground for digital experimentation. Long before blockchain and bitcoin came on the scene, there were virtual worlds like *Second Life* (launched in 2003) and massively multiplayer games like *World of Warcraft* (launched in 2004).[13] Both games have their own digital currencies that players trade for digital and real-world resources. And like the real world, gaming economies have real economic issues, such as resource hoarding, inequality, currency devaluation, digital coin hacking, bank runs, and fraud.[14] This confluence of high tech, entertainment, economics, and social experimentation makes the gaming industry a hotbed of token innovation and a place to watch, given the technical knowledge of gamers and their historical propensity to innovate in-game currencies beyond the currencies' original purpose. Within this fertile ground, e-sports—tournament-driven video game competition—is emerging as a lead contender in blockchain innovation.

E-sports have an estimated viewership of 380 million people worldwide.[15] The market is structured across a global community of game developers (creative studios and thousands of independent game designers), publishers (like Activision and Electronic Arts), distributors (Google Play, Apple Store, Microsoft, and game-dedicated sites like GameStop), gamers competing across hundreds of games (*Clash of Clans, Fortnite, Call of Duty,* etc.), and platforms (console, PC, and mobile). Likewise, e-sports are vulnerable to the same issues that plague all high-volume transaction environments. The industry faces fraud, high switching costs, long delays before game designers or players get paid, and high fees charged by digital platforms, among other challenges.

Several actors are looking at implementing tokens on a blockchain to solve these challenges. One goal is to help e-sports evolve into a more professional structure, like the one modeled by the Federacíon Internationale de Fútbol Associación (FIFA) and other organizations. One path to this professionalized structure sees e-sports consolidating under the power of the major digital gaming businesses. These include game publishers like Activision, which owns *Call of Duty;* and Electronic Arts, which owns the hugely popular e-sports franchises *FIFA 19, Madden NFL 19,* and *Battlefield.* Both these publishers have in-game token systems for some of their properties. Another consolidating force is Amazon, which has an e-sports platform based on Amazon Web Services called GameOn, through which game developers interact to run tournaments, form leagues, and pay players.[16] Amazon launched the Amazon coin virtual currency in 2013 as a gaming and rewards currency for its digital product ecosystem. Since then there has been ample market speculation that Amazon plans to launch an Amazon cryptocurrency, though the company had not made this move by mid-2019.[17] On other digital platforms, Tencent, of course, has its Q coin, which gamers can use across all games in its ecosystem.

These platforms are seeing competition from blockchain startups evolving inside the gaming industry. Gaming company DreamTeam is a well-funded example that launched in 2017. It has a strong pedigree, with advisers from e-sports tournament organizers Major League Gaming and Electronic Sports League. In its first year, DreamTeam focused on *League of Legends* (100 million players monthly) and *Counter-Strike: Global Offensive* (12 million players monthly).[18] On its blockchain-inspired platform, it enables payment and prevents nonpayment and fraud by using the DreamTeam token. DreamTeam reported more than 1 million players by the end of 2018.[19]

Another tokenized solution comes from GameCredits, launched in 2015 to solve the problem of fraud and time lags in payment in e-sports. A key goal of GameCredits is to increase the amount and speed of the payout to developers as an incentive for them to make their games available in the GameCredits store. The company says that the payout can increase from 70 percent of the game purchase price (the typical share offered on Google Play and Apple Store) to 90 percent on its platform.

DMarket moves further away from the centralized platform model with a blockchain-based gaming token designed to be used across games and platforms, so that assets associated with one game can be purchased or traded for assets associated with another. Launched through a connection to Steam, a game distribution platform for hundreds of games, DMarket does for the gaming economy what we hypothesized can happen with airline rewards earlier in this chapter. Its token can be used across properties and vendors, enabling more flexibility, loyalty, and repeat business from buyers.

A final notable gaming coin comes from Enjin, a platform that allows users to create their own tokens to support their games. To limit fraud and double-counting, the Enj coin uses a design element to validate that the gamers own the items they purchase.

The social aspect of e-sports highlights a crossover between social media and gaming. Tokens that allow viewers to reward the gamers have an echo in social media *credits*, tokens designed for use on social media platforms to allow participants to monetize likes.[20] There are a number of new blockchain-based social media platforms aiming to disrupt Facebook, YouTube, and the like, with models that reward participants for their posts and likes. ConnectSocial, for example, doles out rewards whenever users upload content; the company's vision is to facilitate active engagement between influencers and brands they choose to promote.[21] Steemit, another blockchain-based social media site, also rewards content creators with a certain number of coins when they upload content and with more over time as participants view and like the material. Extend this concept to e-sports, and platforms could reward gamers for winning, for popularity with the e-sports audience, or for their sportsmanship. Extend it again for retail or experience brands, you could see ways to cultivate brand loyalty by rewarding customers for posting pictures of themselves using a product.

High user volumes and rapid innovation make the gaming sector a test ground for innovative token development, a place to see how users push the adaptability of tokens and thereby strengthen less centralized models. From DMarket's token, usable across multiple games, to Enjin's approach of custom token development, these companies and others offer appealing alternatives to the ecosystem approach of Amazon, Google, or Apple and model a new approach for companies in other industries.

DATA MONETIZATION

Tokenization can also produce rewards through data monetization.[22] The initial revelations about the vast troves of data captured by large digital companies and exposed to third parties (think Cambridge Analytica) or hacked (think Equifax and Marriott Hotels & Resorts) has helped motivate businesses and individuals to get control over their data.[23] This focus on data control has been a long time coming. Internet users have become increasingly aware that their digital behaviors are captured, stored, analyzed, and sold to advertisers and product developers. This data treasure box is only bigger now with IoT collecting and digitalizing, and artificial intelligence analyzing, information about the physical and digital world.

Blockchain technology also enables users to pragmatically assess when, whether, where, with whom, and how to trade data for value. Already, new data-oriented blockchain solutions are in development. These solutions utilize tokens to value and trade data assets. On a blockchain, tokens can also allow decentralized peer-to-peer data exchange on a global scale using a mechanism that equips data owners with the ability to keep the data they own private until they give explicit consent to a peer to view or use it.

One blockchain solution that provides users more control and oversight over data comes from Datawallet, a US-German startup with a token-enabled blockchain-inspired solution and mobile app that allows participants to agree to share pieces of personal information with marketers in exchange for a digital exchange token. Datawallet's pitch to participants is that they will be paid; the pitch to advertisers is that the information will be timelier and more relevant than the information they can get from some data brokers. (Brokers pull information from a mix of online resources and government census databases like departments of motor vehicles, and many of these sources have inaccuracies and significant time lags). Datawallet anonymizes the data it sells to advertisers.[24]

Datawallet's solution uses smart contracts that capture and enforce the intent and consent of the data owner. In this way, the users are connected with their data, the ownership recorded in the blockchain. These are fundamental requirements for data markets. From the perspective of regulatory compliance, tracking data ownership and consent also provides a way for organizations to comply with privacy regulations such as the European Union's Global Data Protection Regulation (GDPR). For example, in a blockchain, the link from the root information (the personal data) to the corresponding record in the ledger can be severed. Because the separation is auditable, participants can confirm that the right to be forgotten has been respected, as required by the GDPR.

Such tools would help companies involved with data monetization avoid the hefty fines associated with privacy breaches.[25] As more data is generated by IoT, and that data is more readily understandable through the use of artificial intelligence, the role of tokens for monetizing data, managing consent, and enabling data markets will become more important.

Beyond the sheer volume of data and the variety of sources, there will also be a gradual evolution in the technology solutions that enable data ownership and control. To demonstrate how this could work, we return to the vacation scenario we laid out in figure 4-1. Our original scenario involved a digital travel platform acting as the data broker in the exchange, creating and controlling the digital wallet through which the data and currency tokens flowed. The broker has preferred access to traveler data and preferences, thus earning a dominant market position. If it used tokens, they would contribute to more centralization and control over the value created.

Figure 4-2 revisits this example, but this time in the context of a blockchain-complete solution that decentralizes customer data and allows the participant to retain it locally and share it selectively. The traveler can define parameters for how the tokens are used and, with those parameters, how they are captured using a smart contract.

In this scenario, the traveler coordinates the sharing of relevant data with travel providers (airlines, hotels, etc.) in tokenized form and receives offers back directly through a digital wallet or some other interface that only the traveler can access. Coordinating these interactions on a blockchain-complete platform would also create opportunities for the traveler to selectively share data across multiple marketplaces and, as a result, to receive better or more-diverse offers.

Being at the center gives the traveler sovereignty over the data. Decentralization would improve the ability of providers trusted by the consumer to stipulate their own terms and conditions. These companies could negotiate and set their own prices, rather than have their prices guided by the platform's terms. This freedom could drive their participation and innovation. Decentralization of data monetization would favor market competition.

A wave of blockchain startups such as the Sovrin Network, Peer Mountain, Civic Technologies, SelfKey, and Blockpass is showing data owners—be they persons, organizations, or things—how to keep control over their data. These companies allow participants to tokenize personal or corporate information, maintain personal sovereignty over it, and overtly exchange it. In time, the existence of sovereign data will facilitate the creation of new data markets built on consent and rewards

FIGURE 4-2

Tokens in a blockchain-complete solution

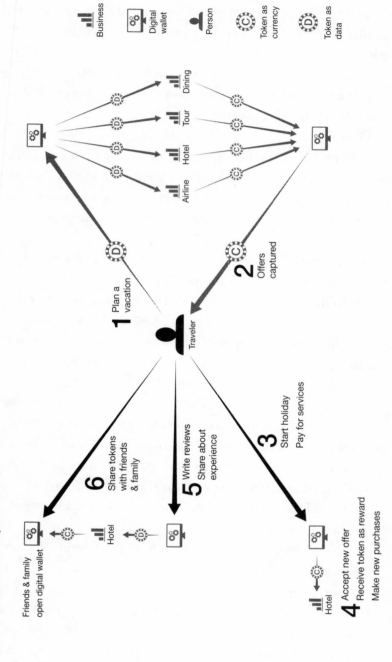

for data owners, while leveling the playing field for a range of companies looking to compete in digital markets.

STRATEGIC TOKENIZATION PATHWAYS

Since tokens can be used in both centralized and decentralized environments, they could follow several evolutionary pathways in the next few years. Digital platforms, for instance, are well positioned and are making investments to exploit tokens (with or without blockchain) to monetize customer data, identity, and other nonmonetary assets and, through these assets, broaden the influence of their digital ecosystems. Besides the aforementioned token experiments by Amazon and Tencent in the context of gaming, Facebook, Google, and Alibaba among others have also been active in tokenization.

Facebook, for instance, is developing its own digital currency, allegedly using a blockchain solution and issuing the Libra as a stablecoin.[26] A possible intention for the Facebook Libra is to create a settlement currency that supports peer-to-peer payments on WhatsApp, Facebook Messenger, and Instagram. Facebook Libra could also function as a reward for users who post (i.e., who share data) and as a payment mechanism across the Facebook domains. None of these scenarios is compatible with a blockchain-complete model, however, since Facebook would control the coin and its use. Moreover, tokens in the hands of any of the digital platforms could be used to nudge customers toward the platform's products and services over those of third-party suppliers. Proprietary tokens could likewise be used to compensate content providers, product developers, and service companies that sell through their platforms. In a centralized context, tokens build market power.

Figure 4-3 plots a selection of tokens on the four-quadrant model of degree of decentralization versus the degree of digitalization/programmability introduced in chapter 1. For tokens, "programmable"—represented as the northernmost end of the digitalization continuum—includes

FIGURE 4-3

Strategic tokenization pathways

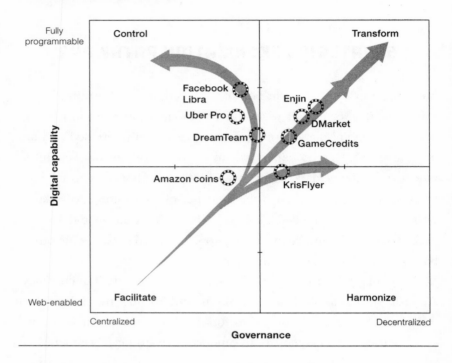

token adaptability. A token is adaptable if its purpose can adjust to changes in the business environment, the underlying asset, demand, supply, ownership, or transferability. (Note that the figure is not mapping the quality of the token programs but is simply showing their relationship to decentralization and digitalization.)

A large proportion of existing tokens aim to facilitate legacy operational processes and modes of exchange (the southwest quadrant). These tokens are playing a tactical role. More strategic use of tokens is underway now. A token that is both centralized in design and programmable will afford the issuer a high degree of control. To build adoption, a digital ecosystem might embrace some aspects of decentralization in the initial token implementation. The decentralization elements are likely to be temporary, however, since the objective is *control* (the northwest quadrant of the figure). Once token adoption reaches critical mass—and lock-in—we predict that the use of the token in a centralized context will evolve to have more restrictions and therefore become more centralized. For example, Uber Pro (the reward program for Uber drivers) has some programmability in its tokens but also a high level of control by Uber, as only drivers with a satisfaction rating of at least 4.85 and a low cancellation rate can participate.[27] The token will only be slightly decentralized because the rules of access aim to influence the behavior of both customers and business partners inside Uber's ecosystem. The destination is the northwest quadrant for this token. This quadrant is also the logical direction for gaming tokens from Amazon, Facebook, and the centralized-platform expansion under way by DreamTeam.

For their part, blockchain-inspired solutions seldom include tokens, but those with tokens could enable a slight easterly move toward more decentralization before reversing course. The token may become more centralized when a consortium or provider achieves its operational objectives or as a way to gain more control over the velocity and fungibility of a token. Jurisdictional factors could also influence exchange, storage, legality, and other characteristics of tokens.

Singapore Airlines, with its experimental blockchain-inspired rewards solutions, could follow that path. The current solution limits the level of decentralization to a few partners. On this platform, the main purpose of tokens is to *harmonize* processes among partners (the southeast quadrant). Tokens in this quadrant have a natural limit on their adaptability. To become more programmable, the network would have to accommodate the business requirements of all partners; that is not the goal of Singapore Airlines and its KrisFlyer program, however. As a result, the token program could eventually become less decentralized.

For e-sports, another pathway is emerging. The tokens of Game-Credits, DMarket, and Enjin are more decentralized than past gaming tokens and more programmable. Their level of decentralization is a direct response to the attempts by digital giants to control the industry and to the diverse requirements of gamers, fans, and developers. These more decentralized tokens enable gaming networks to create value during the *transformation* of an emerging industry (the northeast quadrant). As agents of disruption, these tokens will undoubtedly travel to the domain of game streaming. Google announced its Stadia streaming service in March 2019, and some blockchain-enabled alternatives are already planning to challenge it.[28]

YOUR REAL BUSINESS LENS

WHAT DID YOU LEARN?

Tokenization, the creation and representation of assets using tokens, is not new. Fiat tokens issued by central banks and governments have been used for years side by side with process tokens, such as those supporting Apple Pay, and complementary tokens, such as reward points. Blockchain amplifies the usability and adaptability of tokens, turning them into flexible and dynamic mechanisms for creating and exchanging value in peer-to-peer networks. On blockchains, different token types will be used for different purposes. Cryptocurrencies designed to replace fiat, such as bitcoin, will look to challenge centralized currency models. Utility and security tokens will facilitate new models of crowdfunding, financing, and investing.

Tokens reach beyond finance to enable the monetization of illiquid assets such as personal data. Tokens also offer new ways to manage old problems. For example, they help organizations comply with data privacy regulations, such as GDPR in Europe (important for B2B and IoT data). Tokens can also prevent fraud, accelerate payout (e.g., for gamers in e-sports), and reduce intermediation fees.

WHAT SHOULD YOU DO ABOUT IT?

The maturity of your organization and your industry affects the type of tokens needed. Identify your direct competitors or the adjacent companies that already have token strategies. Once you understand where you are today, you should start to experiment with using tokens as agents of digital business transformation. For example, you could develop a tokenized mechanism that gives your customers sovereignty over their data; this authority will encourage them to participate in data markets, because they know they have control over their information. Ceding personal data control to the data owner has the side benefit of supporting your efforts to observe data privacy laws. You could also explore tokens as rewards and incentives. Rewards serve to nudge network participants to share data and create new markets. These examples show how tokens in a decentralized, blockchain-complete environment could become dynamic and versatile economic agents that expand your market power.

WHAT'S NEXT?

Tokens depend on decentralization to reach their full potential to encourage market participation, data sharing, asset creation, and token diversity and adaptability. In the next chapter, we take another step along the blockchain spectrum to more fully explore decentralization, the fifth design element of blockchain.

CHAPTER 5

EMBRACING CONSENSUS THROUGH DECENTRALIZATION

Decentralization is, in many ways, the beating heart of blockchain. When combined with tokens, the metaphorical blood coursing through the commercial ecosystem, decentralization determines whether you and other network participants operate as true peers with equal ability to derive value or whether some actors reap benefits out of proportion to their contribution. If you hope to participate in blockchain-driven digital markets and derive the maximum benefit from blockchain, decentralization is not optional.

Although the blockchain-complete phase of the spectrum won't begin until about 2023, experiments in decentralization are already under way. If your customers are frustrated about something, we guarantee that some blockchain startup is working on a decentralized solution to relieve their frustration.

For example, Golem is developing a solution for computer users who need a lot of processing power for specific purposes, but whose needs are irregular, and therefore are ill served by cloud service providers like Amazon or Google, which require long-term contracts because of the sunk costs of running a distributed, centralized computing network. Golem's solution allows participants in a peer-to-peer network to rent out the unused processing power on their servers and computers to users who need large amounts of processing capacity. Think of its model as a decentralized version of Airbnb for excess computing power. And like Airbnb, Golem is building a platform with the potential to broker today's illiquid supply. Unused computing supply is a huge market: global server use is just 70 percent of total capacity, which translates into $30 billion in idle servers in data centers.[1] Golem's approach also offers new relationship possibilities. Instead of requiring long-term contracts, Golem can access resources as they are needed and can reward asset owners using tokens.

The company is marketing its first use case, Brass Golem, to computer graphics designers, who need significant power in the short term to render two-dimensional designs so that they appear three-dimensional on screen. Golem has raised more than $17 million since it was formed in 2016.[2] It joined blockchain peers Sonm, Ethernity Networks, Conduit, and others in offering decentralized computing power, as well as Filecoin and Storj—two blockchain startups focused on decentralized storage—to reimagine cloud computing in a decentralized model.

As blockchain startups like Golem gain traction, and as blockchain-inspired solutions of the evolutionary or native archetype expand their user base, legacy organizations will need to explore decentralized solutions more actively. Yet even with these clear competitive nudges, business leaders we've talked to have voiced concerns about decentralization and everything it entails. These challenges span the domains of technological, economic, and social systems and commercial governance.

In this chapter, we tackle a wide range of topics on decentralization. We define the components of decentralization in blockchain, outline the business value of decentralization in an increasingly digital environment, and show how legacy organizations are evolving and embracing decentralization along the spectrum. We also walk you through the major challenges that decentralization poses. We start with the basics of decentralization.

THE EIGHT COMPONENTS OF DECENTRALIZATION

On the surface, the technological aspects of decentralization are straightforward. Instead of a central authority, the design of blockchain gives each participant in the network *one equal vote* on whether other participants are authentic and transactions are valid, according to the business rules that dictate interactions on the blockchain. Participants, can operate as nodes, which are the machines owned or used by participants to run a blockchain consensus algorithm each time a block of transactions passes through.[a] If at least 51 percent of the full network nodes conclude that a transaction is good, it gets cleared and then appended independently by each node to its copy of the ledger.[3] Duplications, double-counted assets, and fraudulent transactions that one node might miss or intentionally overlook are unlikely to be missed by the consensus. The one node, one vote, policy is *the way* that blockchain gets around the challenge of authentication and validation in the absence of a centralized authority.

But decentralization is not just about technology. It is also about how the blockchain defines and executes on the business rules for a solution. It is about who gets to participate as a full node in the network. Decentralization is also about allocating participants' rewards according to their contribution. Overall we see eight primary ways

---

a. Not every person or entity that transacts on a blockchain runs a node; a person can own bitcoin or any other token without operating a node, for example. Only nodes, however, can maintain and update copies of the ledger. Blockchain uses many consensus algorithms. Some of the more common ones are proof of work, proof of state, proof of weight, and Byzantine fault tolerance. Each algorithm operates slightly differently, depending on the purpose of the constituent blockchain.

that decentralization operates in blockchain across the categories of governance, economics, and technology.

GOVERNANCE

Decision making: Participants allow decisions to be codified and executed on the blockchain without a central authority weighing in on them.

Participation: Anyone or anything can act as a full node, assuming the requisite infrastructure and agreement to adhere to the terms of operation.

Commercial ownership and oversight: No single entity or consortium has a majority stake in the value produced on the blockchain. This equitable sharing applies to monetary value and to the currencies of data, access, contracts, and technology.

ECONOMICS

Financing: No single entity or consortium provides or is responsible for the liquidity of the blockchain; a sound economic model sustains the platform.

Rewards allocation: The blockchain fairly distributes rewards to all the nodes running the consensus according to agreed-on and transparent rules.

TECHNOLOGY

Technology architecture: The blockchain relies on a consensus algorithm and a one node, one vote policy to authenticate participants and validate transactions.

Protocol development: Inputs to the solution and the source code come from multiple sources, usually through open-source development.

Network governance: No single entity or consortium has a majority control over the nodes on the blockchain. Participants can have active or passive roles and the freedom to join and exit.

Though each of the eight components can be more or less decentralized, there are clear dependencies between them. For example, a blockchain that has a single owner or group of owners (e.g., centralized commercial governance) is likely to reinforce this centrality with a centrally coordinated technology architecture. Such a design means that the blockchain doesn't rely on decentralized consensus and is thus a blockchain-inspired archetype. Open participation, in contrast, probably relies on a consensus-driven technology architecture to establish trust, since the participants don't know each other.

A CLOSER LOOK AT GOVERNANCE

Despite the current technological limitations of blockchain, these shortcomings aren't, in our experience, the reason why companies hesitate to move toward decentralization. Organizational resistance is.

Leaders like you have told us that they're grappling with how blockchain asks them to hand decision-making control to an algorithm. You and other leaders no doubt have concerns about participating in a network in which you don't know and can't know who is on the other side of your transaction. You are exploring what it means to extract value from a resource (the blockchain) that you don't own or control. The complexity of those governance issues deserves greater attention.

DECENTRALIZED DECISION MAKING

In a blockchain, algorithms execute the business rules and decisions contained in their code. To arrive at that point, leaders have to agree to relinquish control over a respective decision and define the decision with enough detail so that it can be converted into code.

This relinquishing of control may sound like a big jump. However, the journey has already started with some business leaders. Experience gained through the use of AI and the outsourcing of core systems and processes provide stepping-stones into decentralized environments.[4]

Smart contracts hold the code needed to execute decisions in blockchains. Those contracts vary in complexity. Simple smart contracts handle individual decisions or processes; complex smart contracts hold a complete set of rules defining the decisions of an entire operational function, say, all the financial tasks (from purchasing to billing) involved in supply-chain management. These complex contracts are known in the blockchain world as DAOs, or decentralized autonomous organizations. Think of them as avatars for the line of business. In some situations, DAOs will contain all the business rules needed to operate a business, and the interactions, transactions, and value created by the DAO won't have a physical-world equivalent. As an independent business, a DAO will make all the decisions and execute all the processes wired into its programming. Incorporating advanced AI agents will allow these business decisions to be made autonomously by the intelligent systems running over the ledger.

If the idea of handing over decision-making control in this way seems radical, remember that none of this will happen as a first step. Instead, you will begin by decentralizing well-understood decisions such as hiring or staff annual reviews to a blockchain solution before progressing to decentralizing processes like project management or financing and, then, whole corporate functions. The transition to DAOs will likewise evolve first with a focus on processes or parts of a market that are already highly standardized, codified, or automated and that can fit within existing contexts.

DECENTRALIZED PARTICIPATION

As an element of blockchain governance, participation refers to who or what is allowed to act as a node in the network, given the requisite infrastructure. In a fully decentralized blockchain, anyone or anything that wants to can be a full node. A common synonym for decentralized participation is a *public*, or *permissionless*, network. A permissionless network stands in contrast to one with centralized participation, which is called *private* or *permissioned* or even *enterprise* blockchain.

The logic behind centralized participation is that it allows all participants to know who they are dealing with and conform to organizational and operating norms. Many of you have told us you are frankly uncomfortable with the idea of transacting or interacting with an unknown counterparty. Yet maintaining a centralized system with all known participants undermines the foundational benefit of blockchain. In that sense, a permissioned blockchain is like a motorboat with built-in paddles: you're not supposed to need them, so why are they there?

DECENTRALIZED COMMERCIAL GOVERNANCE

Who owns a blockchain? Who oversees its governance? Who takes responsibility if someone is harmed or if other problems arise? In a decentralized blockchain, the answer to the question of ownership is both no one and everyone: no single participant owns the whole, and every participant takes responsibility for its maintenance and operations by operating a full node, running the consensus, and maybe contributing to the open-source protocol and solution development.

On the surface, collective ownership allows for the dispersal of network costs, though decentralization itself carries certain costs. For example, running a consensus algorithm costs the nodes that operate it some computing power and energy (e.g., the bitcoin mining process). Network and system security also carry an associated cost.

Another issue that affects governance is community unity or, as it happens, nonunity. The consensus that enables decentralization at the technical level usually relies on majority rule. If a network introduces a new rule that represents a shift in its vision and goals and some nodes disagree about adopting the rule, then the network can split, or fork. Forks are created when network members disagree on goals and decide to divide into two separate networks (e.g., Bitcoin and Bitcoin Cash). Forks may also happen as a response to an emergency, such as when the Ethereum community chose to fork because of the failure of the DAO project in 2016.[5] In either context, forking has technical, commercial, and legal implications that trouble business leaders who need guarantees about the sustainability of mission-critical systems.

THE EVER-CHANGING STATE OF DECENTRALIZATION

The eight components of decentralization operate both independently and in combination to construct a consensus-driven environment for creating value and distributing it equitably. Importantly, these eight components are dynamic; their degree of decentralization shifts over time. Let's examine that dynamism more closely.

Decentralization in the Bitcoin blockchain—the largest distributed blockchain coordinated through a decentralized architecture—offers a useful view of how a network evolves its decentralized architecture over time. Because of the open, peer-to-peer nature of blockchain, nodes enter and exit as they choose and the technology architecture and the network governance change with those entrances and exits. The reward mechanism of Bitcoin, whereby full nodes are compensated with bitcoin for the work they do maintaining the network and running the consensus, contributes to this trend. Nodes are said to *mine* bitcoin, and the people who run nodes are referred to as *miners*. As the ledger grows, miners need more power executing at greater speed to run the consensus. With bitcoin, miners with the most scalable and cost-efficient operations can mine faster than others. This difference results in market consolidation. The decline in the value of bitcoin compounds the issue by making the rewards no longer worth the work for less efficient miners. They drop out of the mining pool. All this results in the centralization of mining; today, four mining pools run more than 50 percent of the Bitcoin network.[6]

Protocol development is another dimension of centralization in the Bitcoin blockchain. The purported promise of open-source solutions is that because no individual company owns them, they benefit from the diverse contributions of numerous independent programmers. More people catch more bugs and make more improvements in less time than would happen if a central organization were in change. In practice, people have to eat. Developers are more likely to invest in solving a technology problem if they are compensated to do it.

Open-source models also face continuity challenges. When GitHub was acquired by Microsoft in June 2018, for example, the acquisition raised questions about the sustainability of existing open-source solutions in the GitHub library.[7] Some developers will strive to preserve openness such as with the forking of MySQL into MariaDB and Open-Office into LibreOffice after Oracle's acquisition of Sun Microsystems.

Pieter Franken, a senior adviser to Japanese financial services company Monex Group, pointed out, "A lot of contributions to maintaining a blockchain are made on a volunteer basis. How sustainable is this? Who's going to maintain the source code? Who is accountable for a coding bug? What happens if developers have a different view of the world than the company using the related blockchain? How does this impact your business? At Monex Group, we believe that allocating resources to get connected to developers' community is essential."[8]

As a blockchain evolves and its development challenges grow more complex, the skills needed to fix them also become more specialized and thus centralized to a smaller number of developers. The same centralizing tendency applies to Bitcoin. The ongoing development of the platform is being done by fewer people, making it more likely that one developer introduces a vulnerability.[9]

To be clear, there is no evidence that the Bitcoin blockchain has been compromised by the increased centralization of the mining pool or the protocol development. We highlight the example more because it represents a natural experiment in the evolution of decentralized blockchain technology. The lessons offer useful fodder as you attempt to quantify the relative risk and reward of blockchain solutions built with consensus. Keep in mind the comparative small scale of Bitcoin or any of the cryptocurrencies relative to global transaction volumes and business scope. Also recognize the green field in which blockchain began, with no legacy data to transfer, no existing processes to translate, and no established players with vested interests to coordinate and manage.

With this understanding of what decentralization is in blockchain and the multiple ways in which it functions, let's turn to the issues of control and value creation, using the lens of the most pressing question we get from business leaders: what does decentralization allow your organization to accomplish with blockchain?

THE VALUE OF DECENTRALIZATION

Any discussion about decentralization in blockchain must confront an uncomfortable truth: those of you working in legacy businesses face enormous resistance to decentralization. It is the rare legacy business building a blockchain solution today with all five elements. You often hear elaborate justifications for why decentralization won't work. Some of the most common we hear are these:

- A centralized system clears transactions faster than can be achieved with a decentralized system.

- A known actor has to be in control for security or regulatory reasons.

- Your partners won't support it.

- Centralized systems are less energy intensive.

- The volume of data involved in each transaction, or the complexity of the business process, precludes decentralization.

- You need to be centralized (and in control) because your participants lack the technology capability to run a node.

- Participants in a blockchain don't want to expose their transaction data, or perhaps their identity.

None of these arguments are inaccurate or ill informed at face value. Given today's technological capabilities, centralized systems *do* often operate faster. They are also often less energy intensive (depending on the operational architecture) and better able to handle transactions involving huge volumes of descriptive data. Centralization can give regulators single throats to choke, and it does allow powerful actors to manage and control standardized processes and value chains. Finally, centralized systems can be easier for the average information systems team to manage.

The preceding points aren't arguments for centralized design in blockchain, however. They are simply arguments for using traditional data management when you need or want centralized coordination and oversight with trusted counterparts. More to the point, these arguments are self-imposed constraints. Instead of imagining what could be possible in a business environment defined by decentralization, you are shoehorning blockchain into your organization's existing centralized structure, with its top-down hierarchy. This fixed mindset is creating a kind of strategic tautology, whereby legacy organizations are focusing on blockchain as a tool for solving high-cost internal or ecosystem challenges and then rationalizing that the solution they designed does not need decentralization, because the problem it solves applies to a closed network of known participants. To break out of this circular thinking, you can shift perspective. Instead of focusing on why you don't need decentralization, consider what it could do for you.

WHY DECENTRALIZE?

As we described earlier, decentralized systems redefine the terms of engagement away from winner-take-all economics toward a more equitable system in which rewards are distributed according to the participants' contribution and accountability is transparent. Consider what this equitable distribution looks like for the business currencies introduced in chapter 1: data, access, contracts, and technology. As we've noted, data is the primary currency driving the digital economy, so data access and control (as enabled by contracts) are the primary enablers of digital capabilities. Access and control are not the same thing, of course, but they merge in centralized transactional environments. On a digital platform like Amazon or Alibaba or a Trojan horse or opportunistic blockchain-inspired solution, for instance, participants implicitly pay for access by exposing their proprietary data, which the platform owner captures *in addition to* a percentage of each sale or fee for a service. The fee revenue is a onetime input for the platform, but the value of the data repeats multifold as the platform owner exploits it down-market to inform advertising, product placement, product design, supply-chain partnerships, and so forth. In sum, centralized environments operate according to an informal contract that requires participants give up control over their data in exchange for access to customers or technology, or both.

Decentralized environments like blockchain offer an alternative that allows for a separate negotiation of access and control over data in digital contexts. As we demonstrated in chapter 4, tokenization allows participants—whether they are people, organizations, or things—to capture data in a tradable form and then share it in whole or in part with counterparties to generate new sources of revenue. Combining tokenization with decentralization gives participants control over how they share that information and allows the value from that exchange to accrue to them. There is no third party to negotiate a data exchange without the knowledge of the data owner. In a decentralized environment, complementary technologies such as identity and access management tools and confidentiality systems like zero-knowledge proofs give participants even tighter reins on the information they share, who they share it with and how they share it.[b] For example, enterprises can guarantee that confidential data has been delivered to another party without sharing the details of the underlying information. This capability would have wide-ranging implications for every industry sector.

---

b. *Zero-knowledge proofs* are messaging protocols that enable individuals and enterprises to confirm that data related to them is correct without transmitting the information or sharing it with the entire network. These proofs offer an alternative way for participants in a peer-to-peer network to transact and exchange value without exposing proprietary data that they don't want unknown actors to see—even if the information is pseudonymous.

In the corporate banking segment of the financial services industry, trade finance is one domain using such methods to improve the process of issuing purchase orders. Through the use of platforms such as eTradeConnect, financial institutions can avoid overfinancing by cross-referencing financing information between banks without sharing customer data.[10]

Figure 5-1 reprises the image we introduced in chapter 1 to model the potential combinations depending on the degree of decentralization and the degree of programmability in today's business environment. Companies that have achieved an average level of digitalization for their industry and operate with centralized governance—hierarchical

FIGURE 5-1

Programmability versus decentralization

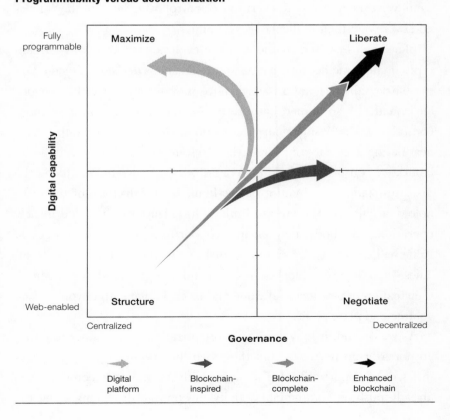

decision making; centrally managed people, processes, and resources; and a centralized business model—operate in the southwest "structure" quadrant. For them, becoming more digital without becoming more decentralized sends them north into the "maximize" quadrant, as in this quadrant, organizations maximize their control over and use of the business currencies. This northerly movement is what blockchain-inspired solutions of the Trojan horse archetype do for you, as described in chapter 2.

Some legacy businesses have managed to claim territory in the northwest quadrant, but the last two decades have made very clear how tough it is to compete head-to-head with digital platforms. Doing so requires exclusive access to a wide variety of data, analysis capabilities, and the ability to convert what you learn into new product development and business models. Those pursuing that path will become *less* decentralized over time as a way to exert more control over the data they amass and over what their audience sees and buys.

Blockchain-inspired solutions of the evolutionary and native archetypes invite some decentralization of the business decisions executed on the blockchain, driving a partial move into or just above the "negotiate" quadrant, so named because in this quadrant, actors have more control over the business currencies and create a new environment for negotiating access to and use of these resources. Participation in a collaborative consortium could help organizations drive further along the decentralization continuum, but without decentralization of the technology architecture, there are limits. Organizations interested in new operational methods, new business opportunities, or new sources of value will therefore aim to move northeast to the "liberate" quadrant. These decentralized blockchains with full programmability facilitate the creation of new forms of value and its exchange with anyone at any volume and price point.

As we've said, it may seem that organizations can choose to either go north or go northeast, but these two directions are not equivalent in terms of opportunity. IoT, coupled with AI and edge computing, is already pushing commercial activity in opposite directions along the centralization-decentralization continuum.[11] On the one hand, the expansion of IoT and edge computing is pushing decentralization by locating computing and decision-making power with widely distributed things. On the other, digital platform providers are reinforcing their hold on power by enhancing their capabilities with AI algorithms that leverage the vast quantities of data they collect from customers, things, their data centers, and other sources.

The competitive gap is ever widening. For the vast majority of companies, the ability to compete at all will depend on their ability to profit from their processes and data using decentralized business models.

THE IMPORTANCE OF STARTING SOONER THAN LATER

Decentralization will offer greater competitive opportunities for the vast majority of companies. That does not mean, however, that an embrace of decentralized governance, technology, and economics will be easy for all organizations.

On the contrary, legacy organizations carry significant metaphorical weight that drags them down and makes it very difficult to change. Rigid organizational processes, out-of-date products and services, old technology, fixed mindsets, and inflexible cultural and hierarchical structures all act as sources of resistance. These sources are why John Childress, an expert on organizational change, focuses on the need for sustained and dedicated effort to change organizational cultures.[12]

Applying this effort to decentralization, figure 5-2 illustrates how an organization must use force to move against the various sources of resistance to achieve business benefits. Organization 1 has more operational and technical sources of friction dragging it down than does Organization 2. For those reasons, Organization 1 takes longer to begin decentralizing its decision making, its other processes, and its business models. The result is a decentralization lag. The longer the lag, the further an organization falls behind those with less internal resistance. Furthermore, the learning cost is strongly correlated with a company's culture and cannot be easily replicated by another company.

FIGURE 5-2

The decentralization inflection point

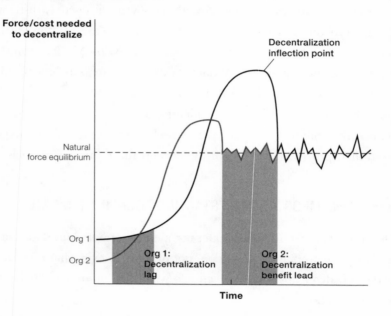

This difference can prevent the laggard from catching up, thanks to the technical experimentation of the leading organization in a given industry. Likewise, time imposes higher costs, since with time, processes and technology grow older and mindsets ossify. As a result, an organization must impose even more force over time to achieve progress.

These factors collectively keep Organization 1 from reaching its decentralization inflection point until long after Organization 2 has reached its respective point. The *decentralization inflection point* is the time when the forces of resistance weaken in your organization and the benefits of decentralization begin to accrue. On the other side of this inflection point is improved competitiveness, efficiency, value creation, and profitability, collectively termed the *decentralization benefit*. Maintaining the benefits of decentralization requires ongoing and dynamic effort, as with any set of competitive activities. In summary, the transition to decentralization will bring challenges, but the challenges only get worse with time if other organizations and competitors start their decentralization journey sooner.

More experimentation is needed to ascertain exactly the best practices for achieving greater decentralization. Incentives and rewards structures will play an important role in decentralization. Tokens can be used to distribute rewards to the people and things that act in ways consistent with the goals of change.

The collaborative software developer Loomio offers an example of using tokens inside an organization to reward group-oriented behavior. For some background, Loomio grew out of an Occupy movement in New Zealand. Benjamin Knight, an Occupy camp manager in Wellington, was inspired by the collaborative decision making process in the movement and hoped to apply it in a distributed environment.[13] From that seed, Loomio was born. Early on, the organization—which operates as a cooperative—created Loomio points and gave them out to reward its first members. The cooperative's founders describe these points: "We have a separate system to acknowledge the work people did for free to get the project off the ground, and the opportunity cost staff wear by accepting pay below market rates while we get the business going. We acknowledge the risk workers took giving their time to an early stage startup with no guarantees by putting a multiplier on points earned during the early days."[14] Interestingly, Loomio points have no concrete value. Only when the board decides that Loomio is in a strong financial position will the points be exchanged for cash bonuses.

In other circumstances, tokens could be used to encourage information sharing across organizational functions. Siloed information is one of the known disadvantages of hierarchies. The equating of knowledge with power in organizations and the resulting hoarding of information greatly lengthens the decentralization lag. But if information sharing is encouraged and rewarded through token distribution, could siloed information sources become more open? The answer is unknown, but we encourage you to conduct experiments to find out how knowledge can be priced and shared inside your organization. Blockchain enables this kind of transparent measuring of behavior in real time so that leaders can better understand the incentives necessary to move the organization toward a new way of operating.

CENTRALIZED BUSINESSES EMBRACING DECENTRALIZATION

Despite the advantages of decentralization, blockchain-inspired solutions are the dominant model in development by legacy organizations. Similarly, the startup community is launching solutions that are more evolutionary than fully decentralized because of the current state of the market. Apart from this common intransigence, some highly centralized organizations are now experimenting with some degree of decentralization.

BANQUE DE FRANCE: DECENTRALIZED ISSUANCE OF CREDENTIALS

Payments in the European Union used to be handled by each member state in its own way, but in 2008, EU payment processes were consolidated under the rules for the Single Euro Payment Area (SEPA) initiative, which requires that payment beneficiaries (i.e., creditors) have ID credentials. Banque de France is in charge of issuing SEPA creditor IDs in France. The manual process is cumbersome and error-prone and requires the transfer of information from hard-copy documents into a database. The procedure causes delays and overlaps with bank KYC processes.

Wanting to modernize the ID issuance procedure with blockchain, Banque de France saw an opportunity to experiment with a new technology, address a known problem, and engage with its commercial bank stakeholders. The blockchain it developed was inspired in design, and the solution the new technology offered was basic; a secure digital portal could have achieved the same end. But the bank sees broader benefits for collaboration and the eventual decentralization of interbank processes. Officers we spoke to at Banque de France said the project created a new level of engagement between the Banque de France and the commercial banking community it serves. The project also allowed everyone to understand how decentralization affects decision making, accountability, and data privacy and permissions.[15]

Banque de France currently owns the software, governs the security infrastructure and the private keys, and co-owns the data. Yet its leaders would like to see the governance model shift over time. One of the Banque de France interviewees told Christophe, "Our role is as software provider and gatekeeper. This is not sustainable governance. It is not a priority for commercial banks, but we need collective governance or this will not work."

That is a remarkable comment for a central bank officer to make. As he articulated it, the vision is to have an open community model that enables more decentralized development, shared costs, and the ability to build new complementary solutions. He compared it to open-source projects like those hosted on GitHub; in the case of Banque de France and its customers, the application's code could be open-sourced and accessible by participating banks. Although the original blockchain was built for France, SEPA credential IDs apply to creditors across the eurozone. Likewise, KYC credentialing uses some of the same information, enabling complementary use cases that would exploit the same platform. Together, these factors point to opportunities for European central banks to collaborate on a more progressively decentralized blockchain credentialing model.

UNION OF EUROPEAN FOOTBALL ASSOCIATIONS: SAFE DECENTRALIZATION OF TICKETING

Another example of a highly centralized organization experimenting with controlled decentralization through blockchain is the Union of European Football Associations (UEFA), the European governing body for the Federación Internationale de Fútbol Associación (FIFA).[16] UEFA organizes some of the most prestigious pan-European football competitions, including the annual Champions League tournament. Tickets for UEFA events are in high demand, and there is a robust, decentralized secondary market for reselling them—scalping, basically. UEFA estimates that only 37 percent of tickets go to primary buyers; the rest go to resellers and sponsors.

Secondary sales create several problems for UEFA. One is security. The union loses the record of who enters its event facilities when the person who uses the ticket is not the person who bought it. The ongoing problem of sports-related hooliganism and rising concerns about terrorism have made the identification of ticket users a pressing issue.[17] Price gouging is another concern. Tickets sell out quickly to bots (or brokers) that swamp official channels. Those tickets then appear on secondary markets at precipitously higher prices. UEFA takes the brand hit when the average family can't afford tickets to a football match, but none of the money goes to UEFA or the teams. Instead, it goes to the ticket brokers, some of which are associated with organized crime. Two more issues are counterfeiting, when a scalper sells a fake ticket, and double-counting, when a scalper sells the same ticket to multiple buyers.

In spite of these problems, UEFA sees secondary sales as a reality of its business and a good way of enabling social viewing and word of mouth. Alternative channels have a role in reaching parts of the market that UEFA can't, so the goal is not to stop secondary sales altogether but to limit their negative aspects by using a decentralized economic market. To this end, UEFA is turning to blockchain.

UEFA is working with SecuTix and TIXnGO, Swiss technology companies that are part of the Swiss IT company ELCA Group. The SecuTix and TIXnGO platform saw its first UEFA pilot in Lyon, France, in May 2018. The platform was used in that city to issue and manage twenty thousand tickets to the final game of the UEFA Europa League. A second pilot was conducted with ten thousand tickets for the UEFA Super Cup match in Tallinn, Estonia, in August of the same year. All eyes are now on the main prize for the solution: the Euro 2020, the European soccer world's equivalent to the World Cup.[18]

The platform works by prompting a ticket buyer to download the SecuTix and TIXnGO app. The app is connected to a blockchain, and tickets are tokenized to allow the platform to record the ticket purchase and link its ownership details. If an owner wants to give a ticket away to a friend or family member, he or she can do that through the app, which sends the record of the transfer to the blockchain. When a ticket holder wants to put the ticket on the open market, things get interesting. SecuTix and TIXnGO have developed the capability for a secondary market to operate inside the blockchain app. The SecuTix platform defines the markup resellers are allowed to charge. This practice prevents price gouging and limits the incentives illegal brokers have to participate but maintains the decentralized environment that allows ticket holders of all kinds—whether they are individuals or ticket brokers—to sell to willing buyers.

Since every ticket transfer is recorded on the blockchain, SecuTix and TIXnGO can track tickets and know the identity of the person entering a venue. In theory, this information could go to the security team and allow security people to prevent entry if they believe a ticket holder poses a security risk. In practice, it's unclear how UEFA can or would use this feature. As Frédéric Longatte, CEO of SecuTix explained, "We have an architectural work around to ensure that the ticket holder's privacy is protected, with no personal data resident on the blockchain, a feature which allows our clients to stay compliant with GDPR rules while still maintaining the ability to associate a ticket to a purchaser."[19]

UEFA's effort with ELCA Group demonstrates how blockchain enables the decentralization of business decision making, specifically as it relates to the sales model. The technology solution is blockchain-inspired, but the combined governance and economic capabilities involving the use of tokens, the inclusion of secondary market actors, and the flexibility of ticket holders to freely sell or exchange tickets (within price limits) nudge the solution eastward along the continuum of decentralization (figure 5-3). Over time, the direction could point further east, as the solution aims to integrate secondary ticket marketplaces and thus more participants and market actors with the goal of enabling safer decentralization of the economic system surrounding ticket sales.

Together, Banque de France and UEFA show a few ways that centralized organizations will experiment with decentralization to unlock new opportunities. Yet we opened this chapter with Golem—a native blockchain company—to highlight a market reality: startup companies are already developing decentralized alternatives to existing business models.

FIGURE 5-3

Relatively decentralized ticketing by the Union of European Football Associations (UEFA)

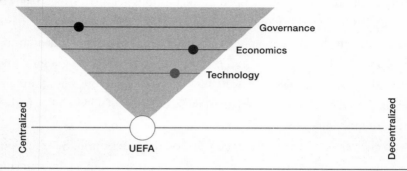

One example is rLoop, a token-enabled DAO focused on connecting decentralized talent in the engineering and design world from all over the globe to create engineering innovations. This model has already won the company a SpaceX Innovation Award for its prototype of the Hyperloop, a high-speed transportation system.[20] The SpaceX competition may pigeonhole rLoop as a futuristic entity, but the group is solving a current problem of talent access in science, technology, engineering, and mathematics (STEM) fields.[21]

Decentralization can happen two ways. Centralized organizations embracing the need for institutional change can make incremental changes. Or new entrants offering alternative ways to create value make a stronger push toward decentralization.

YOUR REAL BUSINESS LENS

WHAT DID YOU LEARN?

The blockchain-inspired phase extends through to about 2025, when technological maturity and business experience enable organizations to make the transition to blockchain-complete solutions. How fast that transition occurs and how fully you benefit from it depend on how quickly you embrace some degree of decentralization.

Decentralization is not just about technology. It has eight components, which fall in three main categories: governance (decision making, participation, and commercial ownership and oversight); economics (financing and rewards allocation); and technology (technology architecture, protocol development, and network governance). These components determine how the blockchain defines and executes on the business rules for a solution; who gets to participate and their roles in the network; and how to allocate rewards to participants according to their contributions.

WHAT SHOULD YOU DO ABOUT IT?

To take advantage of blockchain solutions, you'll need to experiment with decentralization. Begin with simple, administrative decision making, and then progress to more-complex managerial and leadership decisions. Move on to organizational operations and then to organizational business models. Because your organization's capacity for change and its culture will be the biggest sources of resistance, you should consider early on the role of incentives and reward structures using tokens. Even very centralized organizations can adopt some principles of decentralization and create a foundation for new economic systems. Resist the temptation to wait and see what happens in your market. Twenty years of experience with digital disruption reveals a pattern in the way former industry leaders collapse. They fail not just because a new competitor enters the market but also because that competitor taps into a vein of customer disillusionment that the incumbent had been ignoring. Survival and growth will come from participating in your own creative destruction.

WHAT'S NEXT?

The debate over centralization or decentralization is not binary. The blockchain spectrum highlights an evolutionary path. Some aspects of markets, industries, enterprises, and operations may still benefit from aspects of centralization. However, as blockchain capabilities mature, you will encounter more opportunities that encourage you to attack the decentralization inflection point and advance along the decentralization continuum.

In the next chapter, we travel further along the spectrum to examine blockchain-complete solutions and their role in propelling this evolution.

CHAPTER 6

MARKET ACCESS AND PARTICIPATION

Blockchain-complete solutions employing all five elements—including tokenization and decentralization—will begin to have market impact in the mid-2020s. The consensus-driven, decentralized model upends the winner-take-all dynamics that have driven business economics for millennia. The consequences for data alone could be enormous, given the way blockchain-complete solutions will allow customers to tokenize their data (and other assets) and share it selectively with active consent. At the same time, the native creation and exchange of new forms of value allow new markets to emerge and drastically improve the liquidity of illiquid assets. As a leader, you should prepare now.

Some forward thinkers in first-line industries already are preparing. Many blockchain startups have emerged with decentralized commercial models, for example. We gave a preview of such a model in the form of a travel blockchain (chapter 4). Similar models in development for retail include Bleexy, a decentralized marketplace in which individuals, retailers, wholesalers, and manufacturers can directly connect and trade with each other. Such an ecosystem could facilitate more-efficient deals between manufacturers and retailers and could direct sales to consumers in the mode of microbrands like that of Dollar Shave Club in the United States. Another retail blockchain company is Buying.com, which aspires to connect buyers and sellers in the same geographic market for on-demand, short-lead-time purchases. The company is running pilots in four areas in the US state of New Jersey.

If Bleexy and Buying.com are aiming to become blockchain's answer to Amazon or Tmall, then OpenBazaar is the answer to eBay or Taobao. OpenBazaar began as a hackathon experiment to create a decentralized alternative to the centralized and now-defunct dark-web marketplace Silk Road.[1] Today, OpenBazaar presents itself as a free, safe, and anonymous alternative to the digital platforms. Since its 2016 launch, it has reportedly attracted more than seventy-five hundred sellers.[2]

These emerging solutions and others rely on the same currencies that drive digital platforms, but they do so with transparency. The inclusion of tokenization combined with decentralization in their design enables them to deliver the same benefits that attract consumers and sellers to online platforms but without forcing those participants to pay twice to use them—once in the form of real money spent on a purchased item or on transaction fees, and again in the form of personal or organizational data.

In this chapter, we explore what emergent blockchain-complete solutions could look like and how they could challenge existing models. We highlight industries where blockchain-complete models are already having an impact, and we demonstrate how the access they enable could be exploited for competitive advantage.

THE BENEFITS OF BLOCKCHAIN-COMPLETE SOLUTIONS

Retail is just one high-activity sector for startups pursuing blockchain-complete solutions. Other industries with strong blockchain-complete startup activity include ad brokering, data storage, travel brokering, and fintech. These industries have in common a high level of digitalization and a customer subsegment concerned about the exploitation of their personal data. Blockchain startups are offering decentralized, consensus-driven alternatives to the existing centralized, platform-driven models.

One example comes from the blockchain ad-blocking browser provider Brave, which is piloting a digital ad platform that compensates customers for their attention with BATs—basic attention tokens—when they consent to watch an advertisement.[3] BitClave is exploring a similar model using a consumer activity token that rewards users when they agree to share personal data or to view an ad. Consumer browsing and purchasing behavior is unaffected in the sense that people can still go about their web business unimpeded, but with rewards and more transparency and choice associated with how they reveal their identity and preferences.

A decentralized environment could bring about some counterintuitive improvements to data quality. Blockchain is popularly referred to as the *truth machine*, a troubling phrase, given that data can be incomplete, inaccurate, biased, context-specific, or otherwise misleading. On a digital platform, "truth" is established by amassing data over time about what customers look at or buy and then executing on this insight. Granted, this data includes quite a few products, and the number is constantly growing, but it is still only a part of total customer needs and preferences. Who among us hasn't had the experience of looking at a peripherally interesting product on a web platform, only to have ads for that product follow you around the internet for weeks? Platforms use this tainted version of truth to nudge customers toward certain actions and purchases.

An accurate, transparent, and private truth made possible by blockchain-complete solutions could disrupt the market power of digital platforms while also improving trust and allowing widespread opportunity and participation. The consensus algorithm enables "truth" in blockchain-complete solutions. The algorithm will reject transactions based on what it perceives as inaccurate or unverifiable data, and it allows participants to transact, even if they don't implicitly know or trust their counterparts. Participants who don't follow the blockchain's rules won't be authorized to transact. Transactions that go against those rules won't be validated. In addition, record immutability allows a participant to access the transaction record to settle any postsettlement dispute. Blockchain-inspired solutions don't necessarily have those safety mechanisms, or if they do, they are more costly and cumbersome.

Improved accuracy and consensus-driven validation could bring widespread benefits in the form of fairness, in particular as it applies to fair participation and access. Anyone or anything can interact or transact in a blockchain-complete network as long as the party adheres to the shared rules of the network. In this way, blockchain-complete solutions realize the promise of equal access that was part of the World Wide Web at its inception. We are far from that promise today, given the power of digital platforms to act as gatekeepers.[4] To increase their revenue, platforms must capture as much data as possible and limit access competitors may have to the same resources. That capture and control creates a motivation to reverse decentralization (see figure 6-1). Blockchain solutions, in contrast, expand the range of participants to anyone who sees value. Although blockchain does not necessarily produce a green field with wide-open participation, it can increase participation and encourage the fair distribution of benefits.

Fair access refers not just to the right to participate, but also to the practical ability to do so. Efficient, secure, and private sharing of identifying information strongly encourages participation. Portable and decentralized identity credentials will serve as the standard way that blockchain-complete solutions capture and share participant information. In a blockchain-complete environment, these credentials are often tokens that capture a user's relevant information. (The technical approach to capturing credentials will change further along the spectrum.) The tokens may be stored in a digital wallet. Data owners can then share their tokens for single use by designated trading partners. Security clearance is one application for personal data tokens. Your credentials can identify you as a valid owner of a financial account, for example.[5]

This approach could have broad application in many industries. We recently spoke with representatives from the Taipei Medical University

FIGURE 6-1

Programmability versus decentralization with blockchain-complete

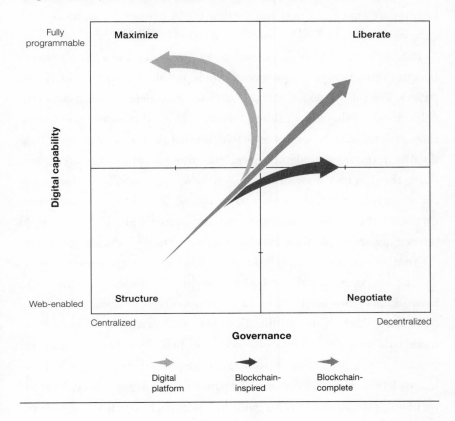

Hospital (TMUH), which is putting patient data on a blockchain to allow more holistic management and sharing of patient records.[6] TMUH sees the potential to give patients control over their "health passport" to improve document protection and enable more efficient information sharing. After patients' consent is captured in a smart contract, providers can access reports of medical tests ordered by another physician in the hospital and thereby prevent unnecessary duplication of tests. Patients can also share their passport with care providers who work outside the hospital system. According to the superintendent of the TMUH, Dr. Ray-Jade Chen, "the benefits in efficiency alone have been staggering, even for the small number of pilot patients on the system.

It used to take three weeks for a health record exchange; now that same exchange can take place within three hours. Likewise, out-of-pocket health-care expenses get reimbursed faster by insurers because the necessary exchange of data is more complete and efficient."[7]

Portability is an important feature. In the TMUH example, patients benefit from having a health record that is portable across providers and payers. For businesses, a portable license or credential could dramatically decrease the cost of doing business. Instead of undergoing separate credentialing processes for each channel partner, a business could document the relevant details once, store them in an identity token, and share them across networks. Smaller, local, or specialized companies could thereby expand their market access. Rather than concentrate their digital activity on one platform, businesses and individuals could participate across platforms and spread access to their data across them.

Another element of fairness in blockchain-complete networks is the fair assessment of value, which is based on the consensus of the entire network, and thus fair pricing. Fair assessment and pricing will emerge from fairer market access. Broader participation allows for wider and more balanced distribution of power and benefits between platforms, product developers, and customers. As described in chapter 4, early hints of this dynamic are evolving in the gaming industry, enabled by blockchain alternatives to game retailers such as EB Games, Sony, Nintendo, Apple, Google, and Microsoft. Blockchain companies promise developers a bigger cut and faster payment for game sales.

Smart contracts would support the fair assessment and exchange of value by capturing rules about acceptable bid and ask prices and the terms of exchange for certain assets. Prediction market solutions such as Gnosis, Delphy.org, Stox, Hivemind, and Augur could play a role in allowing market participants to vote on market activities and gain access to market information related to price and value.

Far from theoretical, these elements of fairness are already emerging in some industries that are embracing decentralized approaches in general and blockchain specifically. Finance, one area of active experimentation, deserves some focused attention.

FINANCIAL INNOVATION THROUGH
BLOCKCHAIN-COMPLETE SOLUTIONS

Central banks exert total control over money supply, interest rates, and the chartering and regulation of commercial banks. The centralization trickles down to the level of the customer, resulting in limited options for businesses (and retail customers) that need financing to launch or grow. An entrepreneur could follow the advice of the billionaire and *Shark Tank* star Mark Cuban, who has famously opined that, "the best equity is sweat equity. The more you can do without raising money, the further you'll go and the more of your company you'll own."[8] Good advice, but not feasible for every business, especially in sectors that require initial investments in supplies or product development. These sectors need capital.

Lack of access to capital is believed to be one of the primary constraints to business growth worldwide.[9] Entrepreneurs can finance their ventures with personal savings or loans and investment from friends or relatives, or they can seek formal finance in the form of debt or equity from the financial sector. There have also always been, and still are, informal sources of finance, such as moneylenders (some quite legitimate, some functioning as loan sharks) and savings groups. In some communities, these informal sources are more common than the formal ones. But for large sums of money, budding entrepreneurs with aspirations of rapid growth and with high capital needs usually turn to commercial banks and, since the 1970s, venture-capital funds, or angel investors.

Formal sources have their limitations. First, they are centralized and thus scarce. Depending on the environment, an entrepreneur could have a few dozen providers they could pitch to for funds. Second, formal sources of financing are expensive. Each lender or investor has its own demands in terms of interest rate, percentage share, or timeline to cash out. Because of large volumes and repeated fund-raising, founders must hand over an ever-larger share of the company they created.

We are hardly the first to point out that finance is ripe for decentralization. In the late 1990s, the San Francisco–based investment bank

WR Hambrecht + Co introduced a Dutch auction model for initial public offerings (IPOs) as a way to give individual investors access to new stocks and to break the monopoly that institutions have enjoyed on IPO access since the 1980s.[10] Spring Street Brewing was one of the first companies to go public with this model.[11] The difference between then and now is that the technology today is cheaper, much more capable, and more widely distributed and accessible.

Digital technology has already been used to facilitate the decentralization of finance. Crowdfunding platforms offer one model with significant traction. Examples of these platforms include 51Give, Ketto, Indiegogo, and Kickstarter, or even Kiva for microlending. In 2017, crowdfunding platforms raised an estimated $33 billion worldwide.[12] Considering the $84 billion in venture capital raised by US businesses alone, crowdfunding was clearly never intended to replace traditional sources, but rather fills the gaps that traditional finance does not serve.[13]

In 2013, the crowdfunding model found a new application in the form of initial coin offerings (ICOs) executed on a blockchain. As discussed in chapter 4, ICOs were one of the first widespread applications of tokens in blockchain solutions. Mastercoin—a cryptocurrency built on the Bitcoin blockchain—is thought to have launched the first ICO in 2013.[14] Ethereum's ICO followed in 2014 and raised more than $2 million in the first twelve hours. In 2017, the ICO market expanded dramatically, with almost nine hundred offerings taking place in the calendar year to raise a total of more than $6 billion. In 2018, there were more than twelve hundred ICOs raising more than $7.5 billion.[15]

In concept, ICOs epitomize the promise of blockchain-complete solutions as enablers of fair access and value exchange. They do this by expanding financial access to a larger variety of aspiring entrepreneurs than could or would be served by commercial banks, angel investors, or venture-capital funds and by potentially accessing a global capital pool. Improved access extends to the supply side as well. ICOs allow any investor to support an entrepreneur at almost any level, even in increments smaller than $0.01. Both sides enjoy a fairer exchange of value at a fair price within a system that takes a little bit of money from a lot of participants. The use of smart contracts as part of the process also facilitates a more accurate and auditable transaction flow. All these elements break the hold that the formal financial sector has on capital. Decentralized finance thus drives down the cost of capital and enables a more equitable exchange—at least in theory.

SMART CONTRACTS AS REGULATORS

Before we explore how these dynamics are playing out in reality, we want to briefly touch on the mechanisms that support blockchain-complete solutions and that ensure their fairness and safety for participants. One foundational enabler is the smart contract. As explained in our discussion of digital currencies, the absence of an explicit contract between users and digital platforms has allowed the latter to capture and store unlimited amounts of data. The presence of a contract would clarify the terms and specify what the participant gets in exchange. The idea of smart contracts originated in 1994 with Nick Szabo, a computer scientist and cryptographer credited with designing a precursor to bitcoin.[16] Ethereum was one of the first blockchains to employ smart contracts; they are now the standard by which many blockchains execute rules.

A simple smart contract captures basic rules and standards to enable an autonomous peer-to-peer transaction. More-complex exchanges involving multiple parties or complicated flows of information would instead use a more sophisticated bit of technology called a *decentralized application*, or *dapp*. Dapps are applications that use smart contracts plus added code to enable the exchange of digital assets (tokens) involving back-end computation and front-end access. At the risk of oversimplification, a smart contract would be used if a transaction were as straightforward as two peers exchanging data tokens. A dapp would be used instead to enable, say, an insurance claim that disburses money from an insurance carrier to a claimant and that involves the exchange and processing of claim information.

Smart contracts and dapps capture and execute the rules of a blockchain. Those rules have the additional safeguard in a public blockchain of the consensus mechanism to ensure they are followed for each transaction equitably. Although the technology capturing those rules is still immature, they will eventually serve the same function that centralized oversight does today—as a safeguard. In fact, smart contracts, dapps, and consensus can be even more effective, cheaper, and faster than the centralized and mediated financial system we have today. But there is a significant learning curve before that promise is realized, as demonstrated by the DAO project.

The DAO project was a decentralized blockchain organization that formed with the goal of funding projects to build decentralized operations, with each project voted for by DAO token holders.[17] The project had no organization to speak of and was designed to be entirely consensus driven. In May 2016, it raised an impressive $150 million. But the following month, a token holder exploited a vulnerability in the smart contract and network code and siphoned the equivalent of $50 million. Thanks to a nuance in the network rules, the community was able to fork the project's blockchain, freeze the currency, and liquidate the remaining DAO funds to the original investors.

The DAO project offered further proof that a resonant idea can raise funds from the crowd without recourse to traditional capital markets. But it also exposed the immaturity of the mechanisms underlying decentralized finance, not least the lack of regulatory recourse. The culprit in the DAO project incident was the smart contract operating on its blockchain. ICOs have fallen prey to more straightforward challenges from old-fashioned currency manipulation and other illegal means.

THE RISKS AND BENEFITS OF ICOs

The impact of ICOs on financial decentralization is captured in the sheer volume of companies that have acquired capital through blockchain-enabled crowdfunding. The challenge is also revealed in the high rate of failure of ICO-backed ventures. An analysis by researchers at Boston College shows that 56 percent of startups that issue ICOs go out of business within four months of finalizing the token sales.[18] This failure rate isn't surprising, given that a large majority of startups with seed or venture funding fail to secure more financing and ultimately go out of business. The accelerated timeline raises questions, however, about whether these companies had a sufficiently rigorous idea to support financing.[19]

ICOs have attracted much attention from legitimate entrepreneurs and investors but also from fraudsters and speculators. Some frauds have been perpetrated by self-declared entrepreneurs. A strong-sounding idea coupled with competent marketing can attract investors to participate in an ICO, resulting in millions of dollars for the issuing organization, even when that organization is vague about what those millions are for. The limited regulation has allowed this ambiguity to persist.

As noted in chapter 4, tokens fall into several categories. Security tokens represent an equity investment in a company, analogous to buying a share of stock in an IPO. Utility tokens, in contrast, purportedly reserve a space in line for the holder to access a technology solution. But few of the early ICOs had an associated contract that required the issuing company to produce a product. Consequently, many ICOs produced nothing. Even legitimate ideas promoted by sincere entrepreneurs can fall prey to ICO manipulation, particularly pump and dump campaigns by investors who talk up the coin price and then dump their coins on the market, causing a crash in value. Also mixed up with the subject of ICOs and manipulation are *cryptocurrency airdrops*, a onetime free distribution of tokens to the wallets of specified recipients; airdrops attempt to create liquidity and interest in a token and its corresponding blockchain. They are the blockchain equivalent of a retail promotional campaign.[20]

Many entrepreneurs operating within this market of hype and ambiguity are sincere businesspeople seeking alternative options to fund their passion. The rise in the coin price of bitcoin and Ethereum helped many see the promise of decentralized access to finance. And yet there have been, and will continue to be, growing pains. The crash in cryptocurrency value in 2018 calmed the ICO fever, resulting in far fewer ICOs in the second half of the year than in the first. The organizations that had already completed ICOs but had not transferred funds into fiat saw the value from the initial ICO drop significantly.[21] Some of these organizations now have insufficient working capital to continue. Others are redrawing their strategic plans in an environment of tighter resources.

None of these challenges reduce the promise of ICOs. On the contrary, the period from 2017 to 2018 was a useful proof of concept for decentralized finance. Adding programmability into company ownership radically changes the models for asset creation, investment, and exchange. The successes and failures of ICOs show that widespread financial disintermediation can expand access to finance and its delivery. ICOs even seem to be lucrative for investors. The aforementioned Boston College report found that ICO investors netted an average return of 86 percent; the researchers also suggest that fraudulent ICOs, though real, had minimum impact, because investors spotted them and underfunded those ICOs.

The ICO hype of 2017–2018 also highlights that organizations need a sound business plan and effective leadership—decentralized or not—around blockchain. Accessing finance isn't the last of a business's challenges. The failure of so many organizations almost immediately after an ICO suggests that some of these founders were ill prepared to run a business. To become sustainable, a blockchain platform or solution must still attract customers and serve them at scale.

ICOs are not just for startups, either. Established organizations are taking advantage of them too, often for funding decentralization initiatives. For these organizations, ICOs represent an opportunity to engage existing and prospective customers on new initiatives (subject to regulation). When organizations draw funds from the user market, they can solidify loyalty and make customers feel more invested in the success of a product or service. Token issues executed by established organizations are often referred to as *reverse ICOs*.

The Canadian messaging app Kik, founded in 2009, held a reverse ICO in 2017.[22] With roughly three hundred million registered users, Kik competes with WhatsApp, Facebook Messenger, and WeChat using the same ad-driven model. The Canadian company had raised significant funds through traditional sources, but in 2017, it decided to evolve its solution to a blockchain-complete model that is tokenized and decentralized. To that end, Kik held a reverse ICO and sold nearly $100 million in Kin tokens, which are also used on the platform to incentivize and reward users when they interact with each other. Ted Livingston, Kik's CEO, said, "Our ultimate vision is for Kik to be one of hundreds or thousands of digital services for Kin. What if we got all these developers to integrate Kin, then, as a consumer, I can earn and spend Kin inside all these places?"[23]

Kik isn't the only company trying this approach. Kodak experimented with a KodakCoin ICO in 2018 as part of the KodakOne rights-management platform, developed to allow photographers to monetize and monitor copyright of their digital works.[24]

REGULATION OF DECENTRALIZED FINANCE

Cryptocurrencies and the consequent rise of ICOs have operated mostly outside the domain of government regulation. Those days appear to be over.[25] The poorly defined rules around ICOs are rapidly organizing under the watchful gaze of regulatory bodies. Some countries, such as China and South Korea, have banned ICOs outright and are keeping a tight fist on cryptocurrency activity. Other countries are taking a more inclusive approach.[26] With no standard policy that applies across borders, the idea of a globally decentralized finance market that operates fully on a blockchain is purely theoretical.

For ICOs, the United States is beginning to regulate security tokens as securities under Securities and Exchange Commission guidelines.[27] Other countries, such as Canada, France, and Germany, are examining the functions of tokens to determine if a given token is a security, a utility, or some other entity and are regulating it accordingly. For example, French regulators have passed the PACTE bill, which includes a clause that would encourage token issuers to obtain a visa to operate in the country.[28]

Tokens that are clear security tokens will increasingly be issued in a hybrid IPO/ICO model called a *security token offering*, or STO.[29] The contracts surrounding STOs are more structured than they are for ICOs, with defined requirements that provide some legal protection to issuers and investors. STOs will also be more regulated and (depending on jurisdiction) will be limited to accredited investors. Greater regulation could hit decentralized participation hard.[30] Yet regulation may also enable the creation of more-diverse securities to facilitate trade in both digital assets and physical ones, such as IoT devices and the data they produce.

STOs would only apply to the issuance of security tokens. ICOs will continue to go forward with utility tokens, but the smart contracts operating the ICO will, in a more regulated future, include requirements for both the issuer and the token holder that define who gets what in the exchange.

The path toward decentralization of finance must also consider stablecoins. Because they aim to stabilize the volatility of cryptocurrencies, stablecoins indirectly participate in the decentralization of finance while creating still another regulatory challenge related to cryptocurrencies. Regulators need to take a holistic view of regulating the market. Signs indicate that some regulators intend to do just that. In the United States, for example, the Justice Department and the Commodity Futures Trading Commission are exploring the role of the Tether stablecoin as a tool to manipulate the cryptocurrency markets, notably bitcoin trading.[31]

MOVIECOIN AND DECENTRALIZED FINANCE BEYOND ICOs

The publicity, activity, and money swirling around cryptocurrencies and ICOs offer a case study in how blockchain-complete models can upend old rules. The blockchain startup MovieCoin is looking to apply this approach to finance big-budget, Hollywood-style films.

Big-budget film production is similar to venture-backed small-business finance in that both depend on huge volumes of capital by a few major investors. In the film industry, each participant involves its own legal counsel to create and review scores of contracts for various aspects of the project, creating added costs. The capital is then locked up for years before anyone sees a return. There is another layer of contracts and licensing to do with distribution in theaters and through DVDs or streaming.

MovieCoin is working on decentralized financial alternatives to make both the production and the distribution sides of the value chain more liquid. The company launched in 2017 and has developed a blockchain platform and an MOV token to automate payment collections and distribution for films in production. MOV is a utility token designed to facilitate cash flow management and financial disbursement. In combination with the smart contracts running on the MovieCoin platform, the tokens will theoretically facilitate payments and eliminate third-party service providers so that the involved contributors (including actors and other creatives, who often wait years to see their money) can get paid faster. Consumers could even buy MOV tokens and use them to purchase film tickets. A 2018 MOV presale received a strong response, precluding public sale of the tokens.[32]

In 2019, MovieCoin plans to launch another token, the MovieCoin Smart Fund token (MSF), a security token designed to allow accredited investors to invest in the purchase and production of original Hollywood-style film content. Founder Christopher Woodrow, former investment banker and film financier, told us that MovieCoin plans to finance sixty films in six years.[33] The MSF effectively enables the digitalization and decentralization of film ownership. Through it, a new class of accredited investors can own a piece of a film. In an interview with *Forbes* magazine, Woodrow said, "One of the key things to consider is access. To previously invest in Hollywood films, someone had to show up with a check for $50 million dollars to be taken seriously. Utilizing blockchain technology can open up an entirely new class to accredited investors who previously couldn't do this."[34]

An investor can also trade his or her shares on a cryptocurrency market before the film moves out of production. Rather than limiting access and locking in investment, MSF tokens on the MovieCoin platform could expand investor participation and improve liquidity in the market. Though the company only has ICO plans for the MOV utility token and, in 2019, the MSF token, Woodrow imagines that his platform could enable project-specific tokens in the future.

SWARM FUND

Swarm Fund is another example of a company looking to utilize tokenization in combination with decentralization to offer investors new ways to access and trade value. This nonprofit blockchain startup created what it calls *blockchain for private equity*. The goal is to democratize investing by enabling individual investors to buy assets that are usually only available to institutions. Private equity, real estate, infrastructure development, and natural resources are all investment areas Swarm hopes to open to a larger pool of people. These sectors usually require a minimum investment that is out of reach for all but the wealthiest individuals. Swarm Fund accesses the sectors by allowing users to buy SWM tokens, which the organization combines into an investor swarm capable of buying an institutional-sized block. If successful, the Swarm model could not only challenge the dominance of major mutual fund and hedge fund companies for a range of consumer investing but also disintermediate part of the investment management sector. For example, by introducing transparency to the fee and pricing structure of funds and offering more-detailed insight into portfolios, the startup could create a more decentralized operating model for fund management and could reshuffle the competitive landscape.

THE FATE OF CENTRALIZED SOLUTIONS

As the technology matures to enable blockchain-complete solutions and as organizations experiment with decentralized decision making, processes, and business models, the value proposition of blockchain-inspired solutions and other centralized approaches will change. There are a number of scenarios that could emerge in the market.

Some of the blockchain-inspired solutions that go live into the mid-2020s will gain acceptance and survive to become standard, even as organizations embrace more decentralized models. For example, a consortia of investment bankers could develop a blockchain for IPOs even as the decentralized ICO environment evolves, with each model serving different levels, sectors, or sensibilities of the financing market.

Blockchain-complete solutions will affect existing blockchain-inspired solutions differently, depending on the archetype of the inspired solutions. Because few FOMO solutions will become operational or will survive long, by the time blockchain-complete solutions are possible, few if any of this archetype will exist. In contrast, opportunistic solutions designed to automate an in-house or industry process will still be relevant as long as the process is. For example, solutions like the new trading platform that the Australian stock exchange is developing to replace CHESS will probably come from the opportunistic archetype (see chapter 2). These solutions will not stay static, however. Opportunistic solutions built by consortia or designed to enable cross-organizational use could veer toward centralization if they are successful, attract users, and begin to consolidate data relevant to the business process. They could, alternatively, become more decentralized as the decisions managed by the solution are captured in and executed by a smart contract. Blockchain-inspired solutions built to be evolutionary or native will have the highest likelihood of staying relevant and coexisting with decentralized blockchain solutions, as long as the business models or digital assets they promote continue to generate long-term interest.

What about other centralized digital environments? Will Amazon, Facebook, Google, Tencent, Alibaba, Airbnb, and Uber still hold as much power when there are blockchain-complete alternatives? As digitalization accelerates, digital platforms will no doubt continue to capture large volumes of data to feed their algorithms and develop new products. The tokenization of personal data in many blockchain-complete solutions will allow customers to keep their data private in digital environments, but whether customers will give up the convenience and speed they get from using digital platforms in exchange for short-term pain is an open question. A strong value proposition coupled with incentives in the form of tokens will be necessary to shift customer activity from digital platforms to alternatives running on a blockchain.

There is a balancing act along the decentralization continuum. Whenever one company has significant control over an industry's business currencies (data, access, contracts, and technology)—notably by mobilizing digital platforms, AI, and IoT—decentralization provides a defense mechanism. Decentralization prevents one company from amassing enough data that it can make correlations, identify patterns, and control business outcomes. A slew of businesses with blockchain-complete ambitions are developing solutions that allow individual stakeholders to maintain control over their information and their share of the value proposition.

One sector engaged in rapid experimentation is travel. Digital platforms like Airbnb have clearly proven the money-making potential of the sharing economy for travel accommodations. A number of new ventures are exploring blockchain alternatives to see if the sharing economy can operate within a model that distributes the value more equitably. Startups such as Cool Cousin, Beenest, and LockTrip are some of the first attempts at disrupting the hospitality industry's digital platforms with decentralized options.

Cool Cousin's model rewards locals for providing tips about their favorite locales, restaurants, or activities; the company can integrate with hotel websites or apps and can function as a digital concierge for visitors. Beenest is angling to supplant Airbnb as a decentralized home-sharing option. The Beenest solution uses the Bee Token to settle all transactions inside its system, thereby avoiding foreign exchange fees. The system also uses tokens to reward renters and visitors for good behavior (thus creating reputation) and as a tool to settle disputes.[35] LockTrip likewise offers a decentralized booking solution for both hotels and private property owners, with zero commission rates.[36]

YOUR REAL BUSINESS LENS

WHAT DID YOU LEARN?

The blockchain-complete phase of the blockchain spectrum will begin in the mid-2020s, though these solutions have existed since the launch of bitcoin in 2009. Indeed, the ICOs that have fostered blockchain start-ups in every geographical location, market, and industry demonstrate widespread interest in decentralized models executed in a blockchain-complete network. Early-adopter industries include finance, of course, but also retail, travel, and social media. Blockchain-complete solutions aim to empower customers by giving them access to a broader range of opportunities, but in an environment in which they control their identity and data.

WHAT SHOULD YOU DO ABOUT IT?

Staying on top of market trends will allow you to time your organization's blockchain-complete activity. Monitor the blockchain startup market continuously. New blockchain-complete companies are already emerging to disrupt incumbent players in various industries. The veins of opportunity these startups hope to mine indicate some of the available opportunities where decentralized and tokenized models could take hold and enable you to scale.

In addition, keep track of activity in the ICO market. Although it has been fraught with legal difficulties, liquidity problems, and volatility, the market's maturity and some increased regulation could help the decentralized finance sector transform into an opportunity to improve capital access, get closer to customers, and potentially restructure financing costs.

WHAT'S NEXT?

The maturation of blockchain-complete solutions will take place concurrent with other technology trends, including the increased application of IoT and AI. When blockchains incorporate things and self-learning algorithms into their protocols, we will see a greater variety of assets that can be exchanged, faster transactions, and broader disbursement of network participants. Networks could even be taken over by things as algorithmic agents begin to interact and transact autonomously on behalf of individuals and organizations. We explore that world of enhanced blockchain solutions in the next chapter.

PART THREE

ENHANCED BLOCKCHAIN SOLUTIONS

CHAPTER 7

UNLEASHING THE POWER OF SMART THINGS

In the current excitement around blockchain, it is easy to lose sight of parallel technology trends poised to explode in the next decade. Most important among them, for blockchain, are IoT and AI. Today we think of organizations as made up mostly of people. Yet in a short few years, the number of intelligent assets in an organization could dwarf the number of people, as organizations embed billions of devices and sensors in their products and infrastructure. Today we think of people making decisions and taking actions. Soon, many decisions will be translated into algorithms and executed autonomously.

IoT and AI will activate new value and drive new innovations. When integrated with blockchain, they create an *enhanced blockchain*, a blockchain in which smart, autonomous things join people as participants capable of identifying, creating, transacting, and negotiating for digital assets. Innovators are already taking tentative steps toward these synergies.

Housing scarcity has created a market for illegal rentals in major Chinese cities. Security guards might "rent" a unit when the real property owners are out of town, or the tenants themselves might allow illegal sublets. The challenge of housing fraud is pushing China to try a different approach. In the northern city of Xiong'an, planners aim to fight housing fraud and improve access to property for tenants with the support of blockchain. A representative from Ant Financial explained the approach: "The blockchain will be used to validate that the property is real. The landlord and the tenant will consent on the blockchain to the terms and conditions of the rental. Another benefit of blockchain is that when tenants apply for a housing loan, they do not need to involve multiple agencies to prove the truthfulness of their rental. As a result, this blockchain rental solution allows tenants to enjoy a more convenient property rental experience."[1] Xiong'an is not any city; it's a smart city in development.[a] In addition to using blockchain, it uses AI and IoT, with the potential to combine all three.[2] Kai-Fu Lee, author of *AI Superpowers: China, Silicon Valley and the New World Order,* spoke of the efforts of the Chinese tech company Baidu: "Baidu is already working with Xiong'an's local government to build out this AI City with an environmental focus. Possibilities include sensor-geared cement, computer vision–enabled traffic lights, intersections with facial recognition and parking lots-turned parks."[3]

IoT and AI don't need blockchain, of course. These technologies are already beginning to influence how we live, work, and interact. Without blockchain, however, the most powerful and ubiquitous IoT and AI solutions will operate invisibly and in the background under the control of central actors—digital platforms, government entities, utility

---

a. Gartner defines *smart city* as a life-cycle approach to urban governance for improving its citizens' lives, stimulating its economy, and protecting its environment. The strategy development and its execution are driven by a group of public-sector and citizen stakeholders. They define and measure the impact of technology through data and analytics to create a user-focused and contextualized experience. See Bettina Tratz-Ryan and Bill Finnerty, "Hype Cycle for Smart City Technologies and Solutions," Gartner Research Note G00340460 (Gartner, August 1, 2018).

companies, and banks, to name a few. With blockchain, in contrast, IoT and AI become more transparent and auditable, and their operations could become monetizable, enabling entirely new ways to create value.

In this chapter, we examine how enhanced blockchain solutions—defined as blockchain applied in an environment made up of people and things and operated with autonomous algorithmic intelligence—could unlock the potential of IoT and AI while ensuring privacy, fairness, and access. The chapter includes some speculation and aspiration, given that the enhanced blockchain phase will not begin for another ten years. Nonetheless, looking at how IoT and AI are advancing in dozens of industries, we will project from today's experiments some scenarios for enhanced blockchain. In particular, we examine how IoT, AI, and blockchain can complement one another and drive a broad range of organizations toward competitive advantage.

A BRIEF PRIMER ON IOT AND AI

Gartner defines IoT as "the network of physical objects that contain embedded technology to communicate and sense or interact with their internal states or the external environment."[4] These embedded objects enable numerous practical applications. In the pharmaceutical sector, for example, sensors in the packaging of temperature-sensitive medication can activate an embedded cooling function if conditions inch above a certain level, saving millions of dollars in inventory and possibly saving lives.[5] In smart cities, IoT could be used in public transportation to observe demand in real time and dynamically change train frequencies, or sensors could be placed on the underground pipes owned by the public utility to detect points of failure and prevent main breaks.

These ideas are not theoretical. Kansas City, Missouri, ran a pilot in 2018 in which it used street cameras to capture data about traffic flows. An algorithm analyzed the data and identified streets at high risk of developing potholes. Street crews were then sent to repave those streets *before* potholes developed. Kansas City CIO Bob Bennett estimates that this preventive-maintenance approach saves money by stopping problems before they get severe.[6]

An analogous example on a blockchain comes from PotholeCoin, a solution that aims to decentralize the financing of repairs to public infrastructure. The PotholeCoin app allows motorists to register a needed road repair and put up a token-funded "bounty" to pay for the fix. When enough tokens have been saved, the blockchain sends a message to a designated repair organization (a municipal infrastructure department or a private contractor). The company gets paid via a smart contract when the repair is done. This approach enables community members to collectively fund repairs that may not be a priority for the city infrastructure department.[7]

AI refers to the use of advanced analysis and other logic-based techniques to interpret events, support and automate decisions, and take action. Though AI approaches and techniques vary, we use the term broadly in a blockchain context to refer to intelligent algorithms that operate *and adjust* autonomously (i.e., without human intervention) to enable more effective data management and thereby expedite transaction flows and interactions. When combined with IoT, AI can examine the data collected by a network of distributed and diverse things, draw conclusions from it, and act on the information in real time. In a city, simple examples of those actions might include changing traffic lights to ease congestion, adjusting energy allocation across the smart grid, dispatching police patrols according to signs of conflict, or, as in Kansas City (which used an AI algorithm in its pothole pilot to analyze the video footage), prioritizing street maintenance.

Where does blockchain fit in all this? IoT, AI, and blockchain are beginning to interact and evolve in mutually beneficial ways. By applying blockchain to the capabilities brought through IoT and AI, a new form of trust infrastructure is enabled. In real-time the data captured through the sensors and analyzed using AI is handled transparently, potentially more securely and without the threat of manipulation. The resulting enhanced blockchain solutions will become stronger and will amplify the effective application of IoT and AI. Both sides of the relationship between blockchain and AI and IoT warrant more detail.

HOW IOT AND AI ENHANCE BLOCKCHAIN

The benefits of blockchain clearly increase when its design is more decentralized and its code can handle greater volumes of more-sophisticated transactions. IoT and AI, individually and together, can act as intelligent agents of decentralization in blockchain. Let's look at how these two technologies can accomplish this role.

SMART CONTRACTS GET TRULY SMART

As outlined earlier, smart contracts are the lines of code that capture and execute the business rules of a blockchain. The original vision of a smart contract took for granted that contracts would operate with intelligent, self-learning algorithms capable of adapting to the environment. In other words, the algorithms could act beyond the original defined rules of the market possibly challenging regulatory frameworks.

Smart contracts as they are used today in blockchain don't look like that. The smart contracts developed for blockchain-inspired solutions and the nascent blockchain-complete solutions are simple if-then rules engines capable of taking only limited specified actions. For example, the smart contract used in an ICO defines what type of token is offered and what the buyers get with their purchase, but it cannot dynamically change outcomes based on market or participant activity.

Today's smart contracts have such limited applications because the technology isn't mature enough to reliably and securely do more at sufficient scale. Another reason is that business leaders are uncomfortable giving control to a line of code. In ten years, both AI and blockchain will have evolved to the enhanced phase of the spectrum, and more-advanced algorithms and protocols will be available. By then, smart contracts will conceivably be smart, reliable, and secure enough to guide and instigate activity autonomously. Humans will likewise have more experience deploying algorithms in a range of business areas.

The blockchain startup Fetch is stepping into this aspirational space with a solution that allows adopters to code and deploy autonomous software agents to fulfill certain tasks. Fetch agents might deliver data from one participant to another or execute on a specific service. Agents are rewarded in this system with Fetch tokens. Interestingly, the Fetch platform allows designers to define the work environment in which Fetch agents operate. Whereas humans think of the work environment in predominantly geographic terms, a Fetch agent may be designed to orient its work space for safety and security, for example.[8]

THINGS BECOME NODES

Just as AI can make blockchain smart, IoT can extend decentralization more widely for a given blockchain, especially with the introduction of 5G.[9] Expanding the number of things distributed in physical environments creates more participants in a blockchain network. Not all things will be able to capture data and run intelligent code, or make autonomous decisions, of course. Doing so requires enough security, local memory, network capability, processing power, and local energy storage, which only some things will have. Yet "sophisticated" things large enough and powerful enough to have local intelligence and to act autonomously could function as participants—even as full nodes with economic and client privileges—in a blockchain and, in that way, expand network size and value potential.

Furthermore, IoT could improve data immediacy, quality, and accuracy, for example, by diversifying and potentially decentralizing the source of the data used in some applications so that no single data point can dictate action. Consider the climate in your home, for example. If you live in an older building, you very likely have one thermostat that measures the temperature of the air in the room where it is located and then tells the heating and cooling system to adjust everywhere according to that reading. If the thermostat is in or near your kitchen, the story it tells about your home's climate is warmer than the reality. If instead you had a set of mobile temperature sensors distributed throughout your home and installed a networked thermostat with which the sensors could communicate, the observable data would give a more complete picture.

By cross-referencing data from multiple sources, IoT can improve the quality of the data uploaded or linked to a blockchain. Having multiple, unbiased sources could in theory provide a more reliable view of the world than humans can. For example, a blockchain collecting data directly from the connected things inside and outside a car can provide a more accurate version of the truth than the car owner could, especially if that owner were inclined to mislead a potential buyer about the condition of the vehicle. IoT in this way could facilitate truth.

IDENTITY BECOMES DECENTRALIZED AND SOVEREIGN

In chapter 6, we describe a scenario in which a person shopping on the internet will be able to monetize personal data and share pieces of it as desired with marketers or retailers. From now into the beginning of the blockchain-complete phase (around 2023), the technology that will enable personal data monetization will still be immature, partly because of the use of static IDs.

Decentralized self-sovereign identity, or SSI, in contrast, is a dynamic and evolving digital identity that people will be able to use flexibly.[10] An individual's SSI will identify the person to digital systems and provide secure access without the loss of privacy. Combined with AI, an SSI could support an autonomous agent deployed by an owner to look for opportunities (e.g., find me a new house in a city where I am moving for work) and take action on them (get a mortgage pre-approval).

The need to establish a digital identity for use in a variety of contexts is an old idea but one that has gained momentum. The World Wide Web Consortia (W3C) has been working to define standards for what it calls a "decentralized identifier" for users on the web.[11] In parallel, the nonprofit Sovrin Network formed in 2017 as an open-source project that aims to act as a public-service utility for creating and managing SSI on the internet. Sovrin aims to create a digital equivalent of a driver's license or passport, a portable, ubiquitously accepted proof of identity. The difference between a passport and an SSI, however, is that the SSI will not be permissioned or maintained by a central entity.

Instead, internet users should be able to supply information to confirm their identity and get an SSI through a decentralized system.

Sovrin is playing multiple oversight roles in this space. First, it is a nonprofit open-source project aimed at coordinating the development of an identity-focused blockchain and corresponding user apps. Second, it administers the decentralized governance framework for SSI—a framework designed to comply with existing legal systems. The Sovrin Network includes fifty organizations known as "stewards," many of which run a node. The stewards include technology companies like Evernym—an SSI solution provider—platform vendors like IBM, network providers like T-Mobile, and identity compliance stakeholders such as city municipalities.[12]

In a parallel move, the government of British Columbia is looking to apply the concept of SSI technology to address a real-world problem. In a recent conversation with us, John Jordan, executive director of emerging digital initiatives for British Columbia, described an identity solution his team is developing for businesses in the province. As Jordan explained, businesses must jump through several hoops to keep their licensing current. The process is expensive and time-consuming, given that businesses might need multiple permits, certificates of incorporation, and other validating documentation, all issued by different governmental offices. Though it may seem like a good idea to consolidate and centralize this information, Jordan thinks that consolidation is the wrong approach.

"We want to move away from having a central data authority," he said. "We don't want to aggregate data in a way that could allow that data to be misused. We want to make it hard to correlate data such as email, phone numbers." He continued, "The internet is broken. When transactions need to be backed by Visa or massive data stores that compromise privacy, there's no way for government to inject trust in the economy."[13]

The solution the province is developing—in cooperation with its counterparts in Ontario and the federal government of Canada—enables organizations such as business registries, permitting services, and contracting authorities to issue authentic data using verifiable credentials, an emerging W3C standard. These verifiable credentials will be posted to a public credential registry (OrgBook BC) that uses Hyperledger Indy open-source software. This initial approach is part of a bootstrapping strategy to prepare for when the market has software that will allow business owners to hold their own verifiable credentials. The provincial governments of British Columbia and Ontario envision that businesses will use this authenticated data to establish trusted peer-to-peer relationships such as those needed with supply-chain partners. Together these new software services interoperate to establish a new global system, the Verifiable Organizations Network. This network will facilitate the formation of new digital relationships that are sustainable and trusted without the need for centralized or intermediary services.

The regional governments in Canada are not the only ones to see administrative value in creating an adaptable ID solution for businesses. In South China, as part of the Greater Bay Area (the name for China's efforts to combine numerous cities, including Hong Kong, Macau, and Shenzhen, into one integrated economic hub), Hong Kong's Applied Science and Technology Research Institute Company (ASTRI) is exploring how to use blockchain technology to facilitate business registration across Hong Kong, Macau, and Mainland China, each of which has its own distinct legal frameworks. Today, registration is complex and businesses have to trust unknown intermediaries to open a subsidiary in another market. In this case, as Dr. MeiKei Ieong, the chief technology officer of ASTRI, explained, "the role of the blockchain is narrow. It only checks that the data is real and certified by matching digital keys. It solves a particular problem but with important implications for economic development."[14]

BODIES BECOME NODES

As SSI technology matures, we will see a merging of SSI with IoT in the form of bio-implants that reside inside human bodies and fulfill certain tasks. Bio-implants are a burgeoning area of medical research. A few current applications include implants that deliver diabetes medication directly under the skin without the need for daily or weekly shots; brain implants for delivering deep brain stimulation to treat specific conditions such as Alzheimer's and Parkinson's disease; and "prosthetic memory," an implant that can copy brain patterns as you practice certain skills and then play them back for you to give you a memory boost.[15] In a breakthrough for people with paralysis or missing limbs, researchers are also developing implants that allow individuals to control prosthetic devices by thinking about the movement they want to make.[16]

These advances are eventually expected to lead to implants that could be put in the brain with sensors to capture brain wave data and perform activities. A brain implant SSI could act autonomously—think of it as the brain becoming a node.

Some private companies aren't waiting for the medical field to deliver solutions. One company has developed an implant for the hand or fingertip to store cryptocurrency or personal data.[17] These experimental efforts are of unclear value today, even as they gesture toward a possible future of body-centric things.

HOW BLOCKCHAIN BENEFITS IOT AND AI

Just as IoT and AI can benefit blockchain, so too can blockchain benefit IoT and AI. Blockchain networks enable a broader variety of transactions, improve the level of truth, and encourage more trust. Let's examine each of those aspects in more detail.

WITH BLOCKCHAIN, SMART THINGS CAN IDENTIFY AND TRANSACT

Most IoT applications today involve companies that build sensors into their manufactured products and offer compatible software to pull the data and analyze it. In this context, things don't interact with each other but instead interact with a central platform. As IoT matures, however, the diversity and volume of interactions will increase significantly. The introduction of 5G technology will contribute to those increases. One outcome will be the ability of things to communicate directly with each other without needing a central platform to mediate that exchange. Another will be the greater variety and therefore value of information collected. Things in an office building, for example, will be able to talk to things in the utility-owned water pipes fifty yards away. These distributed things—owned by different entities and running on different technology—are going to need a way to identify each other, communicate, negotiate, and transact.

A core value proposition of blockchain is to provide an architecture for identifying and microtransacting in distributed, autonomous computing environments. To enable identification, things will have the object equivalent of decentralized SSI.[18] For microtransactions, blockchain will enable more diverse forms of value. As we said in chapter 1, fiat and its proxies (bank accounts, credit cards, automated clearinghouses, SWIFT, etc.) weren't built for the volume, the variety of assets, or the type of machine-to-machine microtransactions that are possible between things. When millions of these things can exchange individual units of energy or items of data, the size of any individual transaction drops well below $0.01, while the number of transactions multiplies to unfathomable scale. Operating in this high-volume, low-per-unit-value environment requires new forms of value and native currencies.

Microtransactional capabilities extend to the exchange of assets that are natively digital. We've provided examples of how data could be exchanged and monetized as individual units or in bundles in a tokenized environment, or how personal attention could be sold to a content creator. The market value of an individual data point or five minutes of human attention will vary by market and context, but in general the value of individual transactions will be tiny—a few cents to a few dollars each. Exchanging that value securely and at extreme speeds between millions, even billions, of participants requires decentralized, autonomous, and tokenized mechanisms. Business leaders must therefore recognize the role of tokenization beyond fiat replacement and payments.

What matters most is the ability to use tokens to *create and represent* new forms of value and enable new microtransactions of this value.

A third transactional effect of enhanced blockchain is the ability to trade assets in parts, not just as wholes. An example of this idea in insurance is adjustable rate pricing. A recent discussion with a client demonstrated the possibility of differential pricing in the shipping industry. A smart contract could negotiate differential pricing for shipments placed in lower-risk or higher-risk sections of the boat (the center is safer), for instance, or shipped via international routes that are more secure or less so.

BLOCKCHAIN PUTS DATA IN CONTEXT

IoT and AI rely heavily on the quality, accuracy, and security of the data that feeds them. Yet business leaders have known for a long time that some of their data is dirty. Differences in source and type, how it is captured and organized, who has access to it, where it is stored, and a host of other issues make data reliability a vexing issue.

The combined ability of IoT and AI to capture and analyze data from multiple sources and build an accurate digital view from the various sources offers one benefit for data accuracy. When combined with blockchain's consensus mechanism that validates the data and its auditable record, these benefits become more reliable and useful. The consensus can refuse data that is inconsistent with normal patterns and system rules. This ability to find inconsistencies in high-volume sources of data is as useful for detecting early signs of equipment failure as it is for detecting data breaches. With this ability to validate via consensus, any tampering of data is more easily auditable.

AI also benefits from reliable data. Specialists use large data sets to teach algorithms. The more accurate the data, the more reliable the performance of the algorithm; the more flawed the data, the more biased the algorithm. While human influence in the programming cycles is also a factor, we need to avoid feeding flawed data sets into these algorithms. If the algorithms are to overcome the evidence of algorithmic bias in widely used applications such as mortgage origination tools, or criminal sentencing algorithms, we need to develop them using the most accurate data we can collect.[19]

One example of the promise of AI and IoT combined with block-chain is *digital twins*, digital representations of real-world objects or systems created from the data collected by sensors.[b] Digital twins allow organizations to represent physical assets in digital form to better manage and trade in them. For instance, the Airport Authority Hong Kong has built a digital twin of the Hong Kong International Airport to help with facility planning and management as the authority executes on the airport's expansion. The digital twin allows airport employees to visualize areas of the airport and model different changes to see the impact of design choices. This modeling feature is especially relevant for engineers of the airport expansion and for retail shop owners, who can more easily visualize how additions will affect passenger traffic flow.

To be clear, the airport authority is a centralized organization, and its twin does not reside on a blockchain. Translate the concept to an environment involving multiple facility owners and stakeholders, and you can see how a digital twin on an enhanced blockchain could benefit from various processes. The facility owners could validate data and protect themselves from bad data, erroneous interactions, and unauthorized users. The participants would also enjoy distribution of access so that those in different locations could interact with the data and base decisions on it. Finally, the blockchain participants would have access to alternative financing options, facilitated by the ability of investors to see the environment and engage with it.

b. A digital twin is a digital representation of a real-world entity or system. Though constructed using software, digital twins mirror the characteristics of the object or space they represent, so the twin changes as the thing changes. A digital twin may hold data about events (e.g., a sensor reading or a change of location), the current state of the thing, and historical reference data. It may also contain the programming logic associated with creating, reading, updating, deleting, or performing calculations (including analytics) on the data that it holds.

DANGER ZONES WITH IOT AND AI

Despite the benefits, there are also potential pitfalls in combining IoT and AI with data and blockchain. One problem comes from having too much data. The presence of multiple sensors collecting the same or complementary data and communicating duplicate information to multiple systems can add complexity and redundancy that results in high costs and little insight. Note that IoT developers use a variation on the digital twin concept to filter redundant data at the edge of a network before bringing it in for centralized analysis.

Another risk is the digital platforms deploying and then using things to promote centralization to the point that blockchain alternatives cannot compete. Consider a model in which, for example, Amazon deploys thousands of delivery drones and then rents their excess capacity to third parties such as insurance companies. When an insurance agent needs pictures of a house, for instance, it can order them, and Amazon can have the drone take pictures en route to a delivery. The convenience and effectiveness of such a service would make it hard for the insurance company to switch to an alternative later, and Amazon gets a new source of revenue—and a new source of data—at a very low cost. In the same way that Trojan horse blockchain-inspired solutions draw in participants by delivering near-term value, a centralized IoT service like this example could turn things into a Trojan herd, driving traffic and value to the owners.

Blockchain solutions could mitigate this issue, however, by enabling new and secure engagement models without prior physical contacts and lengthy contract negotiations. For example, drones would become a shared resource among companies operating across multiple industries, such as retail, logistics, and insurance, generating economies of scope. Thanks to the immutability of blockchain records, this arrangement would improve compliance with air-traffic regulation and facilitate insurance for drones by creating virtual flight-data "black boxes" for them. From a business model perspective, cross-industry value exchanges could be temporary and could transact in minuscule denominations. These exchanges would generate fee revenue governed by a smart contract, enabling the sharing of a data token in exchange for another form of value token, both tokens issued via the blockchain. For example, an investor looking into farming data to price a commodity might request access to data generated by another company using the drone. In this way, a blockchain multiplies business interactions and enables the discovery of new opportunities across industries, even reshaping industry boundaries.

Consumers are also voicing increasing concern over the development of self-driving vehicles after an Uber vehicle hit a pedestrian in 2018.[20] Google's Waymo has likewise been on the receiving end of citizen anger in Chandler, Arizona, where locals are questioning what the company's autonomous cars could mean for jobs and privacy in their city.[21]

Small businesses, especially direct-to-consumer microbrands, may therefore see the most benefit from making their actions transparent. And blockchain's immutability, traceability, and auditability functions offer a way for organizations of all kinds to maintain transparency and prove that their actions fit their intentions—a useful tool in today's environment, given the low levels of trust people have in public and private institutions.[22]

SMART CITIES: A LABORATORY FOR ENHANCED BLOCKCHAIN

Cities operate at a strange crossroads between business and government. Like businesses, cities need revenue and compete to attract people and organizations that will pay local income, property, and sales taxes. But cities are also responsible for a broad range of critical public services, including law enforcement, school systems, safe water, and passable roads. Tensions arise when the needs of those who generate the revenue and those who use the services are at odds with each other.

Urban challenges have taken a new turn in our high-tech era as cities compete for attention from technology companies. That competition comes in various forms, including high-profile battles to attract or keep large employers (e.g., Amazon's HQ2); the city-focused grant activity of tech-oriented foundations (Bloomberg and Gates among them); and the courting of cities by technology companies looking to lock in a market and conduct natural experiments with cooperative regulators.[23] Cities are the newest front in the battle for data. Time, as they say, is short, given that more than half the world's population now lives in cities, a proportion that is expected to grow to 65 percent by 2050.[24]

The idea of a smart city has been touted as a solution to many urban-growth problems. Though there are different definitions of what constitutes at minimum a smart city, Gartner defines it as a life-cycle approach to urban governance focused on improving citizens' lives, stimulating its economy, and protecting its environment, using data and analytics to create a user-focused and contextualized experience for residents.[25] The aspiration is laudable, but smart-city efforts have barely begun, especially as they require continuous intelligence.[26] Still, some cities are already applying a smart-city approach to various problems.

SMART IDEAS IN EXISTING ENVIRONMENTS

Kansas City began implementing a smart-city vision in 2016. In addition to the pothole preventive-maintenance solution described earlier in this chapter, Kansas City's initiative includes efforts to update its transit system to be more efficient and inclusive and to utilize technologies to manage crime. Proposed changes include improvements to a low-income, high-volume corridor; the integration of autonomous vehicles (in particular in and around the airport); and digital connections in and between vehicles. Sensors on buses and on bus-stop signs are intended to provide accurate information about human traffic, travel times, and transportation demand so that the city can better adapt to volume and needs.[27]

Data is an important resource for smart-city efforts. In New York, the mayor's Office of Recovery and Resiliency is using data to inform its priorities for reducing greenhouse gas emissions by as much as 80 percent of the 2005 baseline by 2050; this reduction is one of the mayor's key goals.[28] A data analytics effort by the Office of Infrastructure found that 68 percent of greenhouse gas emissions in the city are produced by building heating and cooling systems.[29] The knowledge has informed city advocacy and investment. One effort under way provides support for decentralized energy generation, in particular, solar arrays and wind turbines installed on buildings for local use.[30] The city is also promoting modern heating and cooling technology with sensors to better monitor energy use; the government is already putting those recommendations into action in municipal buildings.

Consider the benefits of using sensors in an office building to capture data on energy use and using AI to analyze the data and find ways to optimize efficiency. DeepMind, Alphabet's AI arm, did just that in 2016 in a Google cloud server farm and achieved up to a 40 percent reduction in energy use.[31] Applying that kind of innovation in a city could produce powerful benefits for the environment through more-efficient energy production and distribution and for the cost of living. But is the same scale of impact that DeepMind achieved in a closed, proprietary environment feasible in a complex city context?

OLD BUILDINGS, NEW TECHNOLOGY, OBSCURE RULES

Existing environments like Kansas City and New York force IT professionals to confront the real challenges of deploying smart solutions in complex environments. DeepMind had the benefit of working with known, modern equipment. Likewise, it was trying to solve a problem with a limited number of variables. Cities are far more complex, with systems that vary widely according to age and infrastructure.

The ideal in smart buildings is for the sensors associated with different systems—heating versus lighting, for example—to be able to talk to each other. If a building is generating its own energy or accessing energy produced by a neighbor, it also needs to talk to the sensors in the building next door. Both building owners shouldn't have to buy the same hardware or software to enable this communication. Because such an exchange is difficult with today's technology, urban leaders and technology companies are interested in smart projects they can build from the ground up—as Xiong'an did in China. They want to gain experience and demonstrate advances without the staunching effects of complexity.

One example of this kind of greenfield development is under way in Toronto, Canada, where city officials have signed a partnership agreement with Sidewalk Labs, a subsidiary of Alphabet, to build on an underdeveloped area of the waterfront. Branded Quayside and managed by a public-private partnership called Waterfront Toronto, the plan for the area includes mixed-use retail and residential buildings, autonomous vehicles, and outdoor space, all of which will be wired with sensors and cameras to collect data and manage human and vehicular traffic, energy use, waste management, and other realities of urban living.[32]

Toronto's Quayside is something of a smart opposite of John Jordan's decentralized SSI initiative in British Columbia. Whereas Jordan is trying to get the government out of the business of managing citizen data, Quayside—through Sidewalk Labs—seems intent on capturing as much information as it can get. Though officials made all the right noises about protecting privacy, the current data policy has kept many of the data rules undefined. In an October 2018 advisory board meeting, Sidewalk Labs reportedly reiterated its intention to scrub collected data of identifying details but said it couldn't guarantee that other groups participating in the project would do the same. The privacy implications so alarmed Ann Cavoukian—Ontario's former privacy commissioner and an adviser to Sidewalk Labs—that she resigned. The Ontario government later removed three municipal representatives from the Waterfront Toronto board, saying they rushed the process and have not allowed for enough oversight by city, state, and federal stakeholders, as well as citizen commentary.[33]

A Quayside that is built with a single platform and homogenous technology could probably produce better short-term outcomes in energy efficiency, waste management, and human and vehicular traffic. These benefits, however, come at a cost; control over citizen data (and the subsequent monetization of it) would be ceded to a private company. The consolidation of such power is problematic in a democratic society. It's one thing for a person to choose to use Gmail or Google when the person has other competitive options. It is another for a person driving on the street to have his or her actions captured on camera and stored by a third party with which the individual has no agreement.

Privacy advocates are worried about the privacy precedent that such a centralized model sets. So too are the citizens of Kansas City in considering their city's smart efforts. The plan to improve the transit system in one of its low-income neighborhoods includes installation of fiber-optic cable to enable Wi-Fi. But the same project also brought cameras, as well as a gunshot detection system, which has community members concerned about what else the city's new smart systems are capturing about them.[34]

BLOCKCHAIN IN THE SMART CITY

The tension between privacy and technology is not unique to cities. It applies wherever more data merges with more intelligent algorithms capable of extracting insights. The smart-city examples we highlight hint at the different approaches municipal leaders are taking in urban environments. Some efforts are developed with an eye toward improved digitalization in an increasingly decentralized environment facilitated by IoT, AI, blockchain, or all of these together. Others are looking to digitalize as a means to further centralization. Figure 7-1 illustrates these scenarios.

The northwest quadrant represents a highly digitalized environment under centralized control. Call it an urban *digital black box*. The algorithms are the property of a given organization or institution, and they are not visible to the citizens whose behavior and actions the algorithms influence. Examples of smart-city efforts in this quadrant include Xiong'an, with data control held by the Chinese government, and Toronto's proposed model for Quayside as of January 2019, with data control held by Alphabet's Sidewalk Labs and its partners. In cities, control can be held by governments, of course, but also by technology providers or even by large property owners.

FIGURE 7-1

Programmability versus decentralization with enhanced blockchain

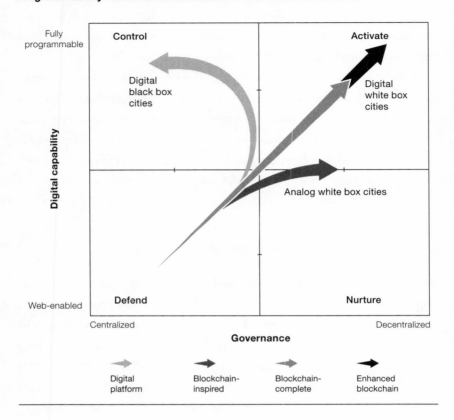

To reiterate, the centralized approach brings benefits in terms of technology efficiency and interactivity, but it has costs in terms of citizen privacy and potentially independence and in the fair distribution of benefits to the inhabitants. In an urban black box, technological things inevitably become agents of surveillance.[35] They provide ways to control community members by nudging them to behave in specific ways.[36] AI accelerates action on the data and may suggests new ideas about what data to collect to monitor and influence citizen behavior.

Social scoring generates mixed reactions. On the one hand, there are behaviors that damage communities and that cities all over the world want to limit. Littering, excessive use of energy or water, dumping of dangerous items, violence, crime, fraud, exploitation—these are but a few. Central actors in the control sector could reasonably argue that their approach allows for faster, more accurate oversight over these behaviors and therefore more relevant policies and approaches to manage them. But the cost to democratic societies that have come to expect privacy may be too much.

One alternative is to make the use of digital tools in urban environments optional—we call this approach the *analog white box*. New York's recommendations for building upgrades fall into this category. The government has published guidelines for building owners who want more-efficient heating and cooling systems; many of these guidelines include sensor technology. Likewise, the city advocates for decentralized energy generation to take pressure off Con Edison, the local utility, and to make the city's energy systems more resilient to storms or coastal flooding. The digitalizing effect of these recommendations is minimal, at the same time that they promote continued decentralization of ownership and decision making. This quadrant represents an interim step. Building owners, companies, citizens, and other stakeholders will feel pressure to become more digital, more centralized, or both if energy use policies become stricter or the city feels increased competition from other cities with more-attractive environments, including those enabled by digital black boxes.

Alternatively, cities could move in the direction of British Columbia's Jordan to hand control of citizen data to the owner—a *digital white box* model. The parameters and intents of the algorithms are the property of the citizens who decide on how to shape them to influence a desired behavior and action. While blockchain combined with IoT and AI cannot solve all the challenges of data privacy and use, it plays a major role. The data collected by things in a digital environment enabled by blockchain with decentralized SSI can inform communities about the availability of resources and development needs in a way that preserves security, accountability, and data privacy. The decentralized digital city can become a more transactional and socially responsive environment, in that citizens get a fair price for sharing data and can see how it is used. These transactions are not just about profit, but also about social goods such as access to housing, public transportation, clean air, and green space. Decentralized digitalization could also improve transparency in local government by making the bidding process for city contracts open and auditable. These systems can still nudge behavior, but they do so in a transparent way that uses tokens to motivate and reward.

Which approach will cities and citizens choose? As blockchain evokes new social opportunities, we are likely to see situations that fit into either the digital white box or the digital black box scenarios worldwide. Fear of losing control over one's data to a digital platform such as Google is a powerful motivator to challenge centralization. As a result, citizen stakeholders—including businesses and their executives—need to stay informed about how IoT and AI algorithms are used in stakeholder environments if they want to influence and advocate for the fair and transparent use of these tools. To do so, citizens have to be motivated and engaged. Thankfully, enhanced blockchain provides business leaders with the tools to achieve sustainable engagement in the form of nudges, via tokens, to provide rewards and incentives to customers, citizens, and other stakeholders. Ultimately, the enhanced blockchain helps people take actions that reap social or community benefits.

YOUR REAL BUSINESS LENS

WHAT DID YOU LEARN?

The parallel developments of blockchain, IoT, AI, and SSI will converge under the umbrella of enhanced blockchain solutions in the middle to late 2020s. IoT and AI individually and together can facilitate decentralization and improve blockchain. IoT can increase the number of nodes on a blockchain network and improve the quality of the data. AI can make smart contracts smarter with self-learning algorithms. Adding SSI solutions elevates the functionality of blockchain by giving all participants—including things—a portable ID; smart things must be able to identify themselves to counterparties and transact with them.

Solutions that take advantage of this symbiosis are already emerging in smart-city projects and elsewhere. The tensions emerging at Toronto's Quayside development and in Kansas City highlight the importance of balancing the need for urban modernization with security and data privacy. Enhanced blockchain solutions designed with decentralized governance could balance these tensions.

WHAT SHOULD YOU DO ABOUT IT?

AI is becoming more broadly embedded in technology and within a few years will enable machines of all kinds to make autonomous economic decisions. This will happen with or without blockchain, but business leaders should explore how enhanced blockchain solutions could uncover new, ethically appropriate business opportunities.

There is an ongoing backlash against AI and IoT by people concerned about both privacy violations and the economic implications of machines replacing the human beings in call centers or the driver's seat of a car. As a leader, you can't underestimate the amount of transparency and corporate social responsibility that will be needed both inside and outside your organization to help stakeholders understand the pros and cons of AI and IoT. Blockchain can help you show stakeholders that your actions are appropriate and compliant and your respect for personal data high using the immutable record.

Also be aware that digital giants can turn IoT and AI into Trojan herds by using proprietary smart things to consolidate a market position. If you invest early in enhanced blockchain solutions, you might establish an alternative market position.

WHAT'S NEXT?

An enhanced blockchain environment governed by consensus has profound implications for how the organizations that build and use them align their various functions. When operational activities and decisions have been coded into a smart contract or, in more-advanced cases, into a DAO, what will the organization look like and do? How will business culture and leadership adapt? Is your organization prepared for a world in which your products, customers, and employees are represented by things or by lines of code? How will you lead when your employees are represented by a mix of humans and algorithms? We explore those questions in the next chapter.

CHAPTER 8

THE BLOCKCHAIN ORGANIZATION

It is hard to overstate how powerful machines and other things could become during and after the enhanced blockchain phase of the spectrum. AI-enabled systems will be able to amass many thousands of lifetimes of business rules and other information and process it in a fraction of a second. On a blockchain, self-executing dapps will process information, draw conclusions, and transact autonomously. In that world, what will it mean for humans to lead, and how will leaders perform that role? What will organizations look like when they are no longer driven from an identifiable center?

For an increasing number of organizations and their leaders, these questions get to the fundamentals of what they want to achieve. Joseph Lubin, CEO of ConsenSys and one of the founders of Ethereum, told us, "If we wrap the world in layers of instant communication and we have consensus technologies like Ethereum and Bitcoin, just that notion of consensus formation has implications for how we set up organizations. The technology we are building inspires us to try a new approach."[1]

As we considered that consensus could function not only on a block-chain but also in the very fabric of an organization, we were inspired by emerging research on computerized swarms. *Swarming* refers to the collective behavior of animals like bees or birds when they engage in a collective activity such as migration. The leadership of a swarm passes to different members during a flight.[2] The bird at the head is sharing the leadership of the group using the natural world's equivalent of a consensus algorithm to determine who participates and what role they take.

Computerized swarms are the subject of experiments by computer scientists. Swarms were on display at the opening ceremonies of the 2018 Winter Olympics in Pyeongchang, South Korea, and at Lady Gaga's Super Bowl 2017 halftime performance.[3] In both these examples, drones were programmed to move in a choreographed way and emit light at prescribed times. But science has since moved past pre-programming toward autonomous collaboration. In June 2018, *Science Robotics* published results from a study in which scientists developed the first swarm of drones that could operate with collective intelligence. The swarm, in other words, was decentralized, each drone deciding autonomously where and how to move.[4]

It is a very short jump from swarming drones to swarming decentralized autonomous organizations (DAOs) on a blockchain coming together to collectively negotiate and execute a business transaction. DAOs or collectives of these organizations could fulfill numerous functions (e.g., finance, legal, compliance, communications) in the same way that a swarm of bees includes a queen, workers, and drones, each doing a different job. Or a swarm of DAOs could consolidate resources and execute a transaction that individual members couldn't pull off independently, similar to how the Swarm Fund consolidates the resources of retail investors to buy institutional assets (see chapter 6).

Swarms offer a useful metaphor for how leadership will evolve away from hierarchical models toward radical, automated, and autonomous collaboration between humans and machines seeking value. Though the exact impact of blockchain on the organization is still a big unknown, within a few decades, many of the tasks that occupy organizational time and resources today will no longer exist or be handled by a machine. Under those circumstances, organizations will need to lead, motivate, and reward people differently from how they do so today. Given the likely changes and the uncertainty about the exact nature of that change, this chapter is a thought experiment on the blockchain organization. We attempt to answer questions such as these: What organizational structures will dominate in a blockchain environment? What leadership approaches will be successful? What kinds of talent can perform in a decentralized environment populated by AI and IoT? How do you motivate and reward stakeholders in a world of decentralized and autonomous organizations and participants?

THE ORGANIZATION ON BLOCKCHAIN

It will be difficult for a great many people who have spent their careers in traditional corporate environments to grasp the concept of a decentralized blockchain organization operating one or many enhanced blockchains built with a consensus-driven design. The way people connect to and engage with a decentralized organization looks radically different from what is common today. There are vast differences in how people are organized; the guidance they receive on what to do, when to do it, and why; and the incentives and compensation for their work. Both the structure of the organization and the styles of leadership that will thrive are likely to be affected in a decentralized blockchain organization.

In an interesting "meta" twist on the possible changes that blockchain makes to the organization, there will also be blockchain solutions designed *for* the organization to realize new ways of structuring, assigning leadership roles, and allowing talent to agree to projects or roles. For example, the London-based startup Colony positions its solution as "the human capital layer" of the technology stack. Colony allows organizations to define what they need to do and to break down the structure and talent needs into doable chunks.

At the first level, users create a colony (i.e., an organization) and then define work domains (e.g., finance, legal, marketing), which are associated with a range of tasks, the smallest unit of work in a colony. Colony uses standard words in a different context to describe the various roles participants play in a colony. Managers define the tasks that need to be done, workers complete the tasks, and evaluators decide whether the task was completed at the requisite level of quality.

Participants rise to their roles (manager, worker, or evaluator) by earning reputation, which they build by performing tasks. The more tasks performed at objectively high quality, the better the reputation. The better the reputation, the more of a leadership role a participant can play in the colony and the bigger the stake the participant gets in the value the colony generates. Crucial to the meritocratic ethos of Colony is the fact that reputation degrades if a participant stops contributing. An early investment does not give participants any stake in the lifetime value of a venture. Nor does charisma, preference, attractiveness, where they went to school, or who their friends are hold sway in an environment organized around who does what to a requisite level of quality. No one can bank their influence. Incentives and rewards are based on ongoing, continuous contribution.

In 2019, Colony was not yet operational with its solution. We highlight the startup not for the organization itself but for the ideas it represents: a meritocratic work environment in which leadership and benefits are fluid. When we intellectually marry the idea of swarming DAOs with blockchain-enabled organizational tools à la Colony, we see major changes in how organizations structure themselves and how leaders rise into positions of authority. Let's look more closely at both.

FROM HIERARCHY TO HOLACRACY

The hierarchy has for centuries been the dominant business leadership standard and the most common organizational approach.[5] It has long worked for us to keep every participant in a system working toward a common goal. We can credit its longevity in part to the applied discipline of corporate management and the influence of many twentieth-century thinkers. For example, Frederick Taylor, Herbert R. Townes, and Henry L. Gantt were all major contributors to scientific management; Frank and Lillian Gilbreth applied the goals of individual efficiency to teams; and Peter Drucker helped lay the foundations of modern management theory. Through their contributions and those of others, centralized and hierarchical organizations have overall enjoyed greater productivity than more horizontal or flat organizations. Scholars have attributed that productivity to the clear network of relationships and the resulting rewards systems inside the organization. These elements allow participants to effectively interact with each other and reap benefits.[6]

Yet hierarchies have their disadvantages.[7] The challenges include a lack of agility in the face of change, bureaucratic decision making that is both slow and ignorant of the realities of how the work gets done, excessive distance between those who make decisions and those who interact most with the customer, and leader bias. Steep hierarchies also tend to perform poorly when the activities they are involved in require a range of expertise and viewpoints. The need for such a range was unusual when the world economy was dominated by companies that made physical products and when connectivity depended on the landline phone and the railways. But the need is the norm in digital environments, in particular those influenced by mobile, digital, social, and, more recently, blockchain solutions. In all these situations, traditional management methods are ill equipped to provide the diverse capabilities needed.

Some organizations saw the limits of hierarchies early. Long before the dawn of the digital age, some radicals saw the agile benefits of flatter, more decentralized structures. In their book, *The Misfit Economy*, Alexa Clay and Kyra Maya Phillips describe the egalitarian organizational structure adopted by nineteenth-century British pirates. Since the risks of piracy were absorbed by everyone, pirates operated as collectives in which everyone got a vote and everyone received equal shares in the plunder. The "captain" only had differential authority during battle.[8]

More modern examples of nonhierarchical businesses include Illinois Tool Works (ITW), long heralded for operating as a federated organization with a central core that sets standards and strategy but lets the individual operating units maintain local leadership and decision making. If a unit of this traditional machine manufacturer gets too big, leaders break it into several smaller parts so that each unit can maintain an entrepreneurial approach to its market. ITW has operated with this model for decades and today is a $14.3 billion company.[9]

Johnson & Johnson is likewise known for its federated model. Former CEO William Weldon explained in 2003 that J&J's decentralized structure is an outgrowth of its diverse product lines in the consumer packaged goods, medical device, and pharmaceutical sectors. The differences in focus, target customer, and regulatory complexity requires each product to operate as its own business with independent leadership.[10] Weldon said that the challenge of keeping so many independent units aligned is worth the effort, because of the increased resilience the decentralized structure gives J&J. If a problem arises in one of the functions, it cannot ripple to the others.[11]

Still further away from hierarchy is Zappos, an online shoe and clothes retailer engaged in a radical experiment with holacracy, an organizational approach that decentralizes decision-making authority to self-organized and self-governing teams. Though observers note that Zappos has seen unprecedented turnover of its labor force since it adopted its holacratic organizational structure, leaders inside the organization see that turnover as a natural by-product of change. Not every employee wants to be part of the experiment.[12]

As Zappos illustrates, people who are used to having clear boundaries may be uncomfortable with the collaborative demands of a decentralized organization. Zappos leaders are sanguine about the challenges of adopting a decentralized organization, but the difficulties of changing one's culture are real for any organization attempting a radical reorganization. While doing research for this book, we spoke with several leaders with experience in decentralized organizations. One interviewee was a former executive of an international manufacturing conglomerate embracing organizational decentralization. The executive, who agreed to share his experience anonymously, reported that the decentralized model worked well at the level of the individual business units, which develop specific products and business models and which operate as collaborative, self-organizing agents in their markets. Their full transformation was hindered, however, by continued hierarchical and centralized behavior from operational service functions such as finance, marketing, and HR. The leaders of these service functions still required a business unit to get approval before they would release budgetary funds, facilitate a new hire or contractor, design a marketing campaign, or provide other centralized functions.

Lubin, the ConsenSys CEO, shared his perspectives on leading a young organization engaged in a radical experiment. "ConsenSys is attempting to eschew top-down command and control. However, this may result in a loss of clarity and accountability that you get for free in a centralized organization."[13] The company will need new processes to ensure clarity and accountability. Lubin also said that operating as a decentralized organization does not mean that it fully rejects hierarchical approaches. For example, a short-term hierarchical structure could develop in a project through an explicit agreement, so that Person A is accountable to Person B in one situation as long as B is accountable to A in another situation.

The experiences of both these executives suggest that operating according to the collaborative ethos of blockchain requires vigilance on the part of leaders. It might otherwise be easy to slip into the practices that bring clarity or accountability "for free," as Lubin put it. Culture attracts certain types of people. Changing an organization's structure while keeping all the people in place regardless of their inclinations creates conflicts. To dig more into this observation, let's look at leadership styles and how they could evolve within the leaderless environment of blockchain.

FROM AUTHORITY TO PARTICIPATION

In hierarchical command and control environments, leaders often rise to their positions because they demonstrate the ability to make strong, independent decisions without input from subordinates. In other words, they can become authoritarian. Alternatively, they may rise on account of their ability to be bureaucratic and follow a playbook of formal or informal rules. Last, they may be charismatic and attract employees and influence their actions because of personal affability.[14]

Authoritarian, bureaucratic, or charismatic styles are unlikely to excel in an enhanced blockchain environment, however, given the ethos of equal participation, open access, and open contribution. Add in all the technological things that will be making autonomous decisions with the help of AI, and you have another layer of self-directed and self-seeking objects that will hold considerable influence. Blockchain empowers those independent moving parts through decentralization, consensus, and individual incentives and rewards in the form of tokens. It is difficult to imagine power in that environment flowing to a leader calling out instructions from the front of the room.

More likely, the advantage will go to people skilled in collaborative forms of leadership, including so-called participative leadership and servant leadership, approaches that date from long before the emergence of block-chain and that have momentum outside the digital sphere.[15] The automotive giant Toyota, for instance, is held up as a model of servant leadership because of its emphasis on coaching and developing others. This is not just talk. Toyota organizes its reporting structure (hierarchical, we should note) so that no leader has more than eight direct reports.[16] The purpose is to give leaders the time they need to coach their direct reports while also receiving coaching from their direct leader for their business-line responsibilities (self-development is another core tenet of Toyota-style leadership).

These collaborative leadership movements don't necessarily depend on blockchain, but this sort of leadership and blockchain are mutually complementary. More so, leaders naturally drawn to collaborate and encourage group-driven consensus will have an advantage in decentralized environments over those who depend on positional authority.

LEADING WHEN THERE ARE NO FOLLOWERS

To consider organizational structure and leadership behavior in relation to blockchain, we'll revisit swarms. These structures demonstrate several qualities relevant to blockchain leadership.

First, a swarm has decentralized coordination. A technological swarm is not a group in the traditional sense. There is no leader, and participants are not chosen. Swarms are holacratic: participants self-select to the swarm and self-manage while in it. This quality suggests that successful blockchain leaders will be skilled at framing goals or problems and encouraging qualified participants to opt in to a project. Clear goal framing, clear definitions of desired outcomes, and clear incentives allow participants to join and take actions that benefit them as individuals and the network as a whole. Blockchain solutions like Colony or Bounty0x, a task-posting blockchain solution, can provide the technical mechanisms by which organizations and participants execute on the vision.[17]

Second, swarms are dynamic in both size and scale of activity. Leaders who have formed or participated in agile teams or whose organizations have taken a bimodal approach to digital transformation will be familiar with this type of team development.[a] Blockchain leaders will need skills similar to those of agile leaders. They must maintain a broad overview, seeing connections between the disparate parts and identifying any needs. Instead of communicating from the top down, a blockchain leader will connect people, things, or resources that might not be

---

a. *Bimodal* is the practice of managing two separate but coherent styles of work: one focused on predictability, and the other on exploration. The predictability mode is optimized for areas that are more predictable and better understood. It focuses on exploiting what is known while reorganizing the legacy environment for a digital world. The other mode is exploratory, experimenting to solve new problems and optimized for areas of uncertainty. Exploratory initiatives often begin with a hypothesis that is tested and adapted iteratively, potentially adopting a minimum-viable-product approach. Both modes are essential for creating substantial value and driving significant organizational change, and neither method is static. The combination of a more predictable evolution of products and technologies (the first mode) with the new and innovative (the second mode) is the essence of an enterprise's bimodal capability and digital transformation.

aware of each other.[18] The leaders will continue doing so until things become smart enough to discover and engage with each other.

Third, swarms respond and adapt to their environment. If members receive new information, they can autonomously shift to an alternative course of action. Leaders in this environment will likewise need to quickly adapt to new information. They cannot get too attached to a five-year strategic plan or any other predetermined outcome if the evidence suggests that context has changed. Figure 8-1 summarizes the leadership styles and behaviors that will be needed in a decentralized and nonhierarchical blockchain-driven environment, as compared with a traditional hierarchy.

FIGURE 8-1

Leadership styles, from hierarchy to holacracy

Hierarchy		Holacracy
	Leadership style	
Physical	**Location**	Virtual
Duty	**Emphasis**	Initiative
Role	**Assessment**	Capabilities
Linear	**Thinking**	Hive
Siloed	**Engagement**	Fluid
Continuous	**Feedback**	Discontinuous

←——————————————————————→

	Leadership behavior	
Instruct	**How to *influence***	Nudge
Authorize	**How to *enable***	Empower
Set goals	**How to *orient***	Seek goals
Direct resources	**How to *manage***	Connect resources
Supervise	**How to *engage***	Mentor
Discontinuous	**How to *reward***	Continuous

COMMUNICATING WHAT YOU ARE THERE TO DO AND HOW YOU WILL DO IT

How will leaders attract and motivate people in progressively decentralized environments? Like all organizations, decentralized ones need to develop methods to attract participants who can thrive in their decentralized culture and deter people who can't. To do that, you "begin with the end in mind," as Stephen Covey advised three decades ago.[19] Laid out in its barest terms, leading in a decentralized enhanced blockchain environment requires a vision.

When your organization is able to autonomously seek value, self-organize, partner and interact with other autonomous organizations, why your organization exists and how it does what it is designed to do must be firmly defined. Traditional organizations, which have the natural checks and balances inherent in the slow cadence of human mental processing and quarterly board meetings, can be more flexible with their rules.

Just consider the amount of business a DAO can undertake in a human workday. Theoretically, the organization will access huge volumes of data, draw conclusions from it, and execute thousands if not millions of transactions before you've made it from your bed to the coffee machine in the morning. There will be no limits on the number or range of interactions the organization could undertake within just a few minutes. The terms of competition between two organizations with these capabilities could hinge on the smallest differences in opportunism—or in ethics. Competitive pressure will be fierce, creating a potential race to the bottom in terms of how low companies are willing to go to create value. Do we really want the DAOs operating in this world to do so with no limits? Do we want these organizations to be able to collude? The short-term experience with algorithms designed to replace human judgment in certain arenas—law enforcement and mortgage approval, to name two—shows that algorithms can carry the same biases that humans do. As a leader, you will need ways to place checks on algorithmic decisions, assess how they change, and determine if those changes are fair.

Beyond fairness and ethics, checks on decentralized businesses on blockchain will exist for the same reason there are checks today—because laws require these checks. Though they often lag technology adoption, laws do eventually encourage certain business behaviors and restrict others. Blockchain could speed up the regulatory reaction, because the immutable record allows regulators to audit your actions more easily and quickly, and any regulatory redress could be equally dynamic, as regulators will have access to the same tools.

Beyond laws, there are also values. Despite Milton Friedman's famous assertion that the sole responsibility of a business is to generate profit for its shareholders, many leaders—and perhaps more saliently, customers—believe that businesses should operate with a baseline level of respect for the people and resources that allow it to flourish.

The challenges inherent in leading an algorithm are as important as the challenges of leading people. Fortunately, these challenges are intimately related. Both will drive leaders to define a vision, mission, and values, because having a reason for why you exist and what you do helps rally the talent and resources you need. It gives you a frame for the rules and terms coded into a decentralized application, or dapp.[b] From those rules, you can then attract participants to help you pursue your organizational goals. This approach gives people the opportunity to participate according to their capabilities. Once people join in, you will need a way to evaluate the quality of their work, compensate them for their contributions, and create incentives for them to stay or return. Blockchain can play a role here, too, making it easy to audit a record of work and reward quality with tokens.

Lubin spoke about some of the blockchain mechanisms ConsenSys is experimenting with in this vein. For example, a ConsenSys "bounty"

---

b. A decentralized application, or *dapp*, is an umbrella term for an application that contains code for executing agreements and includes smart contracts. But unlike smart contracts, dapps execute transactions among fluid sets of participants (not a fixed number) and need not involve financial obligations. Dapps fall into three categories: apps for value; apps for governance, rules, voting, and the like; and apps for processes (e.g., contract settlement).

program lists initiatives that need resources. "We're enabling smart people to join our projects," he told us, "and we can specify the work. On Gitcoin, we can hire those people if the project or the company likes them." On the importance of clear requirements, Lubin suggested that they should be part of a blockchain-based legally enforceable agreement between an organization and a contributor: "Specify vision, mission, operating goals, board of directors, advisory board, the method for getting work done. Identify stories or issues if a software developer team confronts a problem. We need those mechanisms, plus mechanisms for feedback. Teams will have ways to specify what their intended outcomes are and a single accountable person for each intended outcome, as well as dispute resolution, arbitration—all of that is part of an agreement."

The message from Lubin and others we have spoken with reveals that the requirements for clarity in decentralized organizations are very high. Only when you can clearly articulate the resources you need will you be able to attract them. Of course, once you have those resources, you'll need ways to recognize and pay them. Blockchain will play a role in rewarding, too.

EMPOWERING WORKERS THROUGH BLOCKCHAIN

The challenge of talent recruitment and management is perennial. Gartner's 2019 CEO survey reports that 32 percent of respondents believe they will need a substantial or total change in their talent base over the next three years.[20] A 2018 survey of CEOs by the Conference Board put failure to attract the right talent at the top of the list of respondent concerns, above the need to create new business models to compete with disruptive technologies.[21] And the twenty-first annual CEO survey by PricewaterhouseCoopers (PwC) likewise shows that 80 percent of CEOs worldwide believe their organizations do not have the digital skills they need to compete.[22] Blockchain brings new alternatives to the way leaders and talent find each other, work together, create value, and receive compensation.

Talent attraction in a digital environment cannot ignore the growing impact of temporary, contract, and gig models. In the analog world, there is a strong, growing global staffing industry that sources talent on a short-term basis.[23] Gig platforms such as Lyft and Uber for transportation and TaskRabbit, Upwork, and China's Ziwork for nontransport, labor-based activities likewise offer a mechanism for accessing workers. Research by the JPMorgan Chase & Co. Institute shows 300 percent growth in US worker participation on these platforms since 2013.[24] In Western Europe, between 9 and 22 percent of workers by country are believed to have done some work found through digital platforms.[25] Seeing the potential, large organizations are applying the gig model to supplement their own staff. The accounting firm PwC launched the PwC Talent Exchange in recognition of volatile staffing needs, and the Washington Post developed its proprietary Talent Network for finding freelance journalists.[26] All told, more than 16 million workers in the United States alone work in contract, freelance, or contingent roles.[27]

The momentum behind this trend of digitally sourcing freelance and contingent workers is inarguable. So too are the problems with the existing mechanisms for matching workers with available jobs, confirming the work, and compensating the workers. Given these challenges, blockchain startups are, not surprisingly, emerging with new solutions to mediate gig and contingent work.

Heymate launched in Switzerland in 2018 with a solution that facilitates deals between workers and employers, absent the price bidding that is typical on gig platforms like Upwork.[28] Workchain offers a blockchain payroll solution designed to enable immediate payment for completed work, a big issue in the gig economy, given the long lag times on some platforms between when the work is done and when the worker gets paid. Workchain facilitates prompt payments with a solution that allows registered workers to do a job, have the job verified on-chain, and have their money sent immediately to a Workchain wallet that they can cash out onto a Visa prepaid debit card. Workchain also offers a form of payroll loan that allows workers in good standing to obtain an advance on future earnings.

Another blockchain solution aiming at gig-based talent recruitment and management is ChronoBank in Sydney, Australia. ChronoBank's solution, LaborX, is a blockchain labor platform that allows employers and workers to connect and create work arrangements.[29] Employers buy worker time in LH, the labor-hour token, which is pegged to the hourly minimum wage of the home country of a participating employer.[30]

The increasingly global nature of the economy likewise needs solutions that make it easier for an employer to pay workers located in another country. The startup Bitwage is working on that problem with a cross-border payroll blockchain. The payments are made in bitcoin, and Bitwage manages the conversion to the local currencies in which workers are paid.[31] As for finding people for contract or freelance jobs, Bitwage has a recruitment arm that matches workers with advertised roles.

ChronoBank and Workchain are each addressing just one aspect of the complex relationship between organizational leaders and the people who work for them. Think of them as blockchain-inspired at the level of their ambition, given their focus on translating an existing process for a decentralized digital environment. Other organizations, such as the startup Colony described earlier in the chapter, are going further to reimagine talent sourcing and work to address the issue of ongoing engagement enabled through transparency and rewards.

TRANSPARENCY AND REWARDS

One of the most interesting aspects of what a blockchain organization can do is equip both leaders and workers with the same power to choose to work together and the same information about how well each does the work. That's a radical change. Employers like to say that workers with high-demand skills have power, because the organization needs them to meet customer demand. High-demand workers may have some power, but it is diminished by corporate policy limits on employee pay and benefit and where they can work. Evaluation methods likewise dictate, usually from the top down, how a person's output is judged and rewarded. There's little room for the average employee to negotiate; even very senior employees hit hard limits.

The radical transparency possible in a blockchain business could change this hierarchical system. Algorithmic blockchain organizations can only operate if they are open about what they do, the work they need to have done, and the skills they need to do it. The quality of worker outputs will be open to scrutiny, as will the leaders' work. Rewards will likewise be transparent and enabled with tokens.

A blockchain cannot be vague about the requirements needed to achieve a particular output, the relationship between work done and payment, or the basis on which a worker or a leader gets assigned to a position. Transparency, immutability, and auditability ensure this clarity. The definitional discipline required to translate processes (such as employee goals and objectives) into algorithms will force organizations and leaders to be specific. Leaders may sometimes even need to lean toward absolutism in the way they define talent needs to control and limit on-chain activities.

Nor does specificity preclude bias. Organizations will probably unwittingly embed biases into the blockchain and thus into their talent management programs. Leaders need to take great care when they are defining needs and approving participation in blockchain networks. Blockchain organizations—like all organizations—need strong ethical standards.

We are seeing early application of blockchain for talent recruitment and management. HR functions, for example, are exploring blockchain solutions to verify applicant credentials. The blockchain startup APPII is offering a platform for that purpose. Some tools will also allow employees to develop skills and renew certifications, like the solutions we highlighted in the education sector to capture and store student credentials and match students with teachers for skill development. These examples are compatible with hierarchical organizational structures and are designed from the perspective of the organization. Such a perspective is applicable in today's hierarchical environment, though we suggest that Colony's vision of a two-way balance, whereby leaders evaluate workers and workers evaluate leaders, offers a more interesting and valuable model for the future. As seen earlier in figure 8-1, moving from the traditional top-down structure to a more flexible, horizontal one implies a shift toward a holacracy—the organizational model that Zappos has adopted.

Personnel in holacracies take initiative, define and seek their own goals, and shift those goals as they gain skills or see new opportunities. In practical terms, workers (human beings or things) will choose whether to bid on a task or participate in a project; they won't be assigned, as they are in most environments today. Importantly, the opt-in model could be used as easily with an internal talent pool as with a decentralized workforce. The model could operate by having all participants identified with a tokenized set of data that documents their skills, knowledge, credentials, reliability, preferred schedule, and past achievements. Lubin said that ConsenSys is experimenting with a token-reward system that rewards people for filling out onboarding information, for example, or putting their skills profile into a tokenized wallet they could use to get involved in projects. The same approach could apply to you as a leader.

This kind of radical transparency can bring objectivity—dare we say fairness?—to the work environment through access to information. Another option enabled by technology is *futarchy*, a model of governance in which business communities define measures of success for a particular venture and then use prediction technologies to identify which actions are most likely to bring the desired outcomes.[32] Conceived by economist Robin Hanson as a model for government, futarchy has been embraced by the blockchain community, and several prediction markets, including Augur, Stox, Gnosis, AlphaCast, and Hivemind, have already emerged.[33]

These markets could provide more visibility on the requirements and potential contributions of a given project. Both leaders and workers would be evaluated, compensated, and rewarded (via tokens) according to concrete output. Likability, personal connections, and the ability to publicly self-advocate would have less impact on salary levels and bonus rates than would performance. Discrimination on the basis of race, age, sexual orientation, or physical characteristics would be less rampant in an anonymous environment (again assuming that the algorithmic bias that has been identified in anonymous contexts is eliminated as humans get better at writing intelligent code).[34] A big mistake made years before would carry less evaluative weight in the context of consistently high-quality work. Rewards would come not through a leader's "proof of authority" but through a collaborator's "proof of capability." This change in flow and control of rewards could directly influence behavior. If workers know they can get a bigger stake, will they contribute more? Will leaders invest more consistently in the people they work with and the initiatives they oversee?

THE CHALLENGES OF BLOCKCHAIN LEADERSHIP

We have positioned this chapter as a thought experiment on how the widespread use of blockchain could change leadership and organizational structures. Despite its promise, blockchain also has some major challenges as it relates to the organization. Although today's environment gives few indications of what these challenges might be, they include leadership liability, oversight, and default behaviors. Let's take them one at a time.

The subject of liability in blockchain comes up regularly with our clients, mostly in the context of uncertainty. For example, leaders grapple with who is accountable if activity between two anonymous participants is deemed illegal. And if there are multiple owners of a solution that experiences a costly breach, who carries the risk?

When an organization runs afoul of regulatory guidelines in a centralized environment, regulators turn to leaders to make good. In extreme cases, those leaders can go to jail. That's a pretty good motivator to stay on the right side of the law. As we have highlighted throughout this chapter, however, decentralized organizations with operations unfolding autonomously over a network don't have leaders in the same way that hierarchical organizations operating in the physical world do.

Can a DAO in this situation even be regulated? Should DAOs be regulated in the same way that a traditional human-centric organization is regulated? If a regulatory breach—even one caused by a mistake in one line of code out of millions—should occur, who should bear the brunt of the responsibility? We don't know the answers to those questions, and regulators have not publicly weighed in on the regulatory nuances of blockchain governance, beyond some dialogue about cryptocurrencies.

Another big issue with complex implications is decision-making oversight. In a physical environment, where most decisions are made by people, there are natural checks and balances. Leaders hear opinions from their superiors, peers, subordinates, and customers. An algorithm running on a blockchain does not receive such ongoing input. Unintended consequences will become clear eventually, but perhaps only after millions of interactions and transactions.

Blockchain purists believe that the consensus mechanism, if large enough, would throw out bad decisions. We think it unwise to take the safety of this mechanism for granted. Our concern is exacerbated by the paucity of ethical structures and governance surrounding the use of AI. Organizations can decide as a matter of policy to code leadership oversight into the operations of DAOs. But maintaining policy consistency and authority as DAOs grow to millions of lines of code applied in multiple jurisdictions and constantly updated might be challenging. Oversight and governance, in sum, have few simple solutions.

A final issue affecting leadership is default behavior. People's tendency to default to a set of hardwired habits is well documented in behavioral psychology.[35] Organizations are also vulnerable to defaults, as Clayton Christensen highlights in *The Innovator's Dilemma*.[36] Default behaviors are already evident in the current leadership focus on blockchain as a technology to reinforce current business models rather than as a tool to enable decentralization and new business models.

Admittedly, it is still early. Today's leaders have not yet had to change but will do so when computers can hold and analyze the entire history of an industry on a machine the size of a thumb drive. When value-seeking objects can identify entirely new forms of value, will they force organizations to adapt? As long as humans write the algorithms and teach them, the code will reflect human thinking. In principle, if the thinking leans toward fairness, inclusion, and moral red lines, its presence might not be bad. If the thinking leans toward exclusion and maintaining old models or power, then the algorithms could be problematic. Who gets to decide? How do we ensure that algorithmic decisions do not limit the promise of blockchain to unlock new economic value in a less biased and more collaborative environment?

YOUR REAL BUSINESS LENS

WHAT DID YOU LEARN?

The widespread adoption of enhanced blockchain solutions could have profound implications for the way organizations operate and leaders lead, given that the proliferation of autonomous, self-seeking machines and DAOs will create an environment in which humans and algorithms could collaborate to create value.

Swarms offers a useful metaphor for how humans and machines could come together to realize specific goals and then separate and reform into new configurations for new purposes. Organizations like ConsenSys and Colony offer a glimpse into how people will take part in activities, accumulate reputation, and receive rewards based on their contribution.

Holacracies, futarchies, and prediction markets enable more effective participation, collaboration, and decision making, as well as transparent accountability by leaders and organizations. One way they do this is by using data to predict which choices or behaviors are likely to lead to which outcomes. In theory, this information motivates participants to work toward the outcome they want.

WHAT SHOULD YOU DO ABOUT IT?

You need to be clear about your business purpose and goals. In a decentralized environment, talent and resources will decide autonomously to collaborate with you because of their interest in your purpose and goals.

To keep those resources engaged, take steps to assess your leadership style and your organizational structure, and align them to more holarchical ways of working and engaging.

Also seek advice on what it will take to lead, collaborate with and manage algorithms and algorithmic entities like DAOs. Look to legal frameworks and to ethical, moral, and value-based structures for guidance.

Finally, recognize the culture of your organization will change due to the introduction of autonomous agents. Examine your current rewards and incentive mechanisms with an eye for how well they encourage the talent in your organization to collaborate. Make sure you have multidirectional feedback mechanisms in place to improve outcomes, accountability, and dispute resolution. Consider how your reward mechanisms will influence employee behaviors in relation to autonomous agent collaboration.

WHAT'S NEXT?

As important as engagement, collaboration, and incentives are for commercial organizations, so too will they be for government organizations and for civic communities, both local and "glocal" (both global and local). In the next chapter, we widen our frame to examine blockchain at the societal level and explore how decentralized infrastructure and tokenization can open the door for an accessible, participative, and value-creating blockchain society.

CHAPTER 9

THE BLOCKCHAIN SOCIETY

Our goal when we began writing this book was to help business leaders understand how blockchain can be used today and tomorrow to reinvent who your customers and partners are and how you engage with them. Yet even with that business focus, our research into blockchain has always touched on the ways it could fundamentally change the rules of engagement in broader society. After all, enterprises are both dependent on society and enablers of it. Society establishes the infrastructure in which business operates, and businesses, in turn, feed society through employment, economic engagement, and applied innovation. We cannot talk about one without recognizing the influence of the other.

Models for how to forge a new social contract that is technology and business friendly are already emerging in the blockchain world. The highest-profile model among them is taking place in Estonia.[1] The country has built a digital platform known as X-Road and connected Estonia's government agencies to it. X-Road is at once comprehensive and contained: it underpins a variety of private and public services from health care to finance, yet no individual service can access information from another without permission from the person to whom the information refers. Views of given records are also tracked and recorded, and the viewer's right to the information is authenticated.

In just a few short years, X-Road has become so essential and reliable in the eyes of Estonian society that businesses build their platforms on it. The Finnish government is likewise leasing X-Road for its digital infrastructure, raising new questions about the portability of citizenship services, the nature of borders, and government sovereignty. Estonia is pushing those questions with an e-residency model that allows non-Estonians to apply for Estonian residency and thereafter establish their businesses and pay their taxes there. As a small country with limited natural resources and a history of geopolitical vulnerability, Estonia is making a play for long-term economic independence by appealing to EU entrepreneurs.

With Estonia having just 1.3 million citizens, X-Road must accommodate only a fraction of what a comparable platform would need to in London or New York (population more than 8 million), to say nothing of Mexico City or Beijing (population over 20 million). Still, the country is far from alone in its view of the importance of a network that allows for peer-to-peer information sharing. Blockchain can clearly build on this foundation and can be used for its broader set of capabilities for reinventing societal service and engagement. Lithuania—with its high-tech sector, cheap internet access, and sophisticated fintech and regtech (technologies addressing regulatory issues) initiatives—has embraced cryptocurrencies and was third in the world for ICO investment in 2018, behind the United States and China.[2] Malta's government has weighed in to legitimize the development of blockchain by creating a regulatory body to oversee smart contracts and DAOs.[3] In Switzerland, the government of Zug issued digital identifiers based on Ethereum. Japan has implemented regulatory guidelines to permit the trade in cryptocurrencies. The UAE is seeking to implement a blockchain infrastructure as part of its Smart Dubai initiative.[4] These examples and others point to some of the ways that blockchain is gaining traction as a tool to empower society.[5]

This chapter examines the potential impacts that blockchain could have on societies and societal constructs and in turn how societies may react or adapt as blockchain matures. Throughout the chapter, we take both a component-based and a holistic view. We examine how siloed applications of blockchain technology could reinvent practices or constructs and how these components could roll up across hundreds or even thousands of blockchain-enabled ledgers to foundationally alter the fabric of society. We start with a definition: what is the blockchain society?

CHOOSING A BLOCKCHAIN SOCIETY

Some years ago, we began a research effort with colleagues across Gartner to describe the future culmination of technological advances related to the internet, mobile technologies, cloud computing, big data, social media, IoT, AI, and blockchain. We wanted to detail how these technology trends would individually and collectively drive changes in the way humans, things, businesses, and society interacts. At the time, we called this culmination the *programmable society*, as we believed the interactions would depend on digital technology but would influence how people come together to form communities and engage in persistent social interaction.

The programmable society we envisioned resides at the end of a technological, business, and social progression that began with the emergence of the World Wide Web. After a decade, the progression evolved into the early stage of digital business with the adoption of what Gartner called the "nexus of forces" to describe the combined power of mobile computing, social media, cloud computing, and big data.[6] From digital business—the location we occupy now—our economy and communities will pass first through a stage of adaptable business, during which the first AI-enabled smart agents will seek value and transact in ways defined by their algorithms, and then will evolve to autonomous business, when those smart agents will independently adapt and evolve (see figure 9-1).

FIGURE 9-1

The path to the programmable society

	Web	E-business	D-business	Post-blockchain-inspired Adaptive	Post-blockchain-complete Autonomous	Post-enhanced blockchain Programmable
Focus	Build, extend relationships into new markets at lower cost	Sales channels become global	Customers include people & things	Smart things become major customers	Autonomous things enable new forms of value	Value derived from built-in capabilities
Outcome	Optimize, extend relationships	Optimize channels & interactions	New business models	Maximize access, reach & control	Maximize relationships with things	Enable new economic & societal systems
Entities	 People / Business	 Platforms	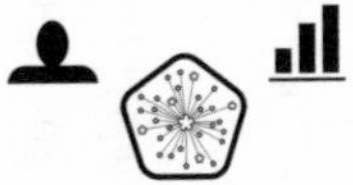 Central things	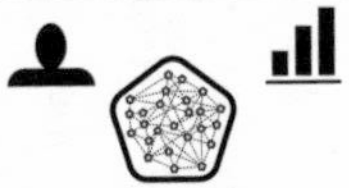 Distributed	 Decentralized	 Programmable
Changes	Technologies leverage the internet of information	Business operations & analytics leverage the internet of content	Distributed manufacturing, financial speed	Things act as proxies for people or businesses	Things act autonomously & leverage the internet of value	Humans & things collaborate on the "internet of me"
Tech	EDI, web, CRM, ERP	Cloud, BI, portals, mobile, social	APIs, apps, sensors, 3-D printing, AI	Robotics, goal-setting machines, IoT, blockchain, digital twins	Goal-seeking & self-optimizing algorithms, smart contracts, blockchain	World Wide Ledger, DAOs, SSI, smart implants

Abbreviations: AI = artificial intelligence; APIs = application programming interfaces; BI = business intelligence; CRM = customer relationship management; DAO = decentralized autonomous organizations; EDI = electronic data interchange; ERP = enterprise resource planning; IoT = internet of things; SSI = self-sovereign identity.

Many technological elements will drive momentum toward a programmable society. For instance, networked things will continue to proliferate, and advanced computational capabilities such as quantum and edge computing will become more viable. Advanced AI will be used in business applications. The volume of micro-interactions and transactions between things will rise steeply. Powerful central actors are investing in all these technologies to ensure their own access to, or ownership of, networks and data. These actors include governments, financial institutions, and powerful corporations (including digital platform providers).

At the same time, the hunger for societal change is strong, and will continue to be so. In the aftermath of the 2008 financial crisis, citizens of all ideological bents began to question the credibility of traditional central intermediaries. Globalism and technological automation had clearly brought dramatic growth but with visible unintended consequences, most notably an increase in income inequality. Fiat currencies have long been considered a symbol of trust, since fiat implies that a trusted authority—a central bank—has made a qualitative judgment about the ability of credited financial institutions to act in the best interest of the system and in turn to make reasoned judgments about the ability of borrowers to repay borrowed funds. When those institutions needed to be saved using taxpayer dollars, with no consequences for their millionaire leaders, it was a breach in the social contract.

Customers and businesses give explicit authority to intermediaries, including banks, insurance companies, and the government leaders that write the laws to regulate them. This authority is conditional; to keep it, institutions have to prove that the world is better off with them than without (acknowledging that different actors define benefits in different ways). Members of society also give implicit authority to the search engines, phones, smart home devices, social media platforms, and GPS that all of us use to manage our lives. As digitalization and social media give democratized insight into the ways that explicit and implicit authority are overlapping and even usurping each other, however, it is now clear that the once-trusted institutions are advancing goals that many citizens neither approve of nor benefit from. Schisms have become more pronounced, and trust at all levels is eroding.

The advances in technological capability coupled with the clear tensions in society suggest that our societal institutions and infrastructure are fragile and perhaps broken. Every country in the world is now experiencing the same political, social, and economic pressures to varying degrees. Most often this is evidenced by citizens who are unable to meet basic needs like food, housing, income, health care, education, and financial services. As consumers of media, we cannot trust the veracity of our newspapers or television news. Our government infrastructure needs repair, upgrades, and expansion. Climate-based events are threatening lives and livelihoods and are displacing people. Trust in and between different groups in society is threatened, and democratic societies are becoming more polarized.

Technological advances could exacerbate these social issues in many ways. Technology could disrupt the sources of value from which businesses have historically earned profit. The advances could also cause job obsolescence and uncertainty around future income opportunities. And the control and application of AI in the social sector could reinforce bias about who has access to societal resources. Of course, the opposite might also be true. Technological advances could ameliorate these issues.

In short, the programmable society has multiple possibilities. How we as leaders and as citizens manage technological disruption and negotiate societal weak points will determine what our future society looks like. In chapter 6, in the discussion of decentralized finance and elsewhere, we have highlighted the impact that decentralized systems could have on enabling fair access to resources and opportunities and ensuring accountability. When we move up to the societal level, the choices that individual businesses and institutions make will produce two possibilities for the programmable society of the future. Figure 9-2 depicts these divergent paths.

A society that runs on programmable yet centralized systems has the potential to be, frankly, Orwellian. In this *programmed society*, a very small number of organizations could own vast stores of information pertaining

FIGURE 9-2

Programmed versus blockchain society

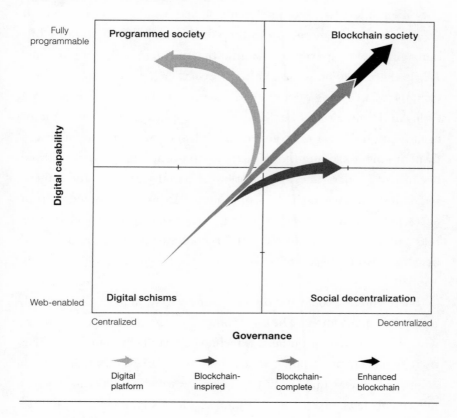

to the behaviors, movements, finances, spending patterns, and even the health and DNA of individuals. Under these circumstances, *choice* would translate to "whatever options the data broker benefits most from promoting." The implicit social contract would be that both individuals and organizations relinquish control over data, access to digital resources, related contracts, and technology in exchange for consumerism and visibility on digital platforms. News organizations could present information in selective and misleading ways. The rewards from work and societal engagement would be unequally distributed. Human rights could be broadly curtailed, for example, by limiting eligibility for health services, admission to certain universities, and home purchases in certain neighborhoods. Organizations could limit hiring to people with desired DNA profiles or according to a social credit system designed by and benefiting an oligopoly.

Some readers will scoff, believing society would never let such an Orwellian world emerge. But others live in that world already. Billions of people experience systemic bias in their daily interactions. While there is some good in almost every society, humans still universally fail at giving all members of a society equal access to societal rights and public resources. This failing applies at all levels, be it an organizational level or a governmental one. Some forms of disenfranchisement are intentional (e.g., when groups are denied suffrage because of gender, race, age, or organizational seniority), and some is incidental (e.g., when the lack of a photo ID prevents someone from accessing health services or voting). In a programmed society, this bias could worsen, because the ability to define privilege and reward or deny it would become easier, more automated, and more broadly applied.

There will be people and organizations who want to see this centralized future come about. They will want to secure rights for some groups while denying them for others. If technology can help these individuals more quickly deny certain people access to resources, they will use it. It could happen very quickly. Just consider how rapidly right-wing populist movements have taken hold in countries such as Hungary, Poland, the United States, and the United Kingdom, even with today's relatively modest level of technological sophistication. These movements give the impression of being for the people—especially for people who feel entitled to power but have been somehow cut off from it.

A society that runs on programmable yet decentralized systems, in contrast, has the potential to be fair and empowered. Societal participants control their own data and are empowered to advocate for their views and their communities through effective and proactive participation. A decentralized societal model will arise only when the technologies we have discussed throughout this book are deployed at commercial scale. Decentralized governance models such as holacracies and futarchies would likewise facilitate a more empowered model. The social contract would enable individuals and organizations to liberate data and give them access to digital resources, related contracts, and other technology in exchange for deeper engagement and an ability to defend and build on their core values.

We call this decentralized model the *blockchain society*. It enables fairness in self-representation, access, value exchange, and distribution of societal benefits. This society is enabled not by one ledger operating in a networked, digital environment, but by a collection of decentralized blockchain networks that overlap with and weave into each other to create a mesh capable of cross-network transactions. Chapter 4 touched on this interoperability, showing how reward points could morph into tokens that are first used with one vendor and then with multiple providers across an ecosystem. In another example of interoperability, gaming tokens could be used across multiple games on new aggregator platforms. At Gartner, we have termed this interoperable mesh of blockchain networks the World Wide Ledger (WWL).[a] The WWL enables dapps and distributed ledgers to power up DAOs independently or as embedded units within any centralized organization. WWL therefore introduces a global trust fabric that allows decentralized and centralized organizational units and operations to coexist.

Of course, two other scenarios are possible. If societies experience a hard limit to digital expansion and maintain their current centralized models, the *societal schisms* so many of us experience in our communities will become more deeply entrenched and increasingly dystopian. Alternatively, societies that see limited digitalization and become more decentralized could experience *social decentralization*. In this scenario, citizens in community or tribal groups might pool data to access limited digital resources and related contracts and technology or as a way to affect social outcomes for those groups. Given the current pace of

a. The WWL is a network of interacting and overlapping blockchains that can be used in a stand-alone manner (e.g., a health-care provider's view of a patient) or combined (e.g., patients can view their medical record across multiple health-care providers), as needed. See Homan Farahmand, David Furlonger, and Rajesh Kandaswamy, "Crypto-Politics and 'World Wide Ledger' Will Rock Your Business Competition," Research Note G00357575 (Gartner, September 17, 2018).

digitalization, and the larger opportunities the blockchain society affords, this scenario seems unlikely to be sustainable.

Which society will rise to the surface with time? Our money is on either a programmed or a blockchain society. Which one we get depends on you as a citizen and as a leader. In a digitally sophisticated environment, societies will form as they always have, on the basis of tribal, geographic, cultural, linguistic, economic, or ideological connections. But in a blockchain society, the participants will choose their affiliations. Societies will likewise hold together or break apart over time depending on the rights, laws, and institutions that enforce the societal contract that participants define and amend. Through universal access to identity, suffrage, and other forms of societal participation, blockchain could offer broader access and engagement for all the participants in society. Let's look at some examples.

IDENTITY IN THE BLOCKCHAIN SOCIETY

A significant portion of the world's population—more than 1 billion people—have no way to prove who they are.[7] Women and young people are particularly affected, as are displaced people, including the more than 670,000 Syrian refugees living in Jordan.[8] Lack of ID makes it difficult to access resources such as food aid provided by the UN World Food Programme (WFP).[9] In response, the WFP has experimented with a blockchain-based iris identification solution that allows refugees at the Azraq refugee camp in Jordan to enter the local partner supermarket, choose their food items, and submit to an iris scan to self-identify to a WFP blockchain platform. The transaction is then verified and authenticated by associating the identity of the buyer with the food vouchers the WFP has allotted to him or her. The solution began as a pilot with a few hundred refugees and is now under consideration for rollout to all 500,000 Syrian refugees living in Jordan and receiving WFP support. Observers note that over time, the blockchain ID solution could extend to other purposes—for instance, verifying credentials for a work program.

FROM AZRAQ, JORDAN, TO AUSTIN, TEXAS

The UN's work with blockchain has inspired other groups around the world to consider blockchain to address similar challenges of access and identification. Like refugees, homeless people usually lack an ID. When you don't have a place to live, it's hard to hold on to possessions, and without a physical ID, you cannot use social services.

"The clearest example is using a pop-up health clinic," said Kerry O'Connor, chief innovation officer for the city of Austin, Texas.[10] "People can go there and sign up there for the city [health-care] program and then go and get a primary care provider. But to continue to see that provider after three months, you have to have an ID; proof of residency, since it's a program for city residents; and proof of income, since these clinics are reserved for low-income people who have below a certain income level."

Anjum Khurshid, head of data integration at Dell Medical School at the University of Texas at Austin, had heard about the WFP experiment in Jordan and told O'Connor about it. When O'Connor looked into it, she saw multiple benefits for Austin's homeless population and the front-line workers who serve them: "Caseworkers spend a lot of time running down documents or details to allow a recipient to access services that the caseworker is not paid to provide," she said.

O'Connor's team began a blockchain effort and identified the primary group it wanted to reach within Austin's population of ten thousand homeless.[11] "If you take it quantitatively," O'Connor explained, "everyone entering homelessness [and who comes in contact with social services] is assessed about their various vulnerabilities. Do they have an addiction? Are they experiencing abuse? Do they suffer from an illness? Et cetera. From that, they get a score. High scores get the most resources, but if the least vulnerable have to wait [for housing or services], their situation will often deteriorate. So my team started asking how we could get to the eight thousand people with low scores faster when their situation is less precarious and maybe get them what they need to transition out of homelessness."

With that population in mind, O'Connor and her team applied for the Bloomberg Philanthropies Mayors Challenge in October 2017 and received first-stage money to conduct tests and create a prototype—a necessary step to apply for the full Bloomberg grant. The team members designed a solution that would include all the social services available and the documentation each service organization needed. They decided to focus on the metadata related to a document: instead of requiring a copy of a birth certificate or a social security card, the blockchain would instead confirm that there was a validated birth certificate or social security card associated with that person. The solution then had a mechanism for the person to sign in and validate himself or herself at a service site.

O'Connor submitted her final proposal for the Mayors Challenge in August 2018. Shortly before our conversation, she had heard that it was not accepted. She has not given up on funding the development of a "minimal viable product" for her city, though.

"When it comes to technology," she said, "we don't spend enough time talking about how it can help the most vulnerable members of our society." She reflected on the time she has spent developing and testing a blockchain identity solution: "We had this idea because we spent time thinking about what it is like for medics, caseworkers, police officers, people working in libraries, and we spent time getting a ground-level view of what it is like to deal with people living with homelessness. It is a systems problem. Every meeting I am in that has workers from different sectors, they say, 'God, if only we could share information!' If you think about their pain points, but also think about the issue of empowerment, it is critical to take a human-centered lens, even for people who you think don't have the resources or wherewithal to take advantage of it."

IDENTITY AS POWER

The ability to use your identifying information for your own benefit is a form of power. We have explored multiple applications of this idea in marketing and data platforms. Extending the idea to the blockchain society, we see the potential for identity-driven solutions to be applied in the health-care, pharmaceutical, and medical research industries— sectors with crossover between social and private markets.

A huge coveted aspect of identification for the health sector is the individual genome. Companies such as 23andMe allow consumers to pay a few hundred US dollars to have a portion of their genome sequenced. Individuals use these kits to learn about their ethnic heritage or to determine if they carry certain gene mutations associated with a disease. For their part, the companies store the sequences and sell access to the data to third parties such as researchers or pharmaceutical companies. The people to whom that genomic data refers are not told when their data is shared; nor are they compensated for its use. This lack of control over genetic information is common in the medical and drug research industries.[12] We aren't saying that people shouldn't share their data, but that the sharing should be a choice each time.

Blockchain makes the choice possible. The UK-based blockchain startup Genomes is building a blockchain platform to which individuals can choose to append their sequenced genome from the minute it is decoded. When a company or research institute has a question about a section of the genome, the owner can selectively unlock access to it in exchange for value. This genome database could benefit private and public research institutions by providing a new and larger pool of data (thanks to incentives for participation and improved privacy guarantees). Citizens also benefit from having a (theoretically) secure way to store genetic information.

Startups are not alone in their embrace of blockchain for securing medical data. The developers of the Taipei Medical University Hospital solution we highlighted in previous chapters have hopes for a blockchain solution. Once they have all the patient data in the system, a blockchain network will create a more flexible way to identify candidates for research studies and then use the platform to capture and track study data.

If blockchain can capture data about cells and DNA, can it do the same with synapses and brainwaves? Philosopher Melanie Swan has developed the concept of *blockchain thinking*, whereby thoughts and other cognitive experiences (perhaps, eventually, consciousness) are collected as "mindfiles" and uploaded to a blockchain.[13] Swan speculates about several applications for this solution. For instance, mindfile blockchains might augment memory in the event of memory loss due to aging, injury, or illness, or they might be used to create a digital twin with which to test future scenarios.

SOCIETY AND REPRESENTATION

Identity is directly related to voting rights. Consequently, the same blockchain activity aimed at verifying identity can also help increase voter participation in elections. Democracies around the world struggle with nondiscriminatory ways to ensure that only those with the right to vote exercise it and to limit voting to one ballot per citizen. Yet flaws in the voting system create uneven access and errors and delays in securing a reliable vote count.

Those challenges have motivated experiments with blockchain voting systems. The US state of West Virginia, for example, developed a system in 2018 to address the issue of low voter participation among military personnel stationed overseas. Deployed citizens are eligible to vote with absentee ballots, but some military members never receive their ballots and only a fraction of those who receive them send them in.[14] In response, the West Virginia government worked with a blockchain startup called Voatz on a mobile voting app for use by West Virginians living overseas.[15] In total, 144 overseas personnel from thirty counties downloaded the app, went through the registration process, and cast their votes in the November 2018 election.[16] These numbers are small by design, and the Voatz approach is blockchain-inspired.[17] But as a proof of concept, the West Virginia experiment points to a future in which more eligible voters can exercise their rights.

Other countries and municipalities are conducting similar experiments with voting-related apps. Vienna, Austria is considering blockchain as a way to secure government data of all kinds, including voting rolls.[18] Officials in the Japanese city of Tsukuba tested a blockchain system for allowing citizens to vote on local development projects.[19] And the city of Zug, Switzerland, is engaged in a multilevel experiment to issue electronic IDs and then allow citizens to use them to identify themselves inside a voting app before casting votes in local government polls. The questions asked in the pilot included whether citizens think electronic systems should be available to pay library fines or parking tickets (the results from the experimental polls were non-binding).[20]

Increased voter participation coupled with an encrypted, immutable, and auditable record of the results paves the way for predictive algorithms to run over voting systems. Predictive tools in a society could enable a futarchical government, a model of governance proposed by economist Robin Hanson. In a futarchical government, societies define broad measures of well-being and use predictive tools to assess which policies or approaches are the most likely to bring about the desired outcomes. There are obvious concerns about voting. For instance, if early votes begin favoring one approach, could they influence people to vote with the crowd even if the result would conflict with the voter's personal beliefs? But the potential to bring societies together more easily and steer monetary investment or policy is intriguing.

Experience with prediction markets have thus far been limited to a few experiments. The idea that a society's members would want to proactively direct local investment according to local consensus, however, is gaining traction, especially to ensure greater levels of accountability and action-oriented policy.

SOCIETY AND INVESTMENT

Financial resources are as important to the functioning of society as they are to business. Yet few topics generate more conflict than does governmental use of financial resources. Giving community members choice over how societal resources are spent could improve buy-in. It may even produce more financial resources: economists have found that if taxpayers were permitted to choose which parts of the budget their tax dollars funded, they would be willing to pay twice as much as they do when funds go into a general pool.[21]

Multiple experiments in local resource control are under way. In Bangladesh, a company called ME SOLshare Ltd, a joint venture with German consulting company MicroEnergy International, is equipping communities in rural parts of the country with solar arrays that can generate energy and enable its trade. In partnership with a local nongovernmental organization (NGO) and Infrastructure Development Company Limited (IDCOL, the Bangladeshi government-owned development bank), ME SOLshare equips communities unserved by central utilities and enables trade using a hardware system that monitors and redirects energy to other consumers. Mobile payment systems and a mobile app (not blockchain) coordinate payment.

One of many blockchain-enabled experiments in decentralized energy is in progress in Brooklyn, New York. With the help of LO3 Energy, a provider of blockchain energy solutions, and Con Edison, the energy utility that serves New York City, a microcommunity has established a microgrid to self-generate solar energy and sell it to others in the vicinity.[22] The Brooklyn experiment is possible because a cluster of homeowners had already made a group purchase of solar panels. LO3 Energy and Con Ed then worked with the panel owners to create platforms and apps that monitor generation and that, instead of feeding excess energy to the Con Ed system, enable locals without panels to buy the excess. The experiment in decentralized energy was explicitly supported by the city government, which is interested in exploring ways to relieve New York's aging infrastructure.

The idea of decentralized resources is not new. NGOs and development institutions have invested significant resources in small-scale mobile solutions for energy, water, medical care, and other social services, with mixed results. One unresolved issue involves the maintenance and repair of physical infrastructure after the donor or installer leaves. Local communities don't always know how to fix broken equipment, or they lack the parts to make repairs. Nor is it obvious who should foot the bill when shared resources break down. NGOs and development finance institutions are therefore investing in community engagement. They are actively collaborating with local representatives so that community investments reflect current needs. A life-cycle view of infrastructure is increasingly part of these conversations, which blockchain can facilitate by improving traceability, visibility, and access and by reducing fraud or corruption. By supporting fair access to, and distribution of, resources, blockchain would make its financial and social impacts more salient.

A different, finance-driven model for community investment comes from Neighborly, which works with municipalities to identify local projects that need funding and then develops a municipal bond issue to raise money for the projects. Local governments can use the platform to raise money for school building maintenance, road repair, public park infrastructure, and other community resources. The blockchain keeps a record of who owns the issued bonds and ensures that those investors receive their returns when the bonds vest. Because the bonds are formally registered and have official ratings, they are low risk and are widely available because of relatively low minimum investment levels. They are also tradable at any time on the secondary bond market.

SOCIETY AND BORDERS

Many human societies are based on borders. We have national and regional borders that define nation states or municipalities. Organizations also have a border of sorts; it defines which people are affiliated with the organization. The issues of identity, voter participation, and local investment discussed in this chapter all take place today within the confines of established governmental borders. But making the processes digital and putting them on the blockchain can sometimes make physical borders more fluid.

In no way are we minimizing the literal and symbolic importance of borders in societal identity and governance. The Palestinians in the

West Bank and Gaza, and the ongoing annexation of the Crimean Peninsula by Russia are just two examples of how deeply borders are linked to power and security in society. From 2014 to 2018, the Islamic State maintained what it referred to as a caliphate in northern Iraq, for instance, creating a symbolic homeland for its version of extremist Islam in and around the city of Kirkuk. Less violent, though perhaps no less disputed, is the country of Liberland, whose existence is based on a difference of opinion over the real borders between Croatia and Serbia.[23]

Yet just as some find deep meaning in borders, others are throwing them into question. The "seasteading" movement, promoted by the Seasteading Institute, aimed to establish an ocean-based society completely outside national borders to pursue technological innovations without the regulatory oversight of government. The concept smacks of *Jurassic Park*–level hubris, and the seasteading movement has lost momentum because of the technical challenges of building safe, livable environments in the middle of the ocean. Still, the idea of by-passing government rule of law endures on nonprofit ocean vessels that travel the world providing medical services such as abortions while anchored in international waters. Greece has likewise used ships to house migrants while they await proper processing.[24]

Blockchain expands the potential for a borderless society by enabling participants to affiliate with one another and access societal resources. Over time, this potential could manifest itself in more granular ways. The casual musings of some Californians on whether the state should declare independence could experience a digital manifestation in the form of a California blockchain. At a smaller scale, blockchain could enable microsocieties made up of micromarkets and microbusinesses.

THE INTERNET OF ME

How far could microdevelopment progress? Gartner's WWL, its proposed global ledger network, could support an ecosystem of agents (autonomous and otherwise) that could facilitate the diverse exchange of value. In our current economic system, actors, assets, customers, and suppliers operate independently from each other and from the enabling mechanisms. In a blockchain society, in contrast, those components could be coded directly within the same system. So, the resources you own, the financing mechanisms you use, the data you own or that refers to you, and your desired contract terms are all coded inside the DAO or dapp that transact as you on the WWL. We refer to this integration of the system and its components as the *internet of me*.

In chapter 7, we introduced the idea of biohacking and human implants that could seamlessly communicate with external components. We've also discussed the potential for thought waves or genomes to be captured and stored on the blockchain. In addition to static storage, our genomes could also be manipulated through more-advanced forms of CRISPR editing.[25] How far do we want these technological advances to go?

In a review of the available literature on gene therapy, David learned that the capability to biologically manipulate behavior, thoughts, and capabilities was closer that he had previously known.[26] He hypothesized that business executives could someday use gene enhancement to gain a competitive edge through genetic procedures that enabled them to think faster and make better decisions.[27] In today's mildly digital society, technology capabilities are *bolt-on*, that is, easily added to a business's functionality. For example, a digital wallet app that requires the user to initiate and authenticate a transaction is a bolt-on capability. With blockchain technology, capabilities could be *built in* to the human form. Combined with SSI, implanted autonomous agents could make decisions on your behalf. This capability raises questions about how the future social contract will be structured. In a time when the machine lives inside humans, how will a social contract between humans be written?

Even without advanced gene editing, the blockchain society can disrupt large, traditional economic institutions in the same manner that social media, microblogging, and peer-to-peer file sharing have disrupted the established content and media industries. The difference between those earlier disruptions and the future blockchain disruptions will depend on the variety and scale of change, as well as its decentralized and programmable nature. The consequences of these changes are significant and widespread, implying a redefinition of moral, legal, ethical, social, economic, and cultural norms.

CHALLENGES IN A BLOCKCHAIN SOCIETY

We see a great deal of promise for enabling participation and fairness in a blockchain society. This society also brings some risks around security, privacy, and data ownership.

In a blockchain society, security becomes both more advanced and much more complex. We have repeatedly tried to debunk the idea of blockchain as an unhackable system. Though aspects of blockchain-complete solutions make them difficult to compromise, there are still vulnerabilities in the peripheral technologies used with or on top of the blockchain ledger. Cryptocurrency wallets, for example, are insecure in their current form, and there have been multiple compromises of token holdings at crypto exchanges as well as hacks to smart contract code. IoT systems are also highly insecure; they currently lack checks and balances to confirm if the data captured and imported reflect reality.

A related issue around security is key management. SSI, cryptocurrency ownership, and network access are all enabled through the use of security keys, which are much like passwords but are issued by the solutions themselves. And just as they do with passwords, participants must keep track of keys. Lose them, and you lose access to your tokens, your IDs, and so forth, and there is no way to recover them. Loss of a key is a major risk in an entirely digital system. A real-world demonstration of the risk took place in February 2019, when the CEO of a crypto-exchange died in possession of the only key to the stored $137 million in tokens.[28]

The question of data ownership will also continue to vex us as society becomes more programmable. Societal systems designed to capture member data will underlie all programmable environments, whether they are programmed or blockchain. How can we as leaders and society members be sure that no single actor gains access to all of it? We can start by building decentralized systems and rejecting the centralized models pushed by powerful corporations. This strategy would require consumers to move en masse away from the proven, centralized platforms that give us so many benefits. Such a change will not happen in democratic societies without strong commercial alternatives. Data decentralization in nondemocratic societies will be even more challenging, since government agencies in these societies have few restrictions on what they can access. The social scoring system described in chapter 7 in the context of smart cities takes on a more sinister cast when a government can use it without limits. China's social credit system is already reportedly influencing who is allowed to travel by airplane or work on certain projects.[29]

Citizen engagement likewise poses a challenge within a blockchain society. Throughout the examples we highlighted, such as voting and involvement in local investments, we have assumed that people will want to be involved. But do they? Voter participation is low in many countries, not just because of the voting challenges we described earlier in the chapter, but because some people don't want to vote, don't think voting is important, or don't believe their vote matters.

Similar questions about participation and behavior apply to the community of technology developers who have so much control over the algorithms that will govern important social infrastructure. Some in the field have proposed a Hippocratic oath for software developers.[30] More recently, B9lab proposed a Satoshi oath as an invitation for blockchain developers to consider how the values of immutability, neutrality, and decentralization will be manifested in each project they touch.[31] The idea is to provide a structure for people to start governing their choices as a blockchain society evolves.

These issues all point to the reality that changing a societal contract is not just about building the infrastructure necessary to do so, but also about attracting people to raise their hands and participate in building it. Just as the blockchain organization requires participants to join the collaboration, so too does the blockchain society. The rewards and incentive model native to blockchain could help drive that participation. The complicated role played by things has great bearing on a blockchain society. Machines that can interact with each other and exchange value may create governance rules for themselves. This self-governing ability gives a whole new angle to the idea of shared intelligence and shared decision making.

YOUR REAL BUSINESS LENS

WHAT DID YOU LEARN?

Customers expect to be able to use technology to shop, manage their finances, and track health behaviors. Why not use it to engage in civic activities as well? The programmable future will touch every aspect of our lives. Blockchain is already gaining traction as a tool to empower societies and citizens. Ongoing experiments are using blockchain in government applications in Zug, Switzerland, and the US city of Austin. In Jordan, blockchain is enabling resource access by Syrian refugees. In Brooklyn, blockchain is part of a crucial experiment in off-grid, decentralized energy generation. The technology is also part of an effort to activate local investment in infrastructure projects through the issuing of blockchain-based municipal bonds. These solutions and others could help drive citizens toward a blockchain society running on decentralized systems that empower participants and encourage transparent and fair access to resources. The alternative is a programmed society in which individuals and organizations relinquish control over data, access, and resources to a centralized power. The choice is still ours to make.

WHAT SHOULD YOU DO ABOUT IT?

In this era of shifting technological capabilities and consequently shifting social and economic norms, you need to decide what role you want to play as a leader. Look for opportunities to take advantage of blockchain to engage citizens and expand access to the societal resources to which everyone has a right.

At a more tactical level, use and promote strong security key management when adopting or promoting blockchain solutions. Security management is especially important in the early years, when people are still learning to trust blockchain. As a way to align blockchain developers around a set of guiding principles, consider adopting a type of Hippocratic oath for your software developers such as the Satoshi oath. You will also gain brand benefit by taking a leadership role in setting the norms and standards of the blockchain society.

Last, prepare for technology to advance to enable the "internet of me." Individuals will interact with blockchain systems as leaders representing an organization, as citizens, and as consumers—the same person could play all three roles. Your ability to recognize these roles, whatever your relationship with them, will help you benefit from the growing social and economic engagement of your customers.

WHAT'S NEXT?

The impulse to wait and see how any new technology evolves is high in risk-averse organizations. We urge you as citizens and as leaders of societal organizations—including businesses—not to wait. The programmable society is not a far-distant dream. Some aspects of it are already here, for example, in the use of the algorithms in law enforcement to determine sentencing.

Programmed systems are reaching further into everyday life than many of us like to consider. If we want our future programmable society to allow for fairness and privacy, we need to lay the groundwork now. The platform leaders are not waiting. The financial institutions that manage the flow of money are not waiting. The largest insurance companies are not waiting. And because they are not waiting, no societal institution, public or private, that hopes to influence the direction of its community and the terms of engagement within it can afford to wait.

CONCLUSION

PURSUING *YOUR* BLOCKCHAIN

You have choices to make for how blockchain will evolve in your organization, your market, and your society. Those choices naturally contain conflicting elements, as we've discussed at various points in this book.

On the one hand, blockchain has been touted as a revolutionary technology to reengineer business processes. On the other, the real business of blockchain creates new markets, industries, types of customer and shapes societal engagement with new organizational models.

On the one hand, enterprises are deploying blockchain in an atmosphere of centralized control. On the other, the real business of blockchain demands decentralization of governance, economics, and technology.

On the one hand, you have risen in your career within a market (and likely an organization) with clear hierarchal lines. On the other, the real business of blockchain drives growth by enabling economic agents to act autonomously in a consensus-driven environment.

On the one hand, societies around the world have experienced a widespread dissolution of citizen trust in public institutions. On the other, the real business of blockchain encourages experimentation with new social contracts and new ways to engage and participate.

On the one hand, the use of AI increases opacity on who controls the business currencies (i.e., data, access, contracts, and technology). On the other, the real business of blockchain provides transparency over smart-machine-based activity and clarifies value exchanges and accountability.

The list of contrasting aims goes on. The biggest difference of all exists in the space between observation and action—between your desire to learn all you can and the need to jump in and experiment for yourself to find blockchain's strategic value. In matters of technology, you're likely to have a strong instinct to wait and see what others do before you make an investment. Received wisdom among enterprise leaders has long held that so-called type B companies—those that wait to invest until pioneers have proven the value of a new technology—usually have the best position.[1] They are supposedly early enough to benefit from some market differentiation, but they avoid the risks absorbed by early adopters.

The type B strategy may have worked in the past. But it won't be as effective as we move toward the programmable society. The business currencies of data, access, technology, and contracts accelerate winner-take-all dynamics. The organizations that control these currencies earn an outsize share of the revenues that flow through a market. These four currencies also define the terms of engagement for customers, including smart machines and other businesses.

The stakes are high in defining a new economic and social model that breaks the hold central actors have over the currencies and that replaces our winner-take-all scenario with a more decentralized, more accessible, more transparent, and fairer alternative. Embracing the real business of blockchain requires not just a vision and new technology skills. Organizations must also evolve toward new organizational models that redefine leadership, enterprise culture, and working practices. Those who wait until blockchain technology matures are guaranteed higher opportunity costs levied from both sides. Thousands of blockchain-native startups will swarm to dilute the competitive capability of type B companies, and centralized powers will keep pushing to maintain their positions.

The window is therefore small. Market actors with a vested interest in maintaining centralized governance models are already pushing blockchain-inspired models as the market status quo. If their efforts succeed and prevent the evolution toward blockchain-complete solutions and enhanced blockchain, you will miss a critical inflection point in the evolution of digital business. Without blockchain-complete solutions, the millions of things emerging as economic agents will be controlled by a central intermediary. The AI and algorithms in development today will therefore convert data into predictive analytics that will benefit only a small percentage of the population.

Leaders who believe that technology should benefit as many organizations and individuals as possible and that advanced solutions should have transparency and accountability cannot wait five, ten, or fifteen years to see how blockchain evolves. They need to define and execute now on their vision of a programmable future with decentralized access, influence, and value, for the benefit of all.

NOTES

CHAPTER 1

1. John-David Lovelock et al., "Forecast: Blockchain Business Value Worldwide, 2017–2030," Research Note G00325744 (Gartner, March 2, 2017).

2. In the Bitcoin blockchain, block size is uniform and determined by the compute size of the cluster of records. In other chains, the size of the block can vary. For example, in Ethereum, block size is based on how computationally intensive the transactions are. As a general rule, any given block holds the records for about 2,000 transactions. See Mitchell Moos, "Bitcoin Transactions per Block at All-Time Highs," *Cryptoslate*, April 8, 2019, https://cryptoslate.com/bitcoin-transactions-per-block-at-all-time-highs/.

3. The concept we now call *blockchain* was first described in a 2008 white paper by a pseudonymous person or group called Satoshi Nakamoto. The white paper describes a digital cryptocurrency that could be safely traded over an open network. Together, blockchain and bitcoin, the cryptocurrency that emerged from Nakamoto's design, solved a problem that had long stymied theorists: how to make sure that two long-distance peers who have no way of communicating with each other both know and agree on the same course of action. (This problem is known in computer science circles as the Byzantine generals' problem.) Nakamoto conceptualized a way to profitably settle transactions below a certain size, prevent "double spending" that can arise with payments that are both nonphysical and decentralized, and confirm and protect the identity of the participants. See Satoshi Nakamoto, "Bitcoin: A Peer-to-Peer Electronic Cash System," Bitcoin.org, November 2008, https://bitcoin.org/bitcoin.pdf.

4. The existing technologies (with their dates or approximate dates of origin) combined to create blockchain include distributed communications networks (around 1964), digital signatures (1976), Merkle trees (1979), complementary currencies (at least as early as 4000 BCE), digital currency (around 1983), proof-of-work consensus algorithms (invented in 1993), Practical Byzantine fault tolerance (1999), and secure hash algorithm SHA-256 (around 2001).

5. Not every person or entity transacting on a blockchain runs a node; a person can own bitcoin or any other token without operating a node, for example. Only full nodes can maintain and update copies of the ledger.

6. Gartner defines *encryption* as the systematic encoding of a bitstream before transmission so that an unauthorized party cannot decipher it.

7. There are different types of forks. Hard forks occur when a software upgrade changes the rules of the network protocol such as a block size change, to which all nodes must agree. Soft forks allow for backward compatibility of the previous protocol operations, to which a majority of nodes must agree. The circumstances under which forks can occur vary. The most common is when a subgroup of participants wants to change or upgrade the protocol operating on the blockchain, and others disagree with the change. In this case, the two groups may "fork" the blockchain to create two separate networks. Forks can also take place when there is a major issue with the blockchain transaction history or the protocol rules that determine network operations, and the network needs to fork to preserve assets or cancel problematic transactions.

8. Tokens can also be considered a form of virtual currency, which the European Banking Authority defined as "a digital representation of value that is neither issued by a central bank or a public authority, nor necessarily attached to a fiat currency, but is accepted by natural or legal persons as a means of payment and can be transferred, stored or traded electronically."

9. Nick Heudecker and Arun Chandrasekaran, "Debunking the Top 3 Blockchain Myths for Data Management," Research Note G00354025 (Gartner, April 19, 2018).

10. Bernard Marr, "How Much Data Do We Create Every Day? The Mind-Blowing Stats Everyone Should Read," *Forbes*, May 21, 2018, www.forbes.com/sites/bernardmarr/2018/05/21/how-much-data-do-we-create-every-day-the-mind-blowing-stats-everyone-should-read/#687bcbdd60ba.

11. Ana Alexandre, "Amazon Granted Patent for Streaming Data Marketplace with Bitcoin Use Case," *Cointelegraph*, April 18, 2018, https://cointelegraph.com/news/amazon-granted-patent-for-streaming-data-marketplace-with-bitcoin-use-case.

12. The "trough of disillusionment" is a phase in the Gartner hype cycle, a construct developed in the mid-1980s to articulate the common phases that new technologies move through on the path to producing mainstream value for the enterprise. The phases of the hype cycle are the innovation trigger, when a new technology comes on the scene; the peak of inflated expectations, when a hyped technology reaches the height of chatter in the market; the trough of disillusionment, when the results of early experiments generate disappointment and enterprises become skeptical about the technology; the slope of enlightenment, when enterprises find effective uses for the technology; and, last, the plateau of productivity, during which technologies realize their potential. To learn more about the hype cycle and how to use it, see Jackie Fenn and Mark Raskino, *Mastering the Hype Cycle: How to Choose the Right Innovation at the Right Time* (Boston: Harvard Business Review Press, 2008).

13. Adam Hayes, "Dotcom Bubble," *Investopedia*, March 19, 2019, www.investopedia.com/terms/d/dotcom-bubble.asp.

14. "Maersk and IBM Introduce TradeLens Blockchain Shipping Solution," Maersk press release, August 9, 2018, www.maersk.com/news/2018/06/29/maersk-and-ibm-introduce-tradelens-blockchain-shipping-solution.

15. Andy Rowsell-Jones et al., "The 2019 CIO Agenda: Securing a New Foundation for Digital Business," Research Note G00366991 (Gartner, October 15, 2018).

16. In practice, this means that blockchain solutions have evolved to offer the following critical capabilities: scalability in transaction throughput, nodes, resources, and so on, according to context; confidentiality and transparency of all transactions; governance (a clear decision-making structure from an industry, a participant, or a data management perspective); technical and business manageability; transaction finality; operational applicability (the solution works with the organization's operations); alignment with legal, accounting, and taxation frameworks and rules; standards for protocols, data, access, and security; interoperability of ledgers and protocols; and defined cost-benefit analysis and frameworks; and clarity about processes, risks, and tokenization.

17. Thomas H. Davenport and George Westerman, "Why So Many High-Profile Digital Transformations Fail," hbr.org, March 9, 2018, https://hbr.org/2018/03/why-so-many-high-profile-digital-transformations-fail.

18. Bay McLaughlin, "How Asia Is Adopting Crowdfunding from the West," *Forbes*, December 1, 2016, www.forbes.com/sites/baymclaughlin/2016/12/01/how-asia-is-adopting-crowdfunding-from-the-west/#446baf2c4102.

CHAPTER 2

1. In David Furlonger and Rajesh Kandaswamy "Understanding the Gartner Blockchain Spectrum and the Evolution of Technology Solutions," Research Note G00373230 (Gartner, October 26, 2018), https://www.gartner.com/en/documents/3892183, we drill down to each of these listed sources of value, among others.

2. ASX, "Daily Trading Volumes," accessed April 28, 2019, www.asx.com.au/asx/statistics/tradingVolumes.do.

3. Dan Chestertman, on-stage interview with authors, Gartner IT Symposium/Xpo, Australia, October 2018.

4. Council of Financial Regulators, Australia, "Review of Competition in Clearing Australian Cash Equities: Conclusions," June 2015, https://static.treasury.gov.au/uploads/sites/1/2017/06/C2015-007_CFR-ConclusionsPaper.pdf.

5. ASX, "ASX's Replacement of CHESS for Equity Post-Trade Services: Business Requirements," consultation paper, September 2016, www.asx.com.au/documents/public-consultations/ASX-Consultation-Paper-CHESS-Replacement-19-September-2016.pdf.

6. For more on misunderstanding in blockchain, see Nick Heudecker and Arun Chandrasekaran, "Debunking the Top 3 Blockchain Myths for Data Management," Research Note G00354025 (Gartner, April 19, 2018).

7. To learn more about leveraging data as a resource in your business, see Douglas B. Laney, *Infonomics: How to Monetize, Manage, and Measure Information as an Asset for Competitive Advantage* (New York: Routledge, 2017).

8. Maersk's blockchain initiative began as an unnamed partnership with IBM and, according to our conversations with executives at Maersk, was built in partnership with IBM. By October 2018, Maersk and IBM had launched the platform as a collaboration between them for a limited number of potential users. The two companies were planning a broader rollout for the first quarter of 2019.

9. For statistics on the merchant shipping industry, see Statistica, "Number of Ships in the World Merchant Fleet as of January 1, 2018, by Type," *Statistica: The Statistics Portal*, December 2018, www.statista.com/statistics/264024/number-of-merchant-ships-worldwide-by-type.

10. TradeLens, "The Power of the Ecosystem," accessed April 23, 2019, www.tradelens.com/ecosystem; Michael del Castillo, "IBM-Maersk Blockchain Platform Adds 92 Clients as Part of Global Launch," *Forbes*, August 9, 2018, www.forbes.com/sites/michaeldelcastillo/2018/08/09/ibm-maersk-blockchain-platform-adds-92-clients-as-part-of-global-launch-1/#2b2c3ff468a4.

11. Escola Europea, "Blockchain Solution for Shipping Has Ports, Container Lines, Forwarding Agents and Customs on Board," *Escola Europa*, August 13, 2018, www.escolaeuropea.eu/news/industry-news/blockchain-solution-for-shipping-has-ports-container-lines-forwarding-agents-and-customs-on-board.

12. Shailaja A. Lakshmi, "Global Shipping Business Network on Blockchain Platform Launched," *MarineLink*, November 6, 2018, https://www.marinelink.com/news/global-shipping-business-network-443587.

13. Matt Smith, "In Wake of Romaine *E. coli* Scare, Walmart Deploys Blockchain to Track Leafy Greens," Walmart, September 24, 2018, https://news.walmart.com/2018/09/24/in-wake-of-romaine-e-coli-scare-walmart-deploys-blockchain-to-track-leafy-greens.

14. Ryan W. Miller, "Romaine Lettuce Warning: CDC Says *E. coli* Outbreak Has Sickened 32 People in 11 States," *USA Today*, November 20, 2018, www.usatoday.com/story/news/health/2018/11/20/romaine-lettuce-cdc-warns-e-coli-outbreak-ahead-thanksgiving/2070654002.

15. Michael Corkery and Nathaniel Popper, "From Farm to Blockchain: Walmart Tracks Its Lettuce," *New York Times*, September 24, 2018, www.nytimes.com/2018/09/24/business/walmart-blockchain-lettuce.html.

16. Charles Redfield et al., "Food Traceability Initiative: Fresh Leafy Greens," Walmart open letter to Leafy Green Supplier, September 24, 2018, https://corporate.walmart.com/media-library/document/blockchain-supplier-letter-september-2018/_proxyDocument?id=00000166-088d-dc77-a7ff-4dff689f0001.

17. Robert Palatnick, telephone interview with authors, November 29, 2018.

18. Anonymous CIO, email correspondence with authors, October 4, 2018.

19. Mats Snäll, interview with authors, Gartner's European IT Symposium/Xpo, November 2018.

CHAPTER 3

1. The four original bank owners are Dexia (now absorbed under Belfius), Fortis (now BNP Paribas Fortis), ING, and KBC Bank.

2. Andrew Grant and Donald M. Raftery, "Large Corporate Banking Relationships Evolving: 2016 Greenwich Leaders U.S. Large Corporate Banking, Cash Management and Trade Finance," Greenwich Associates, December 14, 2016, www.greenwich.com/account/large-corporate-banking-relationships-evolving.

3. Frank Verhaest, telephone interview with authors, September 25, 2018.

4. Gartner, "Blockchain Consortia," Research Note 352092 (Gartner for IT Leaders Tool, 2018).

5. Finextra, "Nordic Banks Explore Shared KYC Utility," *Finextra*, May 31, 2018, www.finextra.com/newsarticle/32178/nordic-banks-explore-shared-kyc-utility; R3, "39 Firms Complete Global Trial of KYC on Corda Blockchain Platform," press release, June 28, 2018, www.r3.com/news/39-firms-complete-global-trial-of-kyc-on-corda-blockchain-platform.

6. Nicky Morris, "Trade Finance Blockchains Consolidate into we.trade," *Ledger Insights*, September 2018, https://www.ledgerinsights.com/trade-finance-blockchain-consolidate-wetrade-batavia.

7. Annaliese Milano, "Russia's Central Bank Mulls Ethereum System for Pan-Eurasian Payments," *CoinDesk*, April 4, 2018, www.coindesk.com/russias-central-bank-mulls-ethereum-system-for-pan-eurasian-payments.

8. Luxembourg, Economic Ministry, "Blockchain and Distributed Ledgers," June 2018, https://gouvernement.lu/dam-assets/documents/actualites/2018/06-juin/13-ilnas-blockchain.pdf.

9. The Hyperledger project is an effort to support collaboration in blockchain development by a wide range of industry players using open-source technology like Corda. The project is supported by influential infrastructure vendors like IBM, Intel, and SAP.

10. Aaron Stanley, "Hyperledger and Enterprise Ethereum Alliance Join Forces in Enterprise Blockchain Boost," *Forbes*, October 1, 2018, www.forbes.com/sites/astanley/2018/10/01/hyperledger-and-enterprise-ethereum-alliance-join-forces-in-enterprise-blockchain-boost/#6267b3f34aa2.

11. Paul Smith et al., "HSBC and ING Execute Groundbreaking Live Trade Finance Transaction on R3's Corda Blockchain Platform," press release, HSBC, May 14, 2018, www.hsbc.com/media/media-releases/2018/hsbc-trade-blockchain-transaction-press-release; Bank of Thailand, "Announcement of Project Inthanon Collaborative Partnership," press release, August 21, 2018, www.bot.or.th/Thai/PressandSpeeches/Press/News2561/n5461e.pdf; Bank of Canada, "Fintech Experiments and Projects," Bank of Canada, Digital Currencies and Fintech, accessed April 28, 2019, www.bankofcanada.ca/research/digital-currencies-and-fintech/fintech-experiments-and-projects.

12. Joseph Young, "Why R3CEV Member Banks Have Left, Abrupt Change in Vision," *CCN*, May 23, 2017, www.ccn.com/r3cev-member-banks-left-abrupt-change-vision.

13. Anna Irrera, "Blockchain Consortium Hyperledger Loses Members, Funding: Documents," Reuters, December 15, 2017, www.reuters.com/article/us-blockchain-consortium/blockchain-consortium-hyperledger-loses-members-funding-documents-idUSKBN1E92O4.

14. Gavin Van Marle, "Maritime Industry Can Now Use Blockchain for Certification of Seafarers," *Lodestar*, November 12, 2018, https://theloadstar.com/maritime-industry-can-now-use-blockchain-certification-seafarers.

15. Richard Spencer, "Two Sentenced to Death over China Melamine Milk Scandal," *Telegraph*, January 22, 2009, www.telegraph.co.uk/news/worldnews/asia/china/4315627/Two-sentenced-to-death-over-China-melamine-milk-scandal.html.

16. Daniel Palmer, "Alibaba Turns to Blockchain in Fight against Food Fraud." *CoinDesk*, March 24, 2017, www.coindesk.com/alibaba-pwc-partner-to-fight-food-fraud-with-blockchain.

17. Anonymous Ant Financial representative, telephone interview with authors, October 18, 2018. Used with permission.

18. Rebecca Hofmann, interview with authors, November 15, 2018.

19. Ibid.

20. Mr. Jean-François Bonald, telephone interview with authors, October 18, 2018.

21. Ana Alexandre, "Insurance Blockchain Startup B3i Raises $16 Million," *Coin Telegraph*, March 25, 2019, https://cointelegraph.com/news/insurance-blockchain-startup-b3i-raises-16-million.

22. Tom Lyons, Ludovic Courcelas, and Ken Timsit, "Scalability, Interoperability, and Sustainability of Blockchains." European Union Blockchain Observatory and Forum, March 6, 2019, https://drive.google.com/file/d/16_IrzddZR84hOs EV6j911gMyO6R1RQpu/view.

23. For international standards, see International Organization for Standardization, "ISO/TC 307, Blockchain and Distributed Ledger Technologies," accessed April 24, 2019, www.iso.org/committee/6266604.html. For Australian standards, see Varant Meguerditchian, "Roadmap for Blockchain Standards Report," Standards Australia, March 2017, www.standards.org.au/getmedia/ad5d74db-8da9-4685-b171-90142ee0a2e1/Roadmap_for_Blockchain_Standards_report.pdf.aspx.

24. RiskBlock Alliance and B3i are separate consortia, but they are also collaborating, and RiskBlock is leading or chairing the new standards for Acord, the Association for Cooperative Operations Research and Development, which is the global standards-setting body for the insurance and related financial services industries.

25. "The Institutes RBA Alliance Launches Canopy, the Risk Management and Insurance Industry's First Blockchain Platform," Institutes Risk and Assurance Knowledge Group, September 12, 2018, www.theinstitutes.org/about-us/media-center/articles/institutes-riskstream-collaborativetm-launches-canopy-risk-management.

26. "French Life Insurer CNP Fined over Unclaimed Funds," Reuters, November 3, 2014, www.reuters.com/article/cnpassurances-fine/french-life-insurer-cnp-fined-over-unclaimed-funds-idUSL6N0ST2L620141103.

27. Andrea Tinianow, "Insurance Interrupted: How Blockchain Innovation Is Transforming the Insurance Industry," *Forbes*, January 9, 2019, https://www.forbes .com/sites/andreatinianow/2019/01/09/insurance-interrupted-how-blockchain-innovation-is-transforming-the-insurance-industry/#71ef837f3ec6.

28. "The Institutes Announces Formation of RBA: The Blockchain Consortium for the Risk and Insurance Industry," Institutes Risk and Insurance Knowledge Group, accessed May 2, 2019, www.theinstitutes.org/about-us/media-center/ articles/institutes-announces-formation-riskblock-blockchain-consortium-risk.

29. Roger Homrich, "Fighting Potholes," *Best Practice* (journal of T-Systems), February 2018, www.t-systems.com/en/best-practice/02-2018/focus/definition/ predictive-road-maintenance-810858.

30. Brendan Gough et al., "Digital Technology: Its Impact on Australia's Road Network Management," *Roads Australia 2017 Fellowship Project—National Team Report*, September 2017, www.roads.org.au/Portals/3/FELLOWSHIP%20PHOTOS/ RA%20Report%20National%20Team%20-%20Final%20with%20Cover%20Page .pdf?ver=2017-12-08-100621-543.

31. Chuka Oham et al., "A Blockchain Based Liability Attribution Framework for Autonomous Vehicles," University of New South Wales, CSIRO, Australia, February 15, 2018, https://arxiv.org/pdf/1802.05050.pdf.

32. Chris Ballinger, quoted in Ian Allison, "BMW, Ford, GM: World's Largest Automakers Form Blockchain Coalition," *CoinDesk*, May 4, 2018, www.coindesk .com/bmw-ford-gm-worlds-largest-automakers-form-blockchain-coalition.

33. Shobha Roy Kolkata, "Why Consortium Lending by Banks Hasn't Delivered," *Hindu Business Line*, March 05, 2018, www.thehindubusinessline.com/money-and-banking/why-consortium-lending-by-banks-hasnt-delivered/article22936118.ece.

34. Dwight Klappich, email exchange with authors. Used with permission.

35. R3, "The R3 Story," R3 web page, accessed May 30, 2019, https://www.r3 .com/about/.

36. Technical debt accumulates when a technological system adds additional functions beyond its core functional requirements. For more detail, see Andy Kyte, Luis Mangi, and Stefan Van Der Zijden, "A Primer on Technical Debt," Research Note G00307777 (Gartner, October 5, 2016; refreshed April 24, 2018).

CHAPTER 4

1. "Definition of Fiat Money," *Financial Times*, accessed April 29, 2019, http://lexicon.ft.com/Term?term=fiat-money.

2. Morten Linnemann Bech et al., "Payments Are A-Changin' but Cash Still Rules," *BIS Quarterly Review*, March 2018, www.bis.org/publ/qtrpdf/r_qt1803g.htm.

3. Michael Joseph, "M-Pesa: The Story of How the World's Leading Mobile Money Service Was Created in Kenya," *Vodafone*, March 6, 2017, www.vodafone .com/content/index/what/technology-blog/m-pesa-created.html#.

4. "Airtime Is Money," *Economist,* January 19, 2013, www.economist.com/finance-and-economics/2013/01/19/airtime-is-money.

5. Julia Wood, "Buyer Beware, Bitcoin's Fate Could Rest with China," *CNBC,* November 28, 2013, www.cnbc.com/2013/11/28/buyer-beware-bitcoins-fate-could-rest-with-china.html.

6. For information on how bitcoin mining works, see Euny Hong, "How Does Bitcoin Mining Work?," *Investopedia,* updated April 27, 2019, www.investopedia.com/tech/how-does-bitcoin-mining-work.

7. See, for example, the valuation on CoinMarketCap, "Bitcoin," accessed April 28, 2019, https://coinmarketcap.com/currencies/bitcoin.

8. Roman Cheng, telephone interview with authors, February 12, 2019.

9. David Floyd, "Tether Just Burned 500 Million USDT Stablecoin Tokens," *CoinDesk,* October 24, 2018, www.coindesk.com/tether-just-burned-500-million-usdt-stablecoin-tokens.

10. Davit Babayan, "Crypto Exchanges Embrace New Stablecoin Systems to Curb Price Volatility," *Newsbtc,* November 28, 2018, www.newsbtc.com/2018/11/28/crypto-exchanges-embrace-new-stablecoin-systems-to-curb-price-volatility/.

11. "KrisFlyer to Launch World's First Blockchain-Based Airline Loyalty Digital Wallet," Singapore Airlines, February 5, 2018, https://www.singaporeair.com/en_UK/sg/media-centre/press-release/article/?q=en_UK/2018/January-March/ne0518-180205.

12. Ledger Insights, "IATA Releases Blockchain Whitepaper for Airlines," *Ledger Insights,* December 2018, www.ledgerinsights.com/iata-blockchain-airlines.

13. See Second Life, "The Beginning of Second Life," *History of Second Life* (blog), accessed April 29, 2019, http://wiki.secondlife.com/wiki/History_of_Second_Life; and Wikipedia, s.v., "World of Warcraft," last updated February 28, 2019, https://en.wikipedia.org/wiki/World_of_Warcraft.

14. Jason Whiting, "Online Game Economies Get Real," *Wired,* November 2002, www.wired.com/2002/11/online-game-economies-get-real.

15. Juree Pannekeet, "Newzoo: Global Esports Economy Will Reach $905.6 Million in 2018 as Brand Investment Grows by 48%," *NewZoo,* February 28, 2018, https://newzoo.com/insights/articles/newzoo-global-esports-economy-will-reach-905-6-million-2018-brand-investment-grows-48.

16. Greg Kumparak, "Amazon's New GameOn API Helps Developers Add Esports Competitions to Their Games," *TechCrunch,* March 19, 2018, https://techcrunch.com/2018/03/19/amazons-new-gameon-api-helps-developers-add-esports-competitions-to-their-games.

17. Bitcoin Exchange Guide News Team, "Amazon Cryptocurrency Possibility Has Much Higher Odds Than Anyone Thinks: Amazon Coin in the Making?" *Bitcoin Exchange Guide,* September 20, 2018, https://bitcoinexchangeguide.com/amazon-cryptocurrency-possibility-has-much-higher-odds-than-anyone-thinks-amazon-coin-in-the-making.

18. Tim Mulkerin, "With Over 100 Million Monthly Players, This Is Officially the Biggest Game in the World," *Business Insider,* September 13, 2016, www.busines sinsider.com/lol-league-of-legends-monthly-active-users-2016-9; and www.statista .com/statistics/808922/csgo-users-number.

19. DreamTeam.gg, "The November DreamTeam Report," *Medium,* December 21, 2018, https://medium.com/dreamteam-gg/dreamteam-report-november-2018-e1bc5ccd16a6.

20. G. Campbell, "APPICS Review: A New Way of Doing Social Media," *Medium,* June 12, 2018, https://medium.com/@GCampbellCrypto/appics-review-a-new-way-of-doing-social-media-607231ed8117.

21. Ashish Mohta, "List of Centralized Social Networks Where You Own Your Data," TheWindowsClub, April 4, 2019, https://www.thewindowsclub.com/decentralized-social-networks.

22. Douglas B. Laney, *Infonomics: How to Monetize Information for Competitive Advantage* (New York: Routledge, 2017).

23. Bloomberg, "Facebook Cambridge Analytica Scandal: 10 Questions Answered," *Fortune,* April 10, 2018, http://fortune.com/2018/04/10/facebook-cam bridge-analytica-what-happened; Alfred Ng, "How the Equifax Hack Happened, and What Still Needs to Be Done," *CNET,* September 7, 2018, www.cnet.com/news/equifaxs-hack-one-year-later-a-look-back-at-how-it-happened-and-whats-changed; Thomas Brewster, "Revealed: Marriott's 500 Million Hack Came after a String of Security Breaches," *Forbes,* December 3, 2018, www.forbes.com/sites/thomasbrewster/2018/12/03/revealed-marriotts-500-million-hack-came-after-a-string-of-security-breaches/#5b1eed54546f.

24. Daniel Hawthorne, Serafin L. Engel, and Alex Norta, "A Data-Ownership Assuring Blockchain Wallet for Privacy-Protected Data Exchange," n.d., accessed May 2, 2019, https://datawallet.com/pdf/datawallet_whitepaper.pdf.

25. Bernard Marr, "GDPR: The Biggest Data Breaches and the Shocking Fines (That Would Have Been)," *Forbes,* June 11, 2018, www.forbes.com/sites/bernardmarr/2018/06/11/gdpr-the-biggest-data-breaches-and-the-shocking-fines-that-would-have-been/#22f2072e6c10.

26. Nathaniel Popper and Mike Isaac, "Facebook and Telegram Are Hoping to Succeed Where Bitcoin Failed," *New York Times,* February 28, 2019, www.nytimes .com/2019/02/28/technology/cryptocurrency-facebook-telegram.html.

27. Uber, "Uber Pro Beta Terms and Conditions," Uber Pro, May 1, 2019, www.uber.com/en-CA/legal/rewards-program/uberpro/us-en.

28. David Their, "Google's New Game Streaming Platform Is Called Stadia, and It's Not a Console," *Forbes,* March 19, 2019, www.forbes.com/sites/davidthier/2019/03/19/googles-new-game-streaming-platform-is-called-stadia-and-its-not-a-console/#4b3d0f838f2d; Derek Strickland, "Square Enix Interested in Blockchain, Game Streaming," *TweakTown,* January 6, 2019, www.tweaktown.com/news/64349/square-enix-interested-blockchain-game-streaming/index.html.

CHAPTER 5

1. Ben Kepes, "30% of Servers Are Sitting 'Comatose' According to Research," *Forbes*, June 3, 2016, www.forbes.com/sites/benkepes/2015/06/03/30-of-servers-are-sitting-comatose-according-to-research/#6ee3a75459c7.

2. Crunchbase, "Golem Factory GmbH," Crunchbase company listings, accessed April 28, 2019, www.crunchbase.com/organization/golem-network#section-locked-marketplace.

3. In Bitcoin, 51 percent of participant nodes have to validate a transaction for it to be approved and appended to a block, and these rules are set in the messaging layer of the Bitcoin blockchain technology stack. In other blockchain networks, the consensus requirements may be set to a higher percentage, but 51 percent tends to be the standard.

4. Ben Rossi, "How Tesco Is Using AI to Gain Customer Insight," *Information Age*, May 17, 2017, www.information-age.com/tesco-using-ai-gain-customer-insight-123466328.

5. Samuel Falkon, "The Story of the DAO: Its History and Consequences," *Medium*, December 24, 2017, https://medium.com/swlh/the-story-of-the-dao-its-history-and-consequences-71e6a8a551ee.

6. Blockchain, "Hashrate Distribution," accessed April 28, 2019, www.blockchain.com/en/pools.

7. Paul V. Weinstein, "Why Microsoft Is Willing to Pay So Much for GitHub," hbr.org, June 6, 2018, https://hbr.org/2018/06/why-microsoft-is-willing-to-pay-so-much-for-github.

8. Pieter Franken, interview with authors, October 2018.

9. Bitcoin Project, "Bitcoin Development," *BitcoinCore*, accessed May 2, 2019, https://bitcoin.org/en/development#bitcoin-core-contributors.

10. Hong Kong Monetary Authority, "The Launch of eTradeConnect and the Collaboration with we.trade," press release, October 31, 2018, www.hkma.gov.hk/eng/key-information/press-releases/2018/20181031-4.shtml.

11. Aapo Markkanen, Thomas Bittman, and Bob Gill, "What Tech Product Managers Must Know about Edge Computing," Research Note G00379625 (Gartner, December 2018).

12. John Childress, "Friction and Culture Change," *John T. Childress . . . Rethinking* (blog), January 22, 2015, https://blog.johnrchildress.com/2015/01/22/friction-and-culture-change.

13. Klint Finley, "Out in the Open: Occupy Wall Street Reincarnated as Open Source Software," *Wired*, April 28, 2014, https://www.wired.com/2014/04/loomio/.

14. Alanna, and Richard D. Bartlett, "Loomio Points," *GitHub*, September 11, 2016, https://github.com/loomio/loomio-coop-handbook/blob/master/loomio_points.md.

15. Banque de France officers, meeting with authors, November 29, 2018.

16. Though UEFA is the administrative body for FIFA in Europe, some of its member countries are geographically transcontinental (e.g., Azerbaijan, Georgia, Kazakhstan, Russia, and Turkey) or Asian (e.g., Israel).

17. See Sonia Avalos, Agence France-Presse, "Argentina Hooligans: The Endless Cycle of Football Violence," https://sports.yahoo.com/argentinas-hooligans-endless-cycle-football-violence-015134453--sow.html, November 26, 2018; and UEFA, "Counter-Terrorism Focus at UEFA Seminar," *Inside UEFA*, April 20, 2018, www.uefa.com/insideuefa/protecting-the-game/security/news/newsid= 2552417.html.

18. UEFA, "All You Need to Know about UEFA Euro 2020," UEFA, April 15, 2019, www.uefa.com/uefaeuro-2020.

19. Frédéric Longatte, telephone interview with authors, December 12, 2018.

20. Wired Brand Lab, "Insider Insights: Coordinating Tomorrow's Fast Lane," *Wired*, February 2017, www.wired.com/brandlab/2017/02/insider-insights-collaborating-tomorrows-fast-lane.

21. Roy Maurer, "Employers Are Frustrated by These 5 STEM Talent Hurdles," *SHRM* (Society for Human Resource Management), July 30, 2018, www.shrm.org/resourcesandtools/hr-topics/talent-acquisition/pages/employers-frustrated-stem-talent-gaps.aspx.

CHAPTER 6

1. Andy Greenberg, "Inside the 'Dark Market' Prototype, a Silk Road the FBI Can Never Seize," *Wired*, April 24, 2014, www.wired.com/2014/04/darkmarket.

2. James Redman, "Under the Tent: A Look at the Latest Openbazaar Marketplace Software," *Bitcoin*, October 3, 2018, https://news.bitcoin.com/under-the-tent-a-look-at-the-latest-openbazaar-marketplace-software.

3. See the Basic Attention Token homepage at https://basicattentiontoken.org. See also Jon Wood, "Blockchain & Advertising: New Solutions to Old Problems," *Medium*, June 28, 2018, https://medium.com/trivial-co/blockchain-advertising-new-solutions-to-old-problems-e7fcbbc16b85.

4. Vauhini Vara, "Amazon's Failed Pitch to Authors," *New Yorker*, July 31, 2014, www.newyorker.com/business/currency/amazons-failed-pitch-authors.

5. Homan Farahmand, "Blockchain: Evolving Decentralized Identity Design," Research Note G00324208 (Gartner, December 2017).

6. Nicky Morris, "Taiwanese Hospital Launches Blockchain Health Record," *Ledger Insights*, September 2018, www.ledgerinsights.com/blockchain-health-records-taiwan.

7. Dr. Ray-Jade Chen, in-person conversation with authors, January 17, 2019.

8. Minda Zetlin, "Mark Cuban Says This Is the 1 Mistake New Entrepreneurs Always Make," *Inc.*, May 23, 2018, www.inc.com/minda-zetlin/mark-cuban-sanyin-siang-entrepreneurship-mistakes-funding-vcs-sales.html.

9. See Jim Duffy, "Zombie Start-ups: Why Are Entrepreneurs Failing to Grow Their Businesses?," *Guardian*, August 7, 2017, www.theguardian.com/small-business-network/2017/aug/07/zombie-startups-entrepreneurs-failing-grow-businesses; and Patrick Musso and Stefano Schiavo, "The Impact of Financial Constraints on Firms Survival and Growth," 2007, https://hal-sciencespo.archives-ouvertes.fr/hal-00973115/document.

10. Alex Frew McMillan, "Sparking an IPO Revolution," CNN Money, January 7, 2000, https://money.cnn.com/2000/01/07/investing/q_hambrecht.

11. Susan Greco, "The Real Legacy of Spring Street Brewing," *Inc.*, September 1, 1999, www.inc.com/magazine/19990901/13720.html.

12. "Volume of Funds Raised through Crowdfunding Worldwide in 2017, by Region (in Million U.S. Dollars)," Statista, September 2018, www.statista.com/statistics/946659/global-crowdfunding-volume-worldwide-by-region/.

13. Digital technology can also be wielded to serve centralizing ends. Digital platforms have ventured into finance with online payment solutions (think PayPal and Amazon Pay) in addition to the vast streams of credit card data they collect as a function of selling. When integrated, this payment data allows platforms to predict future purchases, extend financing offers, and negotiate preferred payment terms—all of which can funnel traffic to them.

14. Laura Shin, "Here's the Man Who Created ICOs and This Is the New Token He's Backing," *Forbes*, September 21, 2017, www.forbes.com/sites/laurashin/2017/09/21/heres-the-man-who-created-icos-and-this-is-the-new-token-hes-backing/#5714be7b1183.

15. Icodata.io, "Funds Raised in 2018," accessed May 2, 2019, www.icodata.io/stats/2018.

16. David Petersson, "How Smart Contracts Started and Where They Are Headed," *Forbes*, October 24, 2018, www.forbes.com/sites/davidpetersson/2018/10/24/how-smart-contracts-started-and-where-they-are-heading/#4af9b13937b6.

17. Samuel Falkon, "The Story of the DAO: Its History and Consequences," *Medium*, December 24, 2017, https://medium.com/swlh/the-story-of-the-dao-its-history-and-consequences-71e6a8a551ee.

18. Hugo Benedetti and Leonard Kostovetsky, "Digital Tulips? Returns to Investors in Initial Coin Offerings," *SSRN*, May 20, 2018, https://papers.ssrn.com/sol3/papers.cfm?abstract_id=3182169.

19. CB Insights, "Venture Capital Funnel Shows Odds of Becoming a Unicorn Are About 1%," *CBInsights Research Briefs*, September 6, 2018, www.cbinsights.com/research/venture-capital-funnel-2/; HM Treasury, "Financing Growth in Innovative Firms: Consultation," UK Publications, August 2017, https://assets.publishing.service.gov.uk/government/uploads/system/uploads/attachment_data/file/642456/financing_growth_in_innovative_firms_consultation_web.pdf.

20. Bitcoin Exchange Guide News Team, "How Cryptocurrency Airdrop Tokens/Coins Work," *BitcoinExchangeGuide*, April 30, 2018, https://bitcoinexchangeguide.com/how-cryptocurrency-airdrop-token-coins-work.

21. Olga Kharif, "How's That ICO Working Out?," *Bloomberg Quint*, December 14, 2018, twww.bloombergquint.com/businessweek/crypto-s-15-biggest-icos-by-the-numbers.

22. Kik, "Learn Our Company Story," Kik web page, accessed April 28, 2019, www.kik.com/about.

23. Jon Russell, "Chat App Kik Takes on Facebook with Developer Ecosystem Built on the Blockchain," *Techcrunch*, May 25, 2017, https://techcrunch.com/2017/05/25/kik-makes-a-move-into-the-blockchain.

24. Ross Eastwood, "KodakCoin ICO Went from a Joke to a Real Blockchain Project in 2019," *Independent Republic*, January 13, 2018, https://theindependentrepublic.com/2019/01/13/kodakcoin-ico-went-from-joke-real-blockchain-project-2019.

25. Adrian Zmudzinski, "OECD Calls for 'Delicate Balance' in Global ICO Regulation," *Cointelegraph*, January 18, 2019, https://cointelegraph.com/news/oecd-calls-for-delicate-balance-in-global-ico-regulation.

26. Alejandro Gomez de la Cruz, "The State of ICO Regulation: Insights from 3 Lawyers," *Medium*, September 4, 2018, https://medium.com/coin-governance-system/the-state-of-ico-regulation-insights-from-3-lawyers-b326164681f9.

27. US Securities and Exchange Commission (SEC), "Spotlight on Initial Coin Offerings (ICOs)," SEC, updated April 11, 2019, www.sec.gov/ICO.

28. Chems Idrissi, "PACTE Bill: A Framework for ICOs and Protection of Foreign Investments in France," *Soulier Avocats*, December 2018, www.soulier-avocats.com/en/pacte-bill-a-framework-for-icos-and-protection-of-foreign-investments-in-france; Pascal Cuche and Tanguy Bardet, "French Parliament Adopts PACTE Law," Lexology, April 16, 2019, https://www.lexology.com/library/detail.aspx?g=8a917a5b-16c6-4242-9a11-e7bb81dcb38f.

29. "Security Token Calendar," TokenMarket, https://tokenmarket.net/security-token-calendar/.

30. Tatiana Koffman and Marc Boiron, "The Game of Regs: The STO Context," *Medium*, September 14, 2018, https://medium.com/@tatianakoffman/game-of-regs-the-sto-context-35d9deed2c4d.

31. Matt Robinson and Tom Schoenberg, "Bitcoin-Rigging Criminal Probe Focused on Tie to Tether," *Bloomberg*, November 20, 2018, www.bloomberg.com/news/articles/2018-11-20/bitcoin-rigging-criminal-probe-is-said-to-focus-on-tie-to-tether.

32. PR Newswire, "MovieCoin Utility Token Presale Overachieves," *Cision*, November 29, 2018, www.prnewswire.co.uk/news-releases/moviecoin-utility-token-presale-overachieves-811115426.html.

33. Christopher Woodrow, interview with authors, December 2018.

34. Rachel Wolfson, "Christopher Woodrow on Blockchain Technology for the Film Industry," *Forbes*, September 17, 2018, www.forbes.com/sites/rachelwolfson/2018/09/17/christopher-woodrow-on-hollywoods-first-security-token-and-blockchain-technology-for-film-industry/#2ebb3fe96f83.

35. Bee Token, "What Is Beenest? How the Bee Token Is Revolutionizing Home Sharing," *Medium*, December 18, 2017, https://medium.com/@thebeetoken/what-is-beenest-how-the-bee-token-is-revolutionizing-the-home-sharing-market-8da32d79bbbb.

36. "LT BlockChain, Ecosystem & Marketplace DAPP," white paper (LockTrip, n.d.), accessed May 2, 2019, https://locktrip.com/whitepaper_vl.2_t.pdf.

CHAPTER 7

1. Representative of Ant Financial, telephone interviews with authors, November and December 2018.

2. Zheping Huang, "Xiongan Calls in ConsenSys to Bring Blockchain Technology to Xi Jinping's Dream City," *South China Morning Post*, July 23, 2018, www.scmp.com/tech/article/2156396/xiongan-calls-us-company-consensys-bring-blockchain-technology-xi-jinpings.

3. Kai-Fu Lee, quoted in Peter Diamandis, "AI Superpowers by Kai-Fu Lee," *Tech Blog*, China series, accessed April 28, 2019, www.diamandis.com/blog/kai-fu-lee-ai-superpowers.

4. Gartner, "Internet of Things," Gartner IT Glossary, accessed April 28, 2019, www.gartner.com/it-glossary/internet-of-things.

5. "The Future of Pharma Packaging Looks Smart," *Packaging World*, April 20, 2017, www.packworld.com/article/trends-and-issues/anti-counterfeiting/future-pharma-packaging-looks-smart.

6. Stephanie Kanowitz, "Analytics Platform Helps KC Anticipate the Needs of Its Citizens," GCN, June 23, 2017, https://gcn.com/articles/2017/06/23/kansas-city-data-integration.aspx.

7. "Can Blockchain Fix Potholes?," Potholes, August 28, 2018, www.pothole.info/2018/08/can-blockchain-fix-potholes.

8. Toby Simpson, Arthur Meadows, and Humayun Sheikh, "Fetch.AI: Token Overview: A Decentralised World for the Future Economy," Fetch.AI Foundation, February 2019, https://fetch.ai/public/pdf/Fetch-Token-Overview.pdf.

9. 5G is the next-generation cellular standard after 4G. It was designed to enable the high-speed, low-cost, massive scale communication necessary for IoT applications and devices to function more effectively. For some thoughts on its relevance, see Matthew Wall, "What Is 5G and What Will It Mean for You?" *BBC*, July 24, 2018.

10. Homan Farahmand, "Blockchain: The Dawn of Decentralized Identity," Research Note G00363110 (Gartner, May 24, 2018); Kai Wagner et al., "Self-Sovereign Identity: A Position Paper on Blockchain Enabled Identity and the Road Ahead," Blockchain Bundesverband (German Blockchain Association), October 23, 2018, https://jolocom.io/wp-content/uploads/2018/10/Self-sovereign-Identity-_-Blockchain-Bundesverband-2018.pdf.

11. Andrew Hughes, Manu Sporny, and Drummon Reed, eds., "A Primer for Decentralized Identifiers: An Introduction to Self-Administered Identifiers for Curious People," W3C Draft Community Group Report, January 19, 2019, https://w3c-ccg.github.io/did-primer.

12. "Sovrin: A Protocol and Token for Self-Sovereign Identity and Decentralized Trust," white paper (Sovrin Foundation, January 2018), https://sovrin.org/wp-content/uploads/2018/03/Sovrin-Protocol-and-Token-White-Paper.pdf.

13. John Jordan, telephone interviews with authors, December 2018 and March 2019.

14. Dr. MeiKei Leong, interview with authors on October 5, 2018.

15. Nicola Davies, "Smart Technology for Diabetes Self-Care," *Diabetes Self-Management*, June 9, 2016, www.diabetesselfmanagement.com/diabetes-resources/tools-tech/smart-technology-diabetes-self-care; Maria Cohut, "Alzheimer's: Brain Implant Could Improve Cognitive Function," *Medical News Today*, January 31, 2018, www.medicalnewstoday.com/articles/320792.php; Brandon Specktor, "Military-Funded Study Successfully Tests 'Prosthetic Memory' Brain Implants," *Live Science*, April 6, 2018, www.livescience.com/62234-prosthetic-memory-neural-implant.html.

16. K. L. Collins et al., "Ownership of an Artificial Limb Induced by Electrical Brain Stimulation," *Proceedings of the National Academy of Sciences of the United States of America* 114, no. 1 (2016): 166–171, www.ncbi.nlm.nih.gov/pmc/articles/PMC5224395.

17. Grace Caffyn, "Meet the Tiny Bitcoin Wallet That Lives under Your Skin," *CoinDesk*, November 11, 2014, www.coindesk.com/meet-tiny-bitcoin-wallet-lives-skin; David McClelland, "Cash in Hand? This Cryptocurrency Body Implant Will Secure Your Cyber-Cash Stash," *Computer Weekly*, January 18, 2018, www.computerweekly.com/blog/Inspect-a-Gadget/Cash-in-hand-This-cryptocurrency-body-implant-will-secure-your-cyber-cash-stash.

18. Farahmand, "Blockchain: The Dawn of Decentralized Identity."

19. For the problems with mortgage tools, see Robert Bartlett et al., "Consumer-Lending Discrimination in the Era of FinTech," Haas School of Business, University of California Berkeley, October 2018, https://vcresearch.berkeley.edu/news/mortgage-algorithms-perpetuate-racial-bias-lending-study-finds. For the problems with sentencing algorithms, see Jeff Larson et al., "How We Analyzed the COMPAS Recidivism Algorithm," *ProPublica*, May 23, 2016, www.propublica.org/article/how-we-analyzed-the-compas-recidivism-algorithm.

20. Daisuke Wakabayashi, "Self-Driving Uber Car Kills Pedestrian in Arizona, Where Robots Roam," *New York Times*, March 19, 2018, www.nytimes.com/2018/03/19/technology/uber-driverless-fatality.html.

21. Simon Romero, "Wielding Rocks and Knives, Arizonans Attack Self-Driving Cars," *New York Times*, December 31, 2018, www.nytimes.com/2018/12/31/us/waymo-self-driving-cars-arizona-attacks.html.

22. "2019 Edelman Trust Barometer," Edelman, January 20, 2019, www.edelman.com/trust-barometer.

23. Eugene Kim, "Amazon's Tear-Long Publicity Blitz for HQ2 Has Backfired," *CNN*, March 2, 2019, www.cnbc.com/2019/03/02/amazon-hq2-publicity-grab-back firing.html.

24. "2018 Revision of World Urbanization Prospects," UN Department of Economic and Social Affairs, May 16, 2018, www.un.org/development/desa/ publications/2018-revision-of-world-urbanization-prospects.html.

25. Gartner defines *contextualized experiences* as "knowing who the customer is, where they are in the moment, what their behaviors are across devices and machines, and how to interact in specific situations." *See* Gartner, "Hype Cycle for Customer Experience Analytics," Research Note G00338646 (Gartner, August 2, 2018).

26. Gartner defines continuous intelligence as "a style of decision management in which real-time analytics are integrated within a business operation. It processes current and historical data to prescribe actions in response to business moments and other events. It leverages multiple technologies such as augmented analytics, event stream processing, optimization, business rule management and machine learning." See Gartner, "Hype Cycle for Customer Experience Analytics," Research Note G00338646 (Gartner, August 2, 2018).

27. "Beyond Traffic: The Vision for the Kansas City Smart City Challenge," City of Kansas City, Missouri, February 14, 2016, https://cms.dot.gov/sites/dot.gov/files/ docs/Kansas%20City%20Vision%20Narrative.pdf.

28. "New York City's Roadmap to 80 × 50," New York City's Mayor's Office of Sustainability, September 2016, https://www1.nyc.gov/assets/sustainability/down loads/pdf/publications/New%20York%20City's%20Roadmap%20to%2080%20 x%2050_20160926_FOR%20WEB.pdf.

29. R. P. Siegel, "How Kansas City, New York and San Jose Exhibit Three Approaches to Smart Cities," *Green Biz*, October 18, 2018, www.greenbiz.com/ article/how-kansas-city-new-york-and-san-jose-exhibit-three-approaches-smart-cities.

30. New York State, "Reforming the Energy Vision," accessed May 2, 2019, https://rev.ny.gov.

31. Richard Evans and Jim Gao, "DeepMind AI Reduces Google Data Centre Cooling Bill by 40%," DeepMind, July 20, 2016, https://deepmind.com/blog/ deepmind-ai-reduces-google-data-centre-cooling-bill-40.

32. Waterfront Toronto, "Quayside," home page, accessed May 2, 2019, https:// waterfrontoronto.ca/nbe/portal/waterfront/Home/waterfronthome/projects/quayside.

33. Associated Press, "Ontario Government Fires 3 Directors after Goo-gle Deal," *NY1*, December 7, 2018, www.ny1.com/nyc/all-boroughs/ap-top-news/2018/12/07/ontario-government-fires-3-directors-after-google-deal; Jane Wakefield, "The Google City That Has Angered Toronto," BBC, May 18, 2019, https://www.bbc.com/news/technology-47815344.

34. Timothy Williams, "In High-Tech Cities, No More Potholes, but What about Privacy?" *New York Times*, January 1, 2019, www.nytimes.com/2019/01/01/us/ kansas-city-smart-technology.html.

35. Shoshana Zuboff, *The Age of Surveillance Capitalism: The Fight for a Human Future at the New Frontier of Power* (New York: PublicAffairs, 2019).

36. René Raphael and Ling Xi, "China's Rewards and Punishments," *Le Monde Diplomatique*, January 1, 2019, https://mondediplo.com/2019/01/05china-social-credit.

CHAPTER 8

1. Joseph Lubin, telephone interview with authors, February 23, 2019.

2. Phil Berardelli, "When Pigeons Flock, Who's in Command?," *Science*, April 8, 2010, www.sciencemag.org/news/2010/04/when-pigeons-flock-whos-command.

3. Brian Barrett, "Inside the Olympics Opening Ceremony World Record Drone Show," *Wired*, February 9, 2018, www.wired.com/story/olympics-opening-ceremony-drone-show; Brian Barrett, "Lady Gaga's Halftime Show Drones Have a Bright Future," *Wired*, February 5, 2017, www.wired.com/2017/02/lady-gaga-halftime-show-drones.

4. Robbie Gonzalez, "How a Flock of Drones Developed Collective Intelligence," *Wired*, July 18, 2018, www.wired.com/story/how-a-flock-of-drones-developed-collective-intelligence.

5. See Harold J. Leavitt, "Hierarchies, Authority, and Leadership," *Leader to Leader*, June 7, 2005; and Joe C. Magee and Adam D. Galinsky, "Social Hierarchy: The Self-Reinforcing Nature of Power and Status," *Academy of Management Annals* 2, no. 1 (2008): 351–398.

6. Ronald Wintrobe and Albert Breton, "Organizational Structure and Productivity," *American Economic Review* 76, no. 3 (June 1986): 530–538.

7. C. Anderson and C. E. Brown, "The Functions and Dysfunctions of Hierarchy," *Research in Organizational Behavior* 30 (2010): 55–89.

8. Alexa Clay and Kyra Maya Phillips, *The Misfit Economy: Lessons in Creativity from Pirates, Hackers, Gangsters, and Other Informal Entrepreneurs* (New York: Simon & Schuster, 2015).

9. See the company website for a description of its organizational approach: www.itw.com/about-itw.

10. Knowledge@Wharton, "Johnson & Johnson CEO William Weldon: Leadership in a Decentralized Company," podcast, Wharton School of the University of Pennsylvania, June 25, 2008, http://knowledge.wharton.upenn.edu/article/johnson-johnson-ceo-william-weldon-leadership-in-a-decentralized-company.

11. This theory is experiencing a real-world test. J&J's consumer division is currently under attack over claims that its Johnson's baby powder contains asbestos, a known cause of the rare cancer mesothelioma and is a suspected factor in thousands of ovarian cancer diagnoses among women who use talcum powder. The crux of the claim is that leaders in the consumer-packaged goods division were aware of the contamination and still kept the product on the shelves. See Lisa

Girion, "Johnson & Johnson Knew for Decades That Asbestos Lurked in Its Baby Powder," Reuters, December 14, 2018, www.reuters.com/investigates/special-report/johnsonandjohnson-cancer.

12. See Zac Guzman, "Zappos CEO Tony Tsieh on Getting Rid of Managers: What I Wish I'd Done Differently," *CNBC*, September 13, 2016, www.cnbc.com/2016/09/13/zappos-ceo-tony-hsieh-the-thing-i-regret-about-getting-rid-of-managers.html; and Bouree Lam, "Why Are So Many Zappos Employees Leaving?," *Atlantic*, January 15, 2016, www.theatlantic.com/business/archive/2016/01/zappos-holacracy-hierarchy/424173/

13. Lubin, telephone interview.

14. Nitesh Pundir, "10 Leadership Styles with Examples," *Iamwire*, November 10, 2017, www.iamwire.com/2017/10/10-leadership-styles-with-examples/167818.

15. Robert Greenleaf, *Servant Leadership: A Journey into the Nature of Legitimate Power and Greatness* (New York: Paulist Press, 1977).

16. For details on Toyota's approach to leadership development, see Jeffrey Liker and Gary Convis, *The Toyota Way to Lean Leadership* (New York: McGraw Hill, 2012).

17. For information on how Bounty0x works, see Bounty0x, "Earning Crypto Made Simple," accessed May 2, 2019, https://bounty0x.io.

18. Jaime Roca and Sari Wilde, *The Connector Manager: Why Some Leaders Build Exceptional Talent—and Others Don't* (New York: Portfolio, 2019).

19. "Begin with the end in mind" is the second of the seven habits Stephen Covey describes in his perennial classic, *The Seven Habits of Highly Effective People: Powerful Lessons in Personal Change* (New York: Free Press, 1989).

20. Mark Raskino, "2019 CEO Survey: The Year of Challenged Growth," Research Note G00385368 (Gartner, April 16, 2019).

21. Shelly Hagan, "Global CEO's Recession Concerns Fade as Talent Shortage Bites," *Bloomberg*, January 18, 2018, www.bloomberg.com/news/articles/2018-01-18/global-ceos-recession-concerns-fade-as-talent-shortage-bites.

22. PwC, "CEOs' Curbed Confidence Spells Caution," *PwC CEO Survey*, 2018, www.pwc.com/gx/en/ceo-agenda/ceosurvey/2018/gx/deep-dives/talent.html.

23. The staffing sector is overall expected to grow by 7 percent in 2018, but the most active countries, such as Japan, China, and India, are experiencing double-digit growth, according to Staffing Industry Analysts (SIA), "Global Staffing Revenue Hits $461 Billion, SIA Forecast Calls for 7% Growth," *SIA Daily News*, June 11, 2018, www2.staffingindustry.com/site/Editorial/Daily-News/Global-staffing-revenue-hits-461-billion-SIA-forecast-calls-for-7-growth-46365.

24. Diana Farell, Fiona Grieg, and Amar Amoudi, "The Online Platform Economy in 2018, Drivers, Workers, Sellers, and Lessors," JPMorgan Chase & Co. Institute, September 2018, www.jpmorganchase.com/corporate/institute/report-ope-2018.htm.

25. Ursula Huws et al., "Work in the European Gig Economy," Foundation for European Progressive Studies, 2017, www.uni-europa.org/wp-content/uploads/2017/11/europeagigeconomy-longversionpdf.pdf.

26. See the exchanges' websites for more information: https://talentexchange .pwc.com and https://talentnetwork.washingtonpost.com/index.html.

27. US Department of Labor, Bureau of Labor Statistics, "Contingent and Alternative Employment Arrangements Summary," economic news release Bureau of Labor Statistics, June 7, 2018, www.bls.gov/news.release/conemp.nr0.htm.

28. Trevor Clawson, "Automating the Gig Economy: Can Blockchain Tech Make Life Easier for Side-Hustling Millennials?," *Forbes*, September 26, 2018, www.forbes .com/sites/trevorclawson/2018/09/26/automating-the-gig-economy-can-blockchain-tech-make-life-easier-for-side-hustling-millennials/#4f2ca2921bba.

29. Osato Avan-Nomayo, "ChronoBank Launches World's First Complete Blockchain-Based Job Platform, LaborX," *Bitcoinist*, May 28, 2018, https://bitcoinist .com/chronobank-launches-worlds-first-complete-blockchain-based-job-platform-laborx.

30. For more on ChronoBank, see Roger Aitken, "ChronoBank 'Crypto' Startup Attracts $3M Bitcoin, Forges Changelly App Partnership," *Forbes*, January 31, 2017, www.forbes.com/sites/rogeraitken/2017/01/31/chronobank-crypto-startup-attracts-3m-bitcoin-forges-changelly-app-partnership/#2d084e722641; and "What Is Chrono-noBank (TIME)?" *CoinSwitch*, accessed May 2, 2019, https://coinswitch.co/info/chronobank/what-is-chronobank.

31. See PYMNTS, "Where the Distributed Workforce Meets the Distributed Ledger," *PYMNTS*, March 29, 2016, www.pymnts.com/news/b2b-payments/2016/where-the-distributed-workforce-meets-the-distributed-ledger.

32. Ryan Hayes, Alexandra Tran, and Henry Xu, "Futarchy Considered: A Guide to Blockchain-Based Prediction Markets and Futarchy," n.d., accessed May 2, 2019, www.ocf.berkeley.edu/~alexandra/Blockchain/Futarchy.

33. To learn more about Robin Hanson and his ideas, check out his blog at http:// www.overcomingbias.com/, and his book *The Age of Em: Work, Love and Life When Robots Rule the Earth* (Oxford: Oxford University Press, 2016).

34. Robert Bartlett et al., "Consumer Lending Discrimination in the Era of Fintech," University of California, Berkeley, October 2018, http://faculty.haas .berkeley.edu/morse/research/papers/discrim.pdf.

35. See, for example, Daniel Kahneman, *Thinking Fast and Slow* (New York: Farrar, Straus and Giroux, 2011).

36. Clayton M. Christensen, *The Innovator's Dilemma: When New Technologies Cause Great Firms to Fail* (Boston: Harvard Business School Press, 1997).

CHAPTER 9

1. Nathan Heller, "Estonia, the Digital Republic," *New Yorker*, December 18, 2017, www.newyorker.com/magazine/2017/12/18/estonia-the-digital-republic.

2. Lubomir Tasev, "Blind Denial of Cryptocurrencies Leads Nowhere, Bank of Lithuania Says," *Bitcoin*, April 14, 2018, https://news.bitcoin.com/blind-denial-of-cryptocurrencies-leads-nowhere-bank-of-lithuania-says.

3. Malta House of Representatives, "Innovative Technology Arrangements and Services Act, 2018" (in Maltese and English), May 22, 2018, https://parlament.mt/media/94207/bill-43-innovative-technology-arrangements-and-services-bill.pdf.

4. "Top 10 Countries to Adopt Blockchain Technology," Blockstuffs, March 28, 2019, https://www.blockstuffs.com/blog/countries-adopting-blockchain; Carlos Terenzi, "11 Countries Working with Blockchain Technology," UsetheBitcoin, February 12, 2019, https://usethebitcoin.com/11-countries-working-with-blockchain-technology/.

5. CM Guest Columnist, "These 5 Small Nations Are Bigger Players in Blockchain Than You May Have Guessed," *Cyprus Mail Online*, August 27, 2018, https://cyprus-mail.com/2018/08/27/these-5-small-nations-are-bigger-players-in-blockchain-than-you-may-have-guessed.

6. David Willis et al., "The Nexus of Forces Changes Everything: Gartner Symposium/ITxpo 2012 Keynote," Research Note G00246019 (Gartner, January 10, 2013).

7. Vyjayanti Desai, "The Global Identification Challenge: Who Are the 1 Billion People without Proof of Identity?," *Worldbank* (blog), April 25, 2018, https://blogs.worldbank.org/voices/global-identification-challenge-who-are-1-billion-people-without-proof-identity.

8. M. J. Altman, "10 Facts about the Syrian Refugee Crisis in Jordan," World Food Program USA, December 26, 2018, www.wfpusa.org/stories/10-facts-about-the-syrian-refugee-crisis-in-jordan/#.

9. United Nations High Commission for Refugees, UN Refugee Agency, "Jordan Fact Sheet," UN Refugee Agency, June 2018, http://reporting.unhcr.org/sites/default/files/UNHCR%20Jordan%20Fact%20Sheet%20-%20June%202018.pdf.

10. Kerry O'Connor, interview with authors, November 24, 2018.

11. O'Connor clarified that different government offices use different metrics for counting the number of homeless people in the city. But, she said, the systemic and often transient nature of homelessness means that the numbers calculated by the US Department of Housing and Urban office might not be accurate. The HUD numbers are based on people who have applied for housing—a figure lower than the total number of people who experience periods when they lack a permanent residence and are forced to move from one informal source of shelter to another over weeks or months.

12. Rebecca Skloot, in her bestselling book *The Immortal Life of Henrietta Lacks* (New York: Crown, 2010), explores the scant rules in the medical industry around the use of a person's cells and other data.

13. Melanie Swan, "Blockchain Thinking: The Brain as a DAO (Decentralized Autonomous Organization)," n.d., accessed May 2, 2019, https://pdfs.semantic scholar.org/ac86/2c394d5233d7fea85cdf45848b354b0a12b4.pdf.

14. Aaron Wood, "West Virginia Secretary of State Reports Successful Blockchain Voting in 2018 Midterm Elections," *Cointelegraph*, November 17, 2018, https://cointelegraph.com/news/west-virginia-secretary-of-state-reports-successful-blockchain-voting-in-2018-midterm-elections.

15. Aaron Mak, "West Virginia Introduces Blockchain Voting App for Midterm Election," *Slate*, September 25, 2018, https://slate.com/technology/2018/09/west-virginia-blockchain-voting-app-midterm-elections.html.

16. Mac Warner, "2018 General Election: A Huge Success for West Virginia," West Virginia Office of Secretary of State, November 15, 2018, https://sos.wv.gov/news/Pages/11-15-2018-A.aspx.

17. Brian Fung, "West Virginians Abroad in 29 Countries Have Voted by Mobile Device, in the Biggest Blockchain-Based Voting Test Ever," *Washington Post*, November 5, 2018, www.washingtonpost.com/technology/2018/11/06/west-virginians-countries-have-voted-by-mobile-device-biggest-blockchain-based-voting-test-ever/?noredirect=on&utm_term=.dd85f309f0b3.

18. SmartCitiesWorld news team, "Vienna Progresses Blockchain Strategy," *Smart Cities World*, August 3, 2018, www.smartcitiesworld.net/news/news/vienna-progresses-blockchain-strategy-3198.

19. Samburaj Das, "In a First, Japanese City Deploys Online Blockchain Voting System," *CCN*, March 3, 2018, www.ccn.com/in-a-first-japanese-city-deploys-online-blockchain-voting-system.

20. Lester Coleman, "Switzerland's 'Crypto Valley' Set to Test Blockchain Voting," *CCN*, October 6, 2018, www.ccn.com/switzerlands-crypto-valley-set-to-test-blockchain-voting.

21. Sherry Li et al., "Directed Giving Enhances Voluntary Giving to Government," *Economic Letters* 133 (August 2015): 51–54, www.researchgate.net/publication/277605021_Directed_giving_enhances_voluntary_giving_to_government.

22. Michael del Castillo, "Brooklyn Blockchain Startup Could Render Power Companies Redundant," *New York Business Journal*, March 2, 2016, www.bizjournals.com/newyork/news/2016/03/02/brooklyn-blockchain-startup-could-render.html.

23. Jolyon Jenkins, "The Man Who Created a Tiny Country He Can No Longer Enter," *BBC News*, November 14, 2016, www.bbc.com/news/magazine-37941931.

24. Rhodri Marsden, "Improbable Ships: From Hospitals to Floating Nuclear Generators," *Independent* (London), August 25, 2015, www.independent.co.uk/news/world/improbable-ships-from-hospitals-to-floating-nuclear-generators-10471677.html.

25. Megan Molteni, "The Wired Guide to CRISPR," *Wired*, March 12, 2019, www.wired.com/story/wired-guide-to-crispr.

26. David Furlonger, "The CIO Gene(s): Selection of the Fittest," Research Note G00316767 (Gartner, October 10, 2016).

27. Jim Kozubek, "Can CRISPR Cas9 Boost Intelligence," *Scientific American*, September 23, 2016, https://blogs.scientificamerican.com/guest-blog/can-crispr-cas9-boost-intelligence.

28. Gregory Barber, "A Crypto Exchange CEO Dies—with the Only Key to $137 Million," *Wired*, February 5, 2019, www.wired.com/story/crypto-exchange-ceo-dies-holding-only-key.

29. René Raphael and Ling Xi, "China's Rewards and Punishments," *Le Monde Diplomatique*, January 1, 2019, https://mondediplo.com/2019/01/05china-social-credit.

30. See, for example, Phillip A. Laplante, "First, Do No Harm: A Hippocratic Oath for Software Developers," *Queue* (Journal of the Association for Computing Machinery) 2, no. 4 (August 31, 2004), https://queue.acm.org/detail.cfm?id=1016991.

31. The vision of the proponents of the Satoshi oath is to ensure that those values are maintained and protected. See Klara Jaya Brekke, "Proposing the Satoshi Oath for Developers," *B9lab Blog*, September 20, 2016, https://blog.b9lab.com/proposing-the-satoshi-oath-for-developers-69003cffb022.

CONCLUSION

1. Hank Barnes, John-David Lovelock, Jonathon Hardcastle, "Tech Go-to-Market: Introducing Gartner's New Enterprise Personality Profiles for Improved Market Planning and Segmentation," Gartner Research Note G00273124 (Gartner, June 26, 2015).

INDEX

ACKNOWLEDGMENTS

Many people have helped us with this book, and we are extremely grateful for their time, ideas, and patience.

First we would like to thank five individuals whose encouragement and inspiration led us to continuously improve our thinking and take risks along the way:

- Laura Starita, who helped us through long days, nights, and weekends. She structured our ideas and conjured editing magic to clarify our arguments. She challenged us well beyond our comfort zones, while deftly managing our delicate nerves and an aggressive publishing schedule.

- Heather Pemberton Levy, who believed in our ability and made this project possible in the first place. Heather provided invaluable editing comments and encouragement and ensured that all parties worked together.

- Vincent Oliva, who in his career at Gartner managed both of us. Then and later, Vincent drove us to think independently. More than a decade ago, he advocated and provided time for us to develop our project on the future of money, which became the foundation for our blockchain research.

- Ray Valdes, for his thought leadership, his impressive technical know-how and research integrity, and the patient dedication he applied to help ground our analysis.

- Mark Raskino, who in 2007 graciously provided the stage in San Francisco for us to show what the future might hold.

Many Gartner colleagues and other collaborators contributed their thought leadership and insights to make the book better than we could have accomplished without them. We particularly acknowledge those who took precious time out of their busy schedules to provide invaluable manuscript reviews. This list includes, but is hardly limited to, the following individuals: Martino Agostini, Mehmet Bozkurt, Henrik Cederblad, Ismail Charkaoui, Hannah Elliott, Homan Farahmand, Thomas Hawley, Rick Holgate, Rick Howard, Richard Hunter, Rajesh Kandaswamy, Phoebe Lam, Susan Landry, Sarah Largier, Ruu-Tian Lawrence, Maggie Lee, Allen Liao, Jorge Lopez, Rich McAvey, Ali Merji, Kristin Moyer, Alistair Newton, Tina Nunno, Don Scheibenreif, Christine Shao, Bart Stanco, Kyle Wu, and Chenkai Zhu. We also want to recognize all our colleagues whose research supported our thinking. And thank you to Gordon Schuit for the beautiful graphics.

Many thanks to the editing team at Harvard Business Review Press, whose professionalism is well known but is worth proclaiming once again: Erika Heilman, who launched our project and has stayed with us throughout; Kevin Evers for his editorial advice and stewardship; Patricia Boyd for her detailed and careful copy editing; Stephani Finks for her excellent cover design, and Allison Peter and Anne Starr for steering us through the production process.

We are grateful to Gartner senior management for supporting this creative project. Particular thanks go to Andrew Spender for supporting the Gartner Books program, and research leaders Mike Harris and Val Sribar for their dedication to rigorous thinking. Our managers, Lee Weldon, John Kost, and Peter Delano have had the difficult task of helping us balance our work on the book and our client commitments— thank you for sticking with us.

This book would not be as strong or as insightful as it is without the help of many professionals who gave of their valuable time to be interviewed: Jean-François Bonald, Dr. Ray-Jade Chen, Roman Cheng, Dan Chesterman, Pieter Franken, Rebecca Hofmann, Dr. MeiKei Ieong, John Jordan, Dwight Klappich, Stephane Kunesch and his colleagues, Frédéric Longatte, Joseph Lubin, Kerry O'Connor, Rob Palatnick, Mats Snäll,

Tony Sun, Ray Valdes, Frank Verhaest, Michael White, Daniel Wilson, Christopher Woodrow, and Guang Zhao.

Finally, we thank our families and friends for their advice and contributions during this intellectual adventure. In particular, we thank our wives, whose patience and good humor we often tested, but who were always available for support and encouragement.

ABOUT THE AUTHORS

DAVID FURLONGER is a Vice President and Gartner Research Fellow, based in North America. He works primarily with CEOs, boards of directors, and other senior leaders and is an accomplished and frequent keynote speaker with extensive international experience. His research focus is as a futurist, analyzing how long-term business and technology trends strategically impact societies, industries, governments, and organizations. In 2007 he initiated Gartner's research theme titled "The Future of Money," and later launched Gartner's blockchain research and Center of Excellence.

Before joining Gartner, Mr. Furlonger worked in multiple business areas of the financial services industry and in the chemical and precious metals manufacturing industry. As an entrepreneur and consultant, he managed, publicly listed, and then helped to sell a software and media business in North America.

CHRISTOPHE UZUREAU is a Vice President at Gartner, based in Asia Pacific. He works primarily with CEOs, chief digital officers, and senior business leaders. His research focuses on how blockchain and tokenization enable new assets, products, and services to generate business and consumer value. His analysis explores the evolution of digital business, taking into account emerging technology and innovations as well as their impact on customer behavior. Mr. Uzureau has extensive experience in the financial services sector. He has lived and worked in many different countries and brings significant local context to his analysis.